GLQ
A Journal of Lesbian and Gay Studies

VOLUME 18   NUMBERS 2–3   2012

Black/Queer/Diaspora
edited by Jafari S. Allen

JAFARI S. ALLEN

Introduction: Black/Queer/Diaspora
at the Current Conjuncture

211

JAFARI S. ALLEN, WITH OMISE'EKE NATASHA TINSLEY

Editorial Note: A Conversation "Overflowing
with Memory": On Omise'eke Natasha Tinsley's
"Water, Shoulders, Into the Black Pacific"

249

OMISE'EKE NATASHA TINSLEY

Extract from "Water, Shoulders, Into the Black Pacific"

263

LYNDON K. GILL

Chatting Back an Epidemic: Caribbean Gay Men,
HIV/AIDS, and the Uses of Erotic Subjectivity

277

XAVIER LIVERMON
Queer(y)ing Freedom: Black Queer Visibilities in
Postapartheid South Africa
297

VANESSA AGARD-JONES
What the Sands Remember
325

ANA-MAURINE LARA
Of Unexplained Presences, Flying Ife
Heads, Vampires, Sweat, Zombies, and Legbas:
A Meditation on Black Queer Aesthetics
347

MATT RICHARDSON
"My Father Didn't Have a Dick": Social Death
and Jackie Kay's *Trumpet*
361

Image Gallery
381

Book Review
ROBERT G. DIAZ
Queer Histories and the Global City
387

Books in Brief

SYLVIA MIESZKOWSKI

After Sex? On Writing since Queer Theory
edited by Janet Halley and Andrew Parker

407

ELLEN LEWIN

*Not in This Family: Gays and the Meaning
of Kinship in Postwar North America*
by Heather Murray

410

PETRUS LIU

*Backward Glances: Contemporary Chinese Cultures
and the Female Homoerotic Imaginary*
by Fran Martin

413

SCOTT LAURIA MORGENSEN

*When Did Indians Become Straight? Kinship,
the History of Sexuality, and Native Sovereignty*
by Mark Rifkin

416

KARMA R. CHÁVEZ

Against Equality: Queer Critiques of Gay Marriage
edited by Ryan Conrad

419

About the Contributors

423

Introduction

BLACK/QUEER/DIASPORA AT THE CURRENT CONJUNCTURE

Jafari S. Allen

*G*iven this queer space we find ourselves inhabiting currently — one in which the past and our futures seem to demand so much of our now: *What sort of moment is this* in which to pose the question of black/queer/diasporas? Following Stuart Hall, who argues that "moments are always conjunctural . . . have their historical specificity; and . . . always exhibit similarities and continuities with the other moments in which we pose a question like this," this introductory essay proposes a genealogy of black/queer/diaspora work.[1] This work emerges from radical black and Third World lesbian feminist art, activism, and scholarship, and builds on the scholarly and programmatic practice of black queer studies and queer of color critique.

Black/queer/diaspora work emerges in a moment in which the terms *black*, *queer*, and *diaspora* — between the porous strokes I have added here — have already begun to be elaborated beyond the metaphors and concepts offered by any one of these constituencies, and beyond false dichotomies of essentialism and anti-essentialism. Such collections as E. Patrick Johnson and Mae Henderson's *Black Queer Studies: A Critical Anthology*, Jennifer DeVere Brody and Dwight McBride's *Callaloo* special issue "Plum Nelly: New Essays in Black Queer Studies," and a number of other works have already drawn on the lineages of black queer studies, which I turn to in subsequent sections. "Plum Nelly" and *Black Queer Studies* each emerge in different ways from the Black Queer Studies in the Millennium conference, organized by Johnson at the University of North Carolina at Chapel Hill in 2000.[2] Roderick Ferguson's *Aberrations in Black: Toward a Queer of Color*

Critique is the first monograph to name and provide a thoroughgoing analysis and example of queer of color critique.³ *Black Queer Studies* more or less followed the conference's parameters, focusing on the black United States, with Rinaldo Walcott's contribution pushing at these borders from "(a) queer place in diaspora" (Canada). However, Michelle Wright and Antje Schuhmann's collection *Blackness and Sexualities*—which emerges from the Europe-based Collegium of African-American Research and was published in Germany—broadens the geographic and thematic scopes of the black queer studies project to Europe (and Cuba), as well as to themes that are not strictly LGBTQ.⁴ Each of these works, characterized by insurgent rereadings of classical or otherwise well-known texts, reclamation of intellectual traditions, and writing into the scholarly record, subjects otherwise relegated to the margins, at once cleared and claimed space.⁵ We are fortunate to coinhabit this space today. Certainly, this is not to say that black queer theory and queer of color critique are closed discourses—quite the contrary. Nor do I want to give the impression that queer theory has unproblematically incorporated the contributions of this work or that black studies, diaspora studies, or any area or regional studies have welcomed queer thinking, themes, or persons into the center of their research agenda.⁶

Recently Omise'eke Natasha Tinsley's *GLQ* article "Black Atlantic/Queer Atlantic" has offered a rethinking of metaphors of ships, oceans as bodies, and performative bodies (offered by Paul Gilroy, Antonio Benítez-Rojo, and Judith Butler, respectively), arguing that the black queer Atlantic "churns differently . . . diffracting meanings . . . (leaving Black queer diasporic subjects) 'whole and broken' . . . brutalized and feeling . . . divided from other diasporic migrants and linked to them."⁷ Apropos of queer of color critique, José Esteban Muñoz's *Cruising Utopia* follows his earlier work's commitment to creating alternative visions of performance and performativity, read through a lens constituted in and through cultural theory that affirms futurity, *with a difference*.⁸ Although queer of color critique and black queer studies are interdisciplinary projects, they both tend to lean heavily toward humanities and performance scholarship. History and the social sciences must not abdicate their responsibility, however. The literary critic Hortense Spillers has already convinced us of the consequences of negated kinship, and the importance of "first order naming" (which she asserts emerges from historical and social science research).⁹ As more individuals trained in social science methodologies contribute to this work, we are beginning to see new possibilities.¹⁰ *Say It Loud: I'm Black and I'm Proud: Black Pride Survey 2000*, Gloria Wekker's *Politics of Passion*, Critchlow's *Buller Men and Batty Bwoys*, Murray's *Opacity*, my own work, and Juan Battle's Social Justice Sexuality Project now under way have begun to provide ethnographic dimensions and empirical data to black queer studies and queer of color critique.[11] This brings us closer to providing *verbs* to animate the continuation of the black radical intellectual tradition, as well as *a name* — or, more precisely, a number of names — *lesbian, transgender, bisexual, gay, batty bwoy, masisi, bulldagger, two-spirited, maricón, same gender loving, buller, zami, mati working, dress-up girls, bois, butches, femme* or *butch queen, gender insurgent, marimacha, branché, homosexual, sexual minority, men, women,* etcetera . . . *of Africa(n descent)* call ourselves. Of course, some eschew explicit naming, preferring to live their verbs, as for example, simply *am, is, are, been, being, be* — or *interrupt, invent, push, question, refuse, serve,* or *shade,* in some cases.

While commentators have astutely cited the Black Queer Studies in the Millennium conference as a watershed moment that provided both a platform for the staging of black queer studies and a foundation for various other related pursuits like collaboration and mentoring that support the work of black queer studies and black queer scholars and artists, an event that preceded it by five years is just as significant yet has garnered little critical attention.[12] The Black Nations/Queer Nations conference — documented by Shari Frilot in a film by the same name — was concerned not only with raising questions about the study of black LGBT two-spirit and same-gender-loving black people, across nationality, class, ability, gender, and sexual expression but also with expanding capacity toward critically engaging political organizing.[13] Black Nations/Queer Nations is thus also an important model for engaged projects, which, like black/queer/diaspora work, attempts to deepen and broaden the ineluctable connections between scholarship, activism, and artistry. Even a cursory look at the foundational works of black queer studies — anthologies, broadsides, chapbooks, poetry collections, and other nonacademic intellectual and political work — demonstrates this connection.[14] Nurturing these connections is a crucial part of ensuring that scholarship is grounded in, and in some ways accountable to, lived experience and nonacademic intellectual tradition.

Black queer studies and queer of color critique is practiced not only in scholarly publication but also in teaching on the graduate and undergraduate levels; in panels offered at local and international conferences and symposia, for example, by the Black Sexual Economies Reading Group and the Black Gay Research Group; in public education work, such as the Caribbean International Resources Network board; in leadership in professional academic organizations; in productive mentoring relationships formed with senior scholars; in crucial peer support; in collaborative teaching and research; and in activist scholarship by independent cultural workers like Herukhuti (*Conjuring Black Funk: Notes on Culture, Sexuality, and Spirituality*).[15] In addition, several critical archival and cultural projects and political organizations, as well as personal connections between individuals whose networks and texts stretch across the globe, instantiate a more widespread and democratic circuit of *black queer here and there*.[16]

I have not undertaken the task of this special issue to rehearse the arguments of any of the fine works, events, or sites of collaboration or contestation I have just invoked. My aim here is to situate the sterling contributions to this volume vis-à-vis *conjunctural moments* in these interlocking discourses and practices and to welcome others into this dynamic conversation.[17] By conjunctural moments, I mean to index the temporal space in which the articulation (or accretion or collision) of sometimes related and other times opposing or unrelated discourses, practices, or trajectories reshape, reimagine, or alter our view of the present. At conjunctural moments, "new" ideas and practices emerge and take on added significance precisely because of this articulation (or perhaps novel rearticulation, or "mash-up"). The conjunctural moment I am meditating on here, for example, is constituted not only by the maturation of black and queer of color studies literatures and the current existential crisis of queer studies, but also by the recognition of the presence of the transnational in every moment, even "at home," and the rapidity of popular forms of (uneven) global exchange.

Black/queer/diaspora is an organic project of multivalent and multiscalar reclamation, revisioning, and futurity (yes, all at once). Hall, quoting Antonio Gramsci, implores us to "turn violently" toward the unvarnished "contradictory ground of the current conjuncture."[18] Still, in this current moment of stark, murderous contradiction, we are also compelled to envision and produce work that is deeply humane and capacious, as well as analyses that not only reflect "real life" on the ground but also speculate on liberatory models from the past and project our imaginations forward, to possible futures.

In this essay, I argue for the recognition of black/queer/diaspora as at once a caution, a theory, and (most centrally) *a work*. Rather than attempt to increase the territory of queer theory or black queer studies, the aspiration here is to push forward the work, in different sites and forms. The creation of another "studies" is not my aim here. My objective for this essay is to secure neither LGBT rights nor academic office space—although both are necessary and even honorable in many circumstances. This accent on work follows Audre Lorde's "fixing" query "Are you doing your work?," which is itself one way to recognize the black radical tradition of holding paid and unpaid intellectual, artistic, and activist labor as a serious, necessary undertaking.[19] Here I hope to begin to sketch the parameters of black/queer/diaspora ethics, aesthetics, and methodologies by contextualizing the works in this special issue. These are "unsettled" questions in an ongoing conversation. To follow the routes of black/queer/diaspora is to interrogate dynamic, unsettled subjects whose bodies, desires, and texts *move*. Our methodologies must therefore be supple, our communication polyglot, our outlook wide and open, and our analysis nuanced. This multiple, luxuriant, and subtle approach is intellectually generative (if not also a bit unsettling for some). In any case, we find that this is more useful and more pleasurable than attempting to fit complex, contradictory, and perhaps fugitive experiences and imaginings into the staid desensitized and sterile boxes of "race," "sexuality," "nationality," discipline, or genre. Of course, Wahneema Lubiano has already made it clear: "Black queer studies serves as a space in which one might experience freedom in the form of pedagogical and epistemological pleasure."[20]

Rather than trace an intellectual lineage in which metaphors of trees, roots, or even complex intersecting strands of heterosexually reproduced DNA are organized in an orderly, temporally rigid trajectory, I offer here an organization of the genealogical matrix of the present moment that is necessarily and deliberately promiscuous. As Jasbir Puar has argued, "Queer times require even queerer modalities of thought, analysis, creativity, and expression."[21] Here we take up the challenge of these queer times by claiming intellectual kin where we find them; speaking to, with, and through discourses appropriate to the conversation rather than those merely expected by convention, while reaching back to foundational works and projecting our imaginations forward.

And of course, yes. Despite popular and scholarly representations of black people as parochial, we live in the world—all of it. And wherever we are. Moreover, *diaspora* is not a place somewhere "out of Africa" seen only from the United States and England, and only by academics. Black folks participate in (uneven) global exchanges, whether with our entire body, or just a mouse-click, page turn, lifting of a fork, or remittance to a romantic fantasy abroad or family at home. The central theme of my own current research project on black queer sociality and movement is that currently, even *in place*, black queer subjects can hardly escape the flow of diasporic black desires. This is evident in neighborhoods where blackness is accented or differentiated by nation or language block to block, and in seatmates on a flight—one "going home" and the other "going down" or "over there" on vacation. It is evident in cyberspace between Twitterers, Orkutites, Facebookers, and Tumblrers, who trade in porn, gossip, sweet and/or nasty nothings, and urgent political news, and can be seen among individuals who will never leave their own town but who nevertheless powerfully imagine their own black/queer "other."

Black diaspora is at once about particular *locations* (actual and imagined); *roots/uprooting* (principally understood as *from* Africa, but just as much *to* and *within* Africa, in other cases); and *routes* that bodies, ideas, and texts travel. By diaspora, we refer to these conditions of movement and emplacement, and to processes of (dis)identification, but also to relationality, as Jacqueline Nassy Brown points out.[22] Commentators often miss this vital piece. The ways in which African (descended) groups (dis)identify as Black (or "black"), Afro-hyphenated, Kreyól, Creole, mixed, or other designations do not occur in a vacuum but are conditioned by particularities of place, in relation to discourses and practices within other places. Witness, for example, the Dominican Republic's official sublimation of the *negro* racial category, in response to its inevitable intimate, Haiti; or Atlantic Coast Nicaraguans' black (and/or) Creole identity, marking not only mixed Afro-Caribbean heritage but also an English linguistic difference vis-à-vis the Pacific coast–oriented nation; or the British designation of black in the 1980s and 1990s. Though currently *disintegrated*, this category included South Asians, as well as Caribbean and African groups, in a conscious response to violent attempts to "keep Britain white." Black diasporic relationality is also at work in the popular race talk of African (descended) immigrants to the United States who often hold several fascinating beliefs at once: that race is unimportant or not discussed (which are in fact not the same thing) in their homelands, or that social class and racialization are "more complex" in their countries than in the United States; or that they only "became black" once they reached the shores of the United States. Among other works, *Globalization and Race*, edited by Kamari Clarke and Deborah Thomas, illustrates the importance of including the historical specificity of racial formations as part of our analyses of complex global processes.[23]

Even with all of this rich contradiction and history, until recently blackness has most often been ignored in queer theory's considerations of globalization, migration, and diaspora. This betrays a brand of scholarly refusal that poses blackness as transparently uninteresting, unchanging, and bound to the United States, while other groups are cosmopolitan — traveling, changing their minds and sex partners, and exchanging goods and ideas on the global market. To appropriate "diaspora" without considering blackness and antiblack racism is to ignore the work of critical scholars of the black Atlantic who provided foundational theorization of the conditions and performances of diaspora on which various scholars of queer globalization, migration, and diaspora depend.[24] The scholarly and ethical consequences of this ignorance are manifold and include capitulation to projects of antiblack racism, which depend on the assignment of "race" to US blackness only, and "ethnicity" to nearly every other group.

Note the strokes (/) separating *black*, *queer*, and *diaspora*.[25] This can be seen to conjoin the terms on either side or to push them apart, toward sharper individual focus. Both *black* and *queer* exert pressure on *diaspora*, just as *black* leans to *queer*—perhaps toward *something else*, or the conjuncture to come. Black/queer/diaspora work explores the cumulative, synthetic force of each, along with various regional and area studies, performance theory, recent entreaties by "public feelings" scholars to be attentive to the political meanings and potential of affect and performative writing, and increasingly, ethnography.[26] Some of these literatures and politics closely articulate to form productive points of analysis, while the high-stakes disarticulation of others provides provocative entry points for much-needed new formulations. However, here the reader should not expect the standard academic spectacle of savaging work that has preceded the author's pen to paper, putatively to "make room" or situate the author's distinctive viewpoint.[27] This work constitutes a palimpsest, another litany (toward) survival (and thriving):

> looking inward and outward
> at once before and after
> seeking a now that can breed
> futures
> like bread in our children's mouths
> so their dreams will not reflect
> the death of ours[28]

For black queers, survival has always been about finding ways to connect some of what is disconnected, to embody and re-member. This is the social erotics of love at work. The intersubjectivity evidenced by black queer love is "that conjure medicine that helps heal the psychic wounds of enslavement."[29] Thus our work here is both a labor of love and evidence of it, perforce. Note once again the *strokes* shared between *black/queer/diaspora*: they are in fact also caresses, Omise'eke reminds me. Chela Sandoval has already elaborated a theory of "love as a hermeneutics of social change" in which "love can access and guide our theoretical and political *movida*s—revolutionary maneuvers toward decolonized being."[30] This consciousness is of course mostly unheard of in academic discourse and left unsaid among academics. Here we have attempted here to remember the chief distinction of our queerness—whom and how we love (and have sex, certainly). The conventions of our guild — steeped in cool reason — avoid love as a *movida*. It is nevertheless evident in the works featured here and in the passion-filled (not easy, uncomplicated, or necessarily romantic) relationships between many individuals who do this work. Practically, this means re-visioning standard academic disengagement and atomization.

The essays, art, and spirit of this special issue constitute a preliminary love offering of the Black/Queer/Diaspora Work(ing) Group and are drawn from our initial meeting, held in spring 2009 at Yale University.[31] Still in formation, this gathering of humanities scholars, social scientists, cultural critics, artists, and activists working in Africa, the Caribbean, Europe, North and South America, and various flows between these sites moves beyond lamenting the aporia of black diaspora scholarship in queer theory and the lack of engagement with queer theory in black diaspora studies. The working group endeavors to develop scholarly, artistic, and political projects that will provoke conversations and interventions in and across a number of sites, including collective research programs and construction of frames of analysis. This work must not only address the current chasms between bodies of literature but also do so in a way that highlights agency of the multiply subaltern, affirms positive human rights, and serves as a corrective to academic practices that "disappear" the work of black scholars and elide critical intersectional discourses and the experiences and imaginations of black subjects. For the working group, this includes scholarship but also must go beyond academe to form symbiotic collaborations with intellectuals, artists, and activists working on the ground: for example, on the stage, screen, page, sea, sand, and, literally, *on the ground* — at a party, lime or fiesta, demonstration or spiritual intervention — in and between a number of places around the globe. In short, the realms of creativity, performance, troubled/contingent belonging, spirituality, and affect are powerfully inscribed within our work. We recognize that *scholar*, *artist*, *practitioner*, *activist*, and *community member* are not mutually exclusive terms.

"All the Things You Could Be by Now, If Jacqui Alexander and Cathy Cohen Were Your . . ."

During the opening discussion of our symposium, Michelle Wright offered that "dominant epistemologies are quite often illogical, in the way in which heteronormativity insists upon certain [fantastical ways of being and becoming], like the way in which Jehosephat begat Jeboth begat . . ." Queer studies and black studies also too often capitulate to lineages of "male autogenesis."[32] As "outside children" of black studies and queer studies, we claim new ways to queerly trace our genealogies beyond patronymic reconstruction. The title of this section both playfully recalls Spillers's foundational (dare I say "seminal"?) essay "All the Things You Could Be by Now, If Sigmund Freud's Wife Was Your Mother: Psychoanalysis and Race" and honors the radical black and feminist of color lesbian genesis of black/queer/diaspora work, here represented by Cohen and Alexander.[33] After the ellipsis in the section heading above, the reader may find a senior sister, wise lover, mentor, friend, or teacher, for example, or maybe a cousin who comes to visit (from the city, the country, or abroad) doing a new dance or wearing a scandalous outfit—precipitating a shift, structuring a conjuncture.

Since her *The Boundaries of Blackness*, Cohen has exposed how the US state and black institutions, academics, and families construct the dangerous vulnerabilities of the deeply and multiply subaltern—an analytic category she later formulated as "punks, bulldaggers, and welfare queens."[34] In her essay "Deviance as Resistance: A New Research Agenda for the Study of Black Politics," Cohen critiques African American studies' politics of respectability and argues that the reputed deviance of lesbians, gays, transgender and bisexual persons, single mothers, and state aid recipients—in the eyes of not just US policy makers but also scholars and civil society leaders—marks us not only as unruly would-be subject-citizens but also as outside cultural boundaries of belonging and care.[35] Similarly, Alexander has argued that *some* bodies, such as those of the lesbian and the "prostitute," cannot be included as citizens in former colonies of the Caribbean precisely because they embody sexual agency and eroticism radically out of step with the aspiration of the nation to advertise itself as independent, developed, disciplined, and poised to join in the number of putatively civilized states.[36] As she beautifully shows, this same "erotic autonomy" is the site out of which individuals and groups have staged various rebellions. Taken together, this work illustrates both a set of nettlesome political problems and a theoretical puzzle across black diaspora: Is there any place where [the benefits and recognition of] citizenship can accrue to the unruly—the "prostitute," the homosexual, "welfare queen," transgender person, or the black? And what calculus emerges when these gendered, raced, and sexed categories of nonnational, deviant, nonethnic/racial subject, nonconforming, or merely "other" are compounded? Alexander has vividly shown what this looks like moving across borders:

> I am an outlaw in my country of birth: a national, but not a citizen. Born in Trinidad and Tobago . . . I was taught that once we pledged our lives to the new nation, "every creed and race (had) an equal place." I was taught to believe "Massa Day Done," that there would be an imminent end to

> foreign domination. . . . In the United States of North America where I live now, I must constantly keep in my possession the immigrant (green) card given to me by the American state, marking me "legal" resident alien; non-national; non-citizen . . . [in] twenty two states, even with green card in hand, I may be convicted of crimes various defined as lewd unnatural; lascivious conduct; deviant sexual intercourse; gross indecency; buggery or crimes against nature.[37]

There are crucial historical and political-economic distinctions that condition and structure both how a state — any state — attempts to regulate particular bodies and how national belonging is reckoned. Still, it seems the state — seemingly every state, though of course in wildly varying scales and intensities — depends on racialized heteropatriarchy (which is always also *classed*) to constitute and maintain itself in the global hierarchy of states. While literatures on globalization and transnationalism have tended to highlight how the state is disappearing or being eclipsed by global capital and new information technologies, even neoliberal (leaning) states retain their power prerogative of surveillance, severe discipline, and in some cases expulsion or extermination of vulnerable persons, even as they continue to disinvest in public health, education, and welfare.[38] My own research in Cuba, Trinidad and Tobago, and Brazil and experiences at home in the United States impel taking seriously distinctions between socialist and liberal states, (post)colonial and imperial nations, North and South.[39] Certainly, "diaspora" does constitute a way out of the nation-state. Still, failing inclusion as a properly hygienic citizen or subject, where is the place for the black queer? Most pressing for me: if in fact black(s and) queers cannot be full citizens in the liberal sense, can they at least be *free*?

While the politics I highlight here continue to insist on the state's responsibility to protect and care for those within its borders, and for families and communities to acknowledge and accept those within them, the stakes of belonging and unbelonging in black/queer/diaspora are high. The strokes I noted earlier can be, of course, (in the) back *slashes* — violently cutting out and cutting off. I query citizenship here not only because of the barriers black queers face when attempting to enjoy the full complement of citizenship — full "rights" within the nation's political body — but more pointedly to ask whether the notion of citizenship, with its obvious rules of exclusion and exception, stands in for a wider range of assurances and freedoms. Complicating this, nonstate actors such as families, and religious and cultural organizations, often *think like a state* — making strange bedfellows in their support for projects of respectability.[40] Their shared project is to discipline individuals into local legibility and particular forms of subjectification. Witness, for example, how disparate black fundamentalist, religious, and middle-class "race leader" rhetorics, in various sites across the Americas, in Africa, and in Europe, seem so perfectly in sync with one another and with the transnational homophobia and sexism of the largely white US Christian Right.[41] Still, observation of the everyday tactics and strategies of black queers, in a number of locations including those visited in this special issue, persuasively suggests that the "larger freedom" we seek may be more available outside the state's purview and will certainly depend on a willingness to expose and articulate forms of deviance, and to be audacious in a variety of ways, at home in our various communities.[42] This certainly does not excuse the state's disinvestment, or civil society's self-righteousness, but rather holds that sites of resistance and self-making must necessarily find air in other spaces. They do, because they must. These spaces include audacious performativity, eroticism, the spectral, and futurity, as many of the contributions to this special issue richly illustrate. Scholarly work does not create everyday resistance within and survival by the most multiply vulnerable among us, but it can give light to it—helping expand recognition of those sites as legitimate political expression.

Thus in this issue—and in our larger individual and collective projects and those of a growing cadre of scholars, activist intellectuals, and artists—we take up the work that Cohen has challenged us to do, shifting research agendas to understand and meet the urgent demands of those who are multiply vulnerable. Furthermore, we follow Alexander's recent proposal that the key epistemological intervention of our work remains to think/live/write contradictions of genre, discipline, materiality, spirituality, and affect, at once.[43] I turn now to consider the genealogical matrixes out of which this work emerges, before introducing each contribution to this special issue. I begin with queer studies, followed by black and women of color lesbian feminism, black queer studies, black diaspora studies, and queer of color critique. Of course, these are not mutually exclusive literatures or sites of work. Following my précis of the essays, I make some comments about the relative political positioning of black/queer/diaspora work, before a few words of conclusion.

Genealogical Matrixes

Black and queer of color work that has already "thrown shade on the meanings of queer" highlights detail, color, and depth within the discourse that make it more incisive and useful.[44] E. Patrick Johnson's rearticulation of race, place, and affect in his brilliant reformulation of "quare" is one of a number of examples of this. Still, *queer* not only marks one of the constitutive academic discourses and historical moments here but is also a critical way of seeing and saying. That is, following Muñoz, for me "queerness is essentially about . . . an insistence on potentiality or concrete possibility for another world."[45] Moreover, notwithstanding the understandable protests of those who reject *queer* as a name for black subjects on the grounds that it extends a white patronym: *queer* does also uniquely capture the sense of the nonnormative status of men, women, and others who identify with or are identified as homosexual or bisexual, and those whose gender self-identification is not resonant with the sex assigned to them at birth. I am not claiming that large numbers of black or African (descended) people currently (or should) use this term to identify themselves. Still, as I have averred elsewhere, no term, even those that may seem self-evidently local, indigenous, or autochthonous, is perfectly stable or synchronous with dynamic self-identification on the ground.

Please allow me to address the big white elephant, resting just outside the margins of this special issue. The repetition of *black* queer theory, queer *people of color* critique, *black* feminist theory, and *black*/queer/diaspora seems to call the question; still here I must explicitly stipulate to the reader: read "queer theory" as "white queer theory produced in the US and Western Europe, and occasionally Australia and New Zealand."[46] To riff on Hall again, "*What is this* whiteness in queer studies?" Nevertheless, this is a topic for another scholar, at another conjunctural moment. Black and queer of color scholars have already pointed out important contributions of the larger enterprise of queer theory, with respect to its ruthless critique of normativity, and have roundly criticized queer theory's proposition of universal heterosexual privilege. Following scholars like J. Jack Halberstam, Muñoz, and Juana María Rodríguez, I have argued elsewhere that queer studies is due for another wave of reconsideration and reinvigoration. Part of the disappointment in/of some streams of queer theory is that having accepted the postmodern (PoMo) understanding of the collapse of categories of experience melting into nothingness, there is little room for anything—"no future," indeed—beyond a yawning pessimism, which queers of color have, time after time, insisted our communities cannot afford.[47]

While queer theory has proliferated numerous studies in which everyday acts of gender or sexual nonconformity are celebrated, this has always been more complex for people of color. Not only are black subjects always already queer relative to normative ideals of the person, but black queers also often seem *a queer too far* for much of queer studies and gay and lesbian popular culture and politics. In addition, sexual minorities and gender-variant individuals from the global

South who negotiate but do not wholly capitulate to what Cymene Howe has called the "universal queer subject" discursively fall, in both time and space, outside narrowly Western and Northern middle-class gay constructions of "family," "lesbian," "gay," "queer," and "Gay Rights."[48] Rather than pose this as a "problem" for queer studies, it is more productive to see it as an enriching, challenging, and ultimately salutary proposition to refine queer theory. Tellingly, here the reader will find that work in this special issue does not take up typical queer theory tropes of "shame" or "pride" or "the closet," or argue false dichotomies of sexuality *or* gender, race *or* sexuality, nationality *or* class, for example. This work has a different focus. It orbits (and in fact, instantiates) black queer audacity. This is ironic because black and other people of color communities are constantly cast as archaic holdouts to progressive "sexual blindness" within emerging neoliberal multiculturalism: the work of black/queer/diaspora and people of color who seek to strategically or tactically use their putative deviance (*quare*ness?) as resistance is therefore one of the most vigorous forces pushing left in queer studies.

Radical black feminists' uninvited interventions in black politics, arts, and letters first demonstrated that submerged, discredited, or "alternative" knowledges produced at the interstices of violence, silence, invisibility, or forgetting exposed a wider horizon of possibilities.[49] Along with "revolution" or "liberation," this work has been written off by some as a "closed discourse" and is commonly attacked as "identity politics," as if the innovation of politicized identity formations as one strategy (or tactic) of resistance is the evil, rather than misogyny, racism, heterosexism, and classism.[50] Likewise, newer work in several realms of scholarly and artistic practice does not always acknowledge how, for example, black feminism can in fact be read as a queer project, one suffused with affect as a central methodology (and mode of exchange), and an Afro-futuristic one, as it imagines and attempts to call into being futures in which black folks exist and thrive (even if on the detritus of the past). The Black/Queer/Diaspora project takes up black feminism's challenge to develop a synthetic vision and methodology of diasporic black queer futurity.

Continuing in the intellectual tradition of radical "Third World" and black lesbian feminisms, black transgender, lesbian, bisexual, and gay artists and activists in the United States — rooted in the civil rights, black feminist, and black liberation movements that raged between the 1950s and 1970s, and responding to important global political and social shifts of the 1980s and 1990s — revealed spaces within blackness that had been concealed and silenced. That is, they "yield[ed] unexpected ways of intervening and . . . [made] space for something else to be," as Ferguson described the earlier black feminist movement.[51] The concept of home, reflected in, for example, Barbara Smith's anthology *Home Girls: A Black Feminist Anthology* and other texts, including Cheryl Clarke's and Ron Simmons's polemical essays that challenge Black Arts movement icons and traditions of black heterosexual respectability, is the primary focus of this work.[52] Joseph Beam famously asserted in 1984:

> When I speak of home, I mean not only the familial constellation from which I grew, but the entire Black community: the Black press, the Black church, Black academicians, the Black literati, and the Black left. Where is my reflection? I am most often rendered invisible, perceived as a threat to the family, or I am tolerated if I am silent and inconspicuous. I cannot go home as who I am and that hurts me deeply.[53]

Of course Lorde had already economically formulated the riddle of "home" in her poem "School Note":

> For the embattled
> There is no place
> that cannot be home
> Nor is.[54]

By 1991, after the black gay movement failed to provide an alternative home in which Beam could have died surrounded by friends, colleagues, and community members, instead of alone and increasingly (self)alienated, the focus seems to shift for Essex Hemphill. It shifts away from an exposition of the vexed multiplicity of blackness and gayness toward a resolution to be at home, unapologetically. Hemphill writes in the original introduction to *Brother to Brother: New Writing by Black Gay Men*:

> I ask you brother: Does your mama really know about you? Does she really know what I am? Does she know I want to love her son, care for him, nurture and celebrate him? Do you think she'll understand? I hope so, because *I am coming home. There is no place else to go that will be worth so much effort and love.*[55]

Love between family members is certainly no panacea. Nor is it uncomplicated or without conflict. It can also be unrequited, even as family or community support is necessary to battle against the extrinsic threat of racism. Black lesbian and gay artists and activist intellectuals developed a trenchant critique of heteronormativity and its intimate connection to racism, sexism, and classism, laying bare the ravages of internalized hatred as well as external threats. Moreover, they practiced their positions through popular education and community organizing. Their work provided the foundation and impetus for black queer studies, which, following the popular movement's insistence on claiming space, has "animate(d) the dialogic/dialectic 'kinship' [of black studies and queer studies] by mobilizing the tensions embedded in the *conjunction* of 'Black' and 'queer,'" as Johnson and Henderson aver in the introduction to their pathbreaking *Black Queer Studies*.[56] One of the most salient moves at the outset of black queer studies was to claim, and even celebrate, blackness and black self-identification in a historical moment in which "the identity politics pendulum had swung in the direction of a PoMo retreat in the name of anti-essentialism."[57] Sharon Holland, in her foreword to *Black Queer Studies*, reminisces about the challenges that faced those who, like her, had been working in and between black studies and queer theory in the early 1990s. Holland writes:

> I moved toward a space that attempted to define a connection between "Black" and "queer" when "queer" had its own controversial orbit . . . would "queer" obfuscate the presence of lesbians in a movement that . . . had its own specific historical struggle over the "inclusion" of women in the story itself? The academic market, at least its emerging "queer" constituency, seemed to be interpreting "Identity politics" as the root of all evil — [suggesting that] simply getting rid of "race" (always too a fiction?) and the category "woman" (already a misnomer?) and we would have our rebirth on the other side of our problem(s).[58]

For Holland, question of identity politics, "woman" as a universal category, and the position of women in activist and nationalist contexts, for example, hardly seemed "new" for someone like herself who had followed such scholars as Hazel Carby, Spillers, Smith, and others. That is, in contrast to what at the time was the fashionable PoMo party line of queer theory, black and women of color feminism had developed an understanding of difference and resistance to normativity that was not only discursive and performative but also grounded in and responsive to everyday *fact(s)* of *blackness* (to invoke Fanon), that is, the materiality of black experiences.

In US black *quare* studies, the focus was indeed on "making an intervention at home," as Johnson and Henderson remind us.[59] Holland notes that black queer scholars and artists began to find "home . . . tucked away in the Harlem

Renaissance, embedded in second wave feminism, and nestled in the heart of the civil rights struggle . . . as backbone rather than anomaly."[60] And of course, currently, as David Eng reminds us, we have come to understand that "*Home* is not private, as theorized under liberalism. Instead, it is a crucial public site of labor within the global restructuring of capitalism."[61] Recently, examinations of African, Caribbean, Canadian, European, and Latin American literature and film have revealed that this theme is indeed global: *home* as a site of ambivalence and potential *conflama* (a US black gay vernacular conjunction connoting confusion and drama), yet at the same time somehow constituting Hemphill's "place that will be worth so much effort and love." It is just as central in black/queer/diaspora literature beyond US borders. Walcott has provided a significant example in his analysis of the reception of the Canadian short film *Welcome to Africville*.[62] In the watershed anthology *Our Caribbean: Gay and Lesbian Writing from the Antilles*, which is just as powerfully read as a diasporic text as it is an Antillian one, Thomas Glave has collected work from as far back as 1956 (but mostly from the 1990s and 2000s) that reveals, like much of Glave's own beautifully evocative lyrical writing, that "home" in (and out of and returning back to) the Caribbean is also a vexed space.[63] Of course Canadian/Trinbagonian Dionne Brand's critically acclaimed oeuvre also layers (im)migration, diaspora, dispacement, and longing.[64] While there is a growing number of works on Africa that sympathetically engage sexuality, including that of Marc Epprecht, Neville Hoad, and the working group's own Graeme Reid, the impressive and very recently published collection edited by Sylvia Tamale, *African Sexualities: A Reader* (which is more of a comprehensive reader on sexualities rather than specific to homosexualities and trans identities) has opened the way toward more work that highlights African sexual minorities and gender insurgents from the perspectives of black African activists.[65] As the work of the photographer and activist Ajamu X and the community arts organization Rukus! shows, Britain continues to be a hotbed of black/queer/diaspora work.[66] This work, of course, follows the work of such British artists as the filmmaker Isaac Julien, the Nigerian photographer Rotimi Fani-Kayode, and the critical cultural scholar Kobena Mercer — whose work in the late 1980s and 1990s spoke to black queer culture pointedly and engagingly across three continents, before focusing more particularly on visual art. This work provided brilliant provocations toward parsing the political and conceptual consequences of gender, racial, and sexual difference, nationality, ethnicity, and aesthetics within Britain and beyond.

Holland's language of embeddedness — "tucked away" — is thus useful to think about the presence of black diaspora consciousness in black queer studies of the 1980s and 1990s. For example, each member of the triumvirate of black queer letters (Lorde, Beam, and Hemphill) was a "diasporic subject." Beam and Lorde, whose transnational work is well known, both have Caribbean heritage, and though his essays and poems illuminate Washington, D.C., and celebrate it as homespace, Hemphill also traveled internationally and began to have a transnational outlook, making important connections and collaborating significantly with black gay British artists. Of course among other important contributions, Robert Reid-Pharr provides delicious insight into the circulation of desire in German clubs he attended, through a black queer transnational lens, in his *Black Gay Man*, and newer work on choice, desire, and the black American intellectual whose work and life is also translocal.[67] Moreover, in popular culture of the black queer "classical era," Grace Jones served Caribbean-cum-European cosmopolitanism better than any other.[68] Her androgyny, high-fashion styling, fabulously affected "continental" speech, and outrageous yet virtuosic avant-garde performance were legible to only a few as examples of a nice Jamaican girl/boy gone global naughty. Club and house music also has always included not only disco, R & B, and gospel but also West African, Latin, and European electronic musics. Moreover, popular forms of Africentricity—another iteration of earlier pan-African movements—are also well represented in black lesbian and gay culture in the United States. Consider, for example, the names, visual imagery, and stated politics of classical-era organizations including Salsa Soul Sisters, which later became African Ancestral Lesbians United for Social Change, and ADODI (a group of same-sex loving men of African descent, founded in Philadelphia in 1986). Of course groups like Wazobia (organized by and for African gays and lesbians in New York) and Caribbean Pride came along in the late 1990s.

The beginning of Phillip Bryan Harper's *Black Queer Studies* essay thus seems an apt coda for that volume's engagement with the world outside the United States and for black queer studies itself. He begins the essay: "I don't travel much, but . . . lately I've been rethinking my position and pondering a little travel, which might be just the thing to ease my anxiety."[69] Harper notes in his essay that African American studies often reacts to black queer studies "with a nearly deafening official silence."[70] Today, with only a few examples of black queer "noise" reharmonizing storied black studies journals and graduate curricula that still echo with the same old voices, this is still too true. Thus metaphorical travel, that is, what Walcott has called "diaspora reading practices," may be precisely what is needed to ease black queer studies's angst.[71] When we engage black queers beyond our borders, we discover new vocabularies and find new conversation partners.

Gayatri Gopinath's theorization of queer diaspora, in her *Impossible*

Desires: Queer Diasporas and South Asian Public Cultures, provides a provocative arrow to follow toward extending the formulation of black/queer/diaspora—that is, what we might garner from these queer diaspora reading practices. She writes: "The concept of a queer diaspora enables a simultaneous critique of heterosexuality and the national form while exploding the binary between nation and diaspora, heterosexuality and homosexuality, origin and copy."[72] In his review of her *Impossible Desires* and Alexander's *Pedagogies of Crossing*, Eng writes that Gopinath "shifts consideration from dominant analyses of gender in transnational feminism by considering what is at stake in focusing critical attention on the category of transnational sexuality developed by a queer diasporic (and queer of color) critique of family, kinship, and nation," thus demonstrating the crucial need for a particularly queer critique.[73] The critical and methodological orientations of queer of color scholars extend the key theoretical contributions of black queer theory and have broadened black studies' understanding of racial formation by exposing mechanisms through which other racialized subalterns are manufactured. The best of this work takes seriously Third World or women of color feminist politics of, for example, Chandra Talpade Mohanty, Chrystos, Gloria Anzaldúa, Cherríe Moraga, Norma Alarcón, Chela Sandoval, and others who consistently made connections in their local scholarship, artistry, and activism, with state practices and sites within and beyond their own ethnic or racial borders. Major works in queer of color critique, such as Gopinath's as well as Muñoz's *Disidentifications*, Rodríguez's *Queer Latinidad*, Larry La Fountain—Stokes's *Queer Ricans: Cultures and Sexualities in the Diaspora*, Fung's "Looking for My Penis: The Eroticized Asian in Gay Video Porn," Eng's *Racial Castration: Managing Masculinity in Asian America*, as well as *Aberrations in Black* and *Impossible Desires*, which I have already cited, represent this tradition.[74] Moreover, apropos of the position of social science work in queer of color critique, Martin Manalansan's award-winning *Global Divas* uniquely uses ethnography to demonstrate the everyday on-the-ground theorizing of his mostly mobile Filipino male subjects, thereby providing one of the central models for queer anthropology.[75] Recently, Carlos Decena's *Tacit Subjects* has broken new ground in its deft rereading of queer and immigration studies, as well as its multilingual illustration of everyday theoretics.[76] Moreover, Urvashi Vaid's historical policy work in *Virtually Equal* and Kenji Yoshino's legal scholarhip in *Covering*, while not often cited as theoretical or germane to queer of color critique, provide unique insights unavailable in other work.[77]

Still, I worry about both the absence of an analysis of race and racism, and the elision or recasting of antiblack racism as a closed question (the reasoning often goes something like: *way back in the bad old days, there was antiblack racism; now this new thing has replaced it*) in some queer of color work.[78] Partly because of African, Caribbean, and Latin America studies' evident stubborn refusal to face race and antiblack racism, black identification has been posed as singularly African American. This not only effaces the transnational structures of antiblack racism but also elides the ways in which antiblack racism provides "new" vocabularies and models for already existing discrimination, xenophobia, and other racisms. The concept of ethnicity has a different historicity and does not do the same work as race. Where ethnicity is legible as dynamic, multiply constituted, and primed for cosmopolitan transformation—and therefore posed as *not race*— blackness is most often misapprehended as static and constructed only out of US political projects of racialization, which is erroneously posed as a polarity of black versus white and therefore less complex than other places around the globe.[79] While Ferguson's *Aberrations in Black* named the stream of work emerging from women of color feminisms "queer of color critique," his and Grace Kyungwon Hong's recent work incisively takes up this necessary work of "identify(ing) and invent(ing) analytics through which to compare racial formations . . . (rather than) . . . simply parallel instances of similarity."[80] Following the "usable tradition" of Third World and women of color feminism, their important intervention shows that "the stakes for identifying new comparative models are immensely high, for the changing configurations of power in the era after the decolonizing movements and new social movements of the mid-twentieth century demand that we understand how particular populations are rendered vulnerable to processes of death and devaluation over and against other populations, in ways that palimpsestically register older modalities of racialized death but also exceed them."[81]

We claim this current moment to move further toward *becoming fluent in each other's histories*, as Alexander has suggested, and becoming fluent in each other's (perhaps disparate or even contradictory) desires. We are certainly implicated politically in these histories and desires, and they are imprinted on us. After all, it is a queer kind of love that connects us across borders and waters and texts. Black/queer/diaspora constitutes a heterotopic love. By heterotopic love, I am certainly invoking Michel Foucault, and Sandoval, but also Ferguson and Hong's recent reformulation of queer of color relationality in women of color feminisms. Using the example of Moraga's preface to *This Bridge Called My Back*, they write:

> Instead of Foucault's heterotopic nowhere, which he places in opposition to the empirically fixed and fixing table, [women of color feminism] gives us the heterotopic somewhere . . . in which the objects of comparison [e.g.,

an upper-middle-class cisgendered male black American college professor; an undocumented queer Haitian artist working in the United States; a Botswanan lesbian scholar; "queer theorists" and "black diaspora theorists"] have an unstable interrelation to each other, because they have changing meanings depending on context. These objects are not merely incongruous, as in Foucault's analysis, and they are not merely uncategorizable under a uniform set of criteria. Their relationality is constantly shifting.[82]

Thus just as Ferguson and Hong find that "Moraga's 'unmolested' passage through the city, her 'protected' status, is complexly determined by, and determining of . . . surveillance and disciplining . . . as well as . . . brutal state repression," our love ethic here must insist that we be aware of and militate against the ways in which US black queer scholars may find ourselves perhaps similarly "unmolested"—or more realistically and to the point, molested in a different way—which allows for openings or impels coalitions.

This resonates with Walcott's claim that a "diaspora reading practice . . . can disrupt the centrality of nationalist discourses within the Black studies project and thereby also allow for an elaboration of a Black queer diaspora project," which lays crucial foundation for our work here apropos his contention that "the reconceptualizing of Black queer and Black diaspora produces both a Black queer diaspora and a new Black queer theory."[83]

The contributors to this special issue and to the larger project of black/queer/diaspora work have certainly taken up this challenge with aplomb. Still, I cannot deny that my aspiration toward a diverse "international" special issue with scholars from at least three continents failed.[84] I hear Walcott's reproof: "What is at stake here is the way in which some Black diaspora queers find African-American queers, yet the reverse always seems impossible," calling "the sexual/textual economy" by which some US black scholars have seemed unaware of or uninterested in engaging across borders "(an) unequal exchange."[85] However, this issue and the expanding project of black/queer/diaspora work is not a project of unrequited love. Black/queer/diaspora announces itself ready and willing to embrace and be embraced—to listen and to negotiate. The notion of ethics or even "good politics" is not strong enough to hold this. Perhaps love is. Still unfinished, our work consciously looks for and finds nonheteronormative people of Africa(n descent), within and outside the United States, as we also lay claim to our position in black studies, queer studies, and feminist studies, as *backbone rather than anomaly*.[86]

The Fabulous Essays

In this special issue we ask a "new" set of questions, conjuncturally related to perennial ones: Do African and African-descended sexual minorities and gender insurgents share common desires, or conditions, across borders and languages? What "erotic subjectivities" and insurgent black queer poetics obtain in sites scholars have previously ignored, or spaces that span across, through, and between? What political or affective strategies might be effective for one place or space but not for others? And, finally, what methodologies must we use to track all of this? By what means should we convey our analysis and reflection? Readers will find ample answers to these queries, and more provocative arrows toward spectral figures haunting these margins, in the essays that follow. In an effort to approximate more closely the conversations and diverse perspectives in which the working group and others are currently engaged, the editorial note "A Conversation 'Overflowing with Memory': On Omise'eke Natasha Tinsley's 'Water, Shoulders, Into the Black Pacific,'" follows this introduction. This not only prefaces Tinsley's piece but also endeavors to inspire or provoke conversations apropos of innovative methods and affective strategies.

Other contributors continue black queer and queer of color theory's dogged assertion of black queer agency and, especially, of an inner realm of individual consciousness and intersubjectivity, which some of us, inspired by Lorde ("uses of the erotic") and Alexander ("erotic autonomy"), have come to call "erotic subjectivity."[87] I am concerned with using the erotic as an embodied human resource, composed of our personal histories and (sexual, social) desires, toward deepening and enlivening individuals' experiences. In one aspect, as I have averred in ¡Venceremos?, this view of the erotic is hermeneutical. In Lorde's words, it is "a lens through which we scrutinize all aspects of our existence, forcing us to evaluate those aspects honestly in terms of their relative meaning within our lives."[88] Although deeply personal, the erotic is also intersubjective — "self-connection shared" — and therefore political. I employ erotic subjectivity as a way to pose the relationship between individual everyday acts of refusal and the intention to build political communities or foment movement. An ongoing process, erotic subjectivity may therefore be used strategically, or tactically. Out of this we may create a counterpublic in which new forms of affective and erotic relations, and rules of public and private engagement, not only inform all our choices, as Lorde suggests, but in fact condition new choices and new politics.

In this issue, Lyndon Gill crafts a sterling example of this theorizing, pushing it significantly forward. While the current trend in queer studies seems characterized by a turning away from sociality and politics, for black and other subjects of color, sociality in the form of love, friendship, and sexual relationships is an indispensable survival tool, which, as Gill's Trinbagonian respondents show, may also be the foundation for life-enhancing and life-saving interventions. The monstrous skeleton of putatively exceptional Caribbean homophobia haunts our perceptions of the region. These incomplete perceptions hide truths about the everyday effects of heterosexism and homophobia, and everyday resistance to it, both here and there. In his "Chatting Back an Epidemic: Caribbean Gay Men, HIV/AIDS, and the Uses of Erotic Subjectivity," Gill adds sinew, blood (indeed), and heart. Centering the islands of Trinidad and Tobago, he asserts that the organization Friends For Life—in its formation, the consciousness of its leadership, and in its most successful program, Community Chatroom—demonstrates the usefulness of erotic subjectivity for activism and community building.

Turning to the continent of Africa, Xavier Livermon contributes another example of erotic subjectivity—black queer action that forces recognition of the politics of culture. His essay "Queer(y)ing Freedom," clarifies what other scholars have claimed is a "paradox" of the representation of homosexuality in South Africa, as at once progressive, un-African, un-Christian, and dangerous. Livermon holds that this representation "rests on the racialization of the queer body as white and the sexualization of the black [citizen's] body as straight."[89] The essay then persuasively argues for an expanded understanding of "the political" that can hold the cultural and affectual. Its analysis of public and participatory gay and bisexual scandals moves us from the realm of the juridical, which dominates scholarly work and public imagination of sexuality in Africa, to the everyday public. Livermon argues that audacious acts in the public sphere garner a new visibility. This "cultural labor of black queerness," he offers, pushes toward freedom in ways the progressive constitution cannot. Here black queer persons deploy their complexly constructed identities for political ends that, without this theorization, observers might not readily recognize as politics.

If, as the Combahee River Collective statement argues, the conditions of our lives are "interlocking"—as well as dynamic, reiterative, related to global processes, and deeply felt, as many scholars have come to agree—standard academic practices simply will not do.[90] Moreover, this dynamism, recursivity, "globality," and affect must be reimagined and described with new vocabularies and fresh metaphors.

Generative and useful water metaphors have shaped black diaspora scholarship since Edward Wilmot Blyden and W. E. B. DuBois.[91] Of course Gilroy, Brand, and recently Tinsley have plumbed these depths. Yet in this special issue

Vanessa Agard-Jones shifts our metaphorical apparatus from water to sand "as a repository both of feeling and of experience, of affect and of history." In "What the Sands Remember," she offers an ecological narrative of *place and emplacement*. Looking up close—just behind a remote sand dune, or at a surfside fete in Martinique—we see local lesbians and gay men who may otherwise be obscured by the blur of distant, unengaged theorization, at the same time that her reading of a small moment in a nineteenth-century novel incisively speculates on black women's agency. The analytic articulation of imagination and observable facts, drawn from ethnography and history, include and go beyond the poetics of relation elaborated by the eminent Martinican literary theorist and writer Èdouard Glissant.

Drawing on what he calls "the queer ideas of Glissant," Walcott expounded a related insight into speculation and literary analysis at our 2009 symposium: what he has theorized as a *homopoetics* "that allows him to read across various spaces and texts and to make some truth claims."[92] Three contributions also serve as important examples of this, in very distinctive ways. First, there is Tinsley's extract from her prodigiously researched historical novel in progress, "Water, Shoulders, Into the Black Pacific"—an intimate look at a probable past of desire and longing among women of color in 1940s Northern California, constructed through marking historical moments, places, contexts, and events recorded in archives, but also carefully crafted through imagination. In Tinsley's gorgeous excerpt, we hear echoes of Saidiya Hartman's project to compose a methodology for memory and a writing form to tell stories that must, somehow, be told (or that cannot be told).[93] Since the imagination—fiction—is too important a structuring genre of black/queer/diaspora work to present this piece bound by "explanation" (which would make it another form), an editorial note prefaces the work, describing its scholarly provenance and intention through a conversation with members of the working group.

Like the personal essay and the poem—black queer genres, par excellence—the meditation is an aesthetic and political end in itself, not merely a means by which to "write up" research findings, or prove or explicate a point (although here, Ana-Maurine Lara makes her case with tremendous skill and verve). In "Of Unexplained Presences, Flying Ife Heads, Vampires, Sweat, Zombis, and Legbas: A Meditation on Black Queer Aesthetics," Lara is able to bring two events and a number of discourses into conversation, methodologically using "the metaphor of the *poto mitan* . . . to locate how my body connects two spaces." Metaphorically, the *poto mitan* is both the pillar around which everything revolves, like the vodou peristyle, and the body of the woman (researcher). The term *vodou* in the formulation she offers is already as deeply African as it is a New World invention, simultaneously incorporating European magic and indigenous American medicines, for example. "Vodoun aesthetics" therefore names not only the work of the *DASH* artists in Austin, Texas, and elsewhere, and the Grand Rue artists and participants in Haiti, but also the everyday arts and spiritual practices of black queer life.

Finally, as Matt Richardson asks, "What would it serve for Blacks to take the crisis imposed by colonialism and capture to (re)name and (re)invent the self?"[94] Through an analysis of the Scottish writer Jackie Kay's *Trumpet*, Richardson's "'My Father Didn't Have a Dick': Social Death and Jackie Kay's *Trumpet*" takes up Spillers's challenge to not futilely follow "the master's" definitions of gender down "the (hetero)patriarchal rabbit hole" toward queer versions of normativity but to gain "*insurgent* ground" by taking a stand outside the "traditional symbolics" of gender. Not only does Richardson's analysis of Kay's novel push us to consider how transgender experience centrally informs or talks back to cisgender black masculinity and Scottish identity, but his critical references also reflect a particularly black queer practice. Following Holland, he queers meanings of blackness as social death; argues with and alongside black nationalist critics; pushes Spillers's notions of flesh and patronymic representation forward; and, perhaps scandalously to some, does not rest this work of black queer theory on "queer theorists." Increasingly, as various interdisciplines and streams of work within and between them mature, scholars and artists refer to, claim, and build on genealogies that had been "submerged" (dismissed, or recast). In this issue, we insist on in-context conversation—that is, for example, the deployment of various black studies works or specific contexts lesser known in queer studies to discuss "LGBTQ topics" or to launch a queer argument. Mapping local and translocal genealogies, trajectories, and commitments of black [and] queer politics and expressive culture, these works therefore stand on the emerging edge where queer theory meets critical race theory, transnationalism, and black and Third World feminisms.

"What Is This Black?": Where in the World?

In these essays and in our work, black identity/identification is understood as hybrid, contingent, and relational. That is, *black* is a useful term for describing the historical, political, and affective ties of many individuals to one another, yet we do not attach mystical, transhistorical, or essential biological valence to this term. Witness how contributors to this special issue deploy blackness, depending on local histories and current exigencies as well as relationships to global racial formations and individual choice. Blackness is explicitly named in both Livermon's and Richardson's work, in the cases of South Africa and Scotland, respectively, which obviously have vastly different proportions of blacks relative to the national population and vastly different histories: violent and protracted struggle against racist state violence and symbolic violent erasure, respectively. Writing about Trinidad and Tobago, Gill deploys the term *Afro-Trinidadian* to describe the subjects on which his ethnographic practice is focused — noting that while not self-consciously marked as a space for African-descended or black Trinbagonians (in fact, in keeping with Caribbean race rhetorics, it is open and multicultural), the day-to-day of Friends For Life (the organization the essay focuses on), finds it largely practiced as Afro-Trinidadian space. Of course, Haiti seems to occupy the space of unambiguous blackness, despite a deep history of "mixing" there as well. Perhaps this is why Lara's "larger framework of . . . vodoun aesthetics" can hold so many blacknesses so elegantly — US middle class, Dominican, European, Whitney Museum exhibitor, self-taught sculptor, Jewish, et cetera. Still, during our symposium, Fatima El-Tayeb averred that the diminishing usefulness of the concepts of blackness and nation for her work in Germany, and the inspiration of queer of color critique, prompted her to develop the concept of Europeans of color as a way to capture more precisely the local political realities she seeks to understand. In Agard-Jones's essay, "ordinary (mostly black) Martinicans" share the space of this overseas department of France with *békés*, *métisses*, and *mulâtres*. One of the startling moments in her narrative is when one locality on the island campaigns to replace the French *tricolore* with *the red, the black, and the green*. It seems here that Martinicans' right to enjoy the benefits of their status as citizens of (an overseas department of) France does not preclude a claim to pan-African belonging.

We're Queer! We're Here! But Why? Whither "Radical"?

As Cohen notes, a truly radical or transformative politics has not resulted from queer theory thus far. In some cases, it has in fact "reinforced simple dichotomies between the heterosexual and everything queer."[95] The radical promise of the antecedents of black/queer/diaspora work is located in scholarship, art, and activism "shaped by the burden of persistent colonialism and the euphoric promise of nationalism and self-determination" (Alexander and Mohanty); by activist intellectuals who had analyzed the "interlocking" spheres of race, gender, sexuality, and class through the prism of antiviolence organizing (Combahee River Collective); who had, in nonacademic spheres and languages, poetically called for *Black men loving Black men* as a revolutionary statement of self- and community preservation (Beam, Marlon Riggs, and Hemphill); and moreover, have blocked the public arteries of London, Paris, Rome, Buenos Aires, and New York with their "dead," tracing bodies and leaving their haunting presence on the streets as a sharp indictment of the callous state (Queer Nation ACT UP). (How) then do we engage (or foment) radical or transformative politics at this particular stony, contradictory conjuncture?

To put a finer point on it, I want to ask what positions have fallen out of our intellectual frames in black studies, women's studies, pan-African studies, and queer studies. Does the absence of a revolutionary or radical (black) queer theory evidence that radicalism is in fact a "closed discourse"? Following Joy James's intervention "Radicalizing Black Feminism," I want to call attention to the existence of different impulses in the genealogies I have been tracing. James's unique critical intervention in black feminist theory, in which she explodes the myth that all black feminisms are, perforce, radical, constitutes a crucial caution for black queer studies, queer of color critique, and black/queer/diaspora to not pose our work as always already "radical" or inherently progressive.[96] Perhaps part of black/queer/diaspora work is to revive, even now and especially when it is not fashionable, (at least) the query, whither "liberation"? Otherwise, we might do well to admit that ours is a bourgeois exercise and desist our popularist reimagination of "home," which without some real connection to those embattled by daily insults of being poor, uneducated, perhaps undocumented, for example, *and* black and queer, amounts to voyeurism or worse. Can a *study* be radical, given what we have learned about the need to decolonize the epistemological lenses through which we define and construct research?[97] What about our pedagogies: what are the best ways to facilitate critical thinking and more ethical, beautiful, and joyful futures for our students (and children, lovers, and friends, wherever we find them)? In any case, the apparent abandonment of these questions and potential accountabilities in some quarters indicates a precipitous shift rightward (toward conservatism) that is neither especially queer nor theoretical, nor studious.

Cohen calls for "a politics where the non-normative and marginal positions of punks, bulldaggers, and welfare queens" is the basis for progressive transformational coalitional work and a concomitant new research agenda for black studies, in which the central theoretic sees "deviance as resistance."[98] Perhaps the transformative politics we have been waiting for will emerge through following and participating in actual political transformations on the ground. A significant part of my own current intellectual preoccupation is observing what this might mean for black queer diaspora research agendas. As one example, the concept of sexual-orientation inclusion advocacy, as practiced in Guyana, and Trinidad and Tobago, may provide fertile ground. This work by and on behalf of vulnerable populations of LGBT persons to be free from violence, harassment, and discrimination is far from a single-minded focus on "sexual rights," as it extends participation and protection for minorities and vulnerable persons of all kinds in these self-consciously multicultural postcolonial countries. Thus these advocates' queer work, which seeks to redeem anticolonial struggle, to borrow the title of a recent Arcus Foundation report that surveyed the field, is at once about "saving lives, promoting democracy, alleviating poverty, and fighting AIDS."[99]

In Conclusion

The work of the Black/Queer/Diaspora Work(ing) Group is to consider the states of diasporic black queer projects, in the context of various shifts in Empire(s) and affiliations. Stretching toward a loving global embrace, and focused on expanding capacity to do this work, our nascent offering of this special issue of *GLQ* is a small reflection (or refraction?) of this ambition. The contributions that follow form lines in the architecture of black/queer/diaspora work, which we draw together. These brilliant authors provide models toward thinking how to best represent our research subjects, and our selves, when our eyes/hands/ears must necessarily "settle" on a surface (to write, sing, act, do) but must also mine multidimensions, experiences, and shores. Agard-Jones suggests a new metaphor in this issue — sand. How many dunes to cross, as our bodies ache with desire? How many friends can we wrap ourselves around as we "chat back" dying and death in circles of belonging and care, such as those Gill offers us? The infectious, unrelenting beat of *kwaito* in a South African township provides the soundtrack for scandalous performances of black queerness on the radio — new subjectivities unfolding on the airwaves and in the streets of Jo'burg in Livermon's account. Across the continent and overseas to Scotland, brass horns blare. Richardson listens in on a group of black men in a coastal town, playing their black masculinity loudly — improvising on a tired old theme to deafen cries of their exclusion. Now, back in time once more, and across another ocean, at a western edge of the North American continent, Tinsley invents black and other women of color who wield not only salty glances at each other but also rivet guns vibrating with the power to create new worlds. Through it all the Ife head flies on, simultaneously in Nigeria, Haiti, Dominican Republic, Texas, Miami, and all the places we visit here — appearing in discarded plastics, sequins, and rusted soda caps: dis/figured and refigured through *refuse* — storytelling and divining, all at once. Here the threads of our mourning clothes are laid down/bare.

Notes

I must thank each of the brilliant intellectual-artist-activists who gathered for the first event (Natalie Bennett, Steven G. Fullwood, Lyndon Gill, Rosamond S. King, Ana-Maurine Lara, Xavier Livermon, Graeme Reid, Matt Richardson, Colin Robinson, Omise'eke Natasha Tinsley, Rinaldo Walcott, and Michelle Wright); our new addition, Vanessa Agard-Jones; and those who joined us later, virtually and in spirit, making this issue so rich and significant. The peer-review process was a charmed exercise in finding the sharpest, most appropriate interlocutors, who turned out to be the most generous, too (I wish that I could print your names, to more openly acknowledge your work: thank you). My sincere and profound thanks for interventions on an early draft go to Ann Cvetkovich.Crucial commentary by Omise'eke Natasha Tinsley and Kamari Clarke pushed me significantly further. Still, the privilege of claiming the errors and foibles here belongs to me exclusively. In addition, I want to express my gratitude to George Chauncey, the Yale Program in Transgender, Bisexual, Lesbian, Gay Studies; Kamari Clarke, the Yale Center for Transnational Cultural Analysis; the Yale University Provost's Office; and Yale University Departments of African American Studies and Anthropology, for their support of the Black/Queer/Diaspora Work(ing) Group.

1. See Stuart Hall, "What Is This Black in 'Black Popular Culture?,'" in *Black Popular Culture*, ed. Gina Dent and Michele Wallace (New York: Dia Center for the Arts, 1992), 21–33. I was reminded that Robert Reid-Pharr begins his "Queer Sweetback" chapter with this quote from Hall, in a similar context at the end of my editing process, while rechecking the source of my citation of Reid-Pharr's *Once You Go Black: Choice, Desire, and the Black American Intellectual* (New York: New York University Press, 2007).
2. While "Plum Nelly" was published by *Callaloo* in anticipation of the conference and distributed to conference attendees, *Black Queer Studies* mostly represents work presented at the conference. "Plum Nelly" includes creative work, critical essays, reviews, and an annotated bibliography of black queer studies: Nicholas Boggs, "Queer Black Studies: An Annotated Bibliography, 1994–1999," *Callaloo* 23, no. 1 (2000): 479–94.
3. Roderick A. Ferguson, *Aberration in Black: Toward a Queer of Color Critique* (Minneapolis, University of Minnesota Press, 2004).
4. Michelle M. Wright and Antje Schuhmann, *Blackness and Sexualities* (Berlin: Lit, 2007).
5. See works cited above, and especially the ambitious collection by Juan Battle and Sandra Barnes, *Black Sexualities: Probing Powers, Passions, Practices, and Policies* (New Brunswick, NJ: Rutgers University Press, 2010). This project heralds a more comprehensive black sexuality studies by including a number of themes and balancing the disciplinary divide by highlighting social science work. Among a number of

important essays, Matt Richardson and Enoch Page's "On the Fear of Small Numbers," in Battle and Barnes, *Black Sexualities*, historically breaks silence about the black transgender experience in the United States. This book was organized through a Ford Foundation–funded project headed by Battle and Marysol Asencio to assess the state of the fields of black and Latina/o sexualities, respectively.

6. While I hesitate to use the word *reciprocal*, because of the unevenness, there seems to be a resistance to taking up important radical theorists of the black world in much black/queer/diaspora work. For example, while Frantz Fanon has been mined by feminist and queer scholars, what might a political economy of black queer diaspora, taking up Walter Rodney, look like? Or a reimagining of Abdias Nascimiento on race making and black erasure; or Claudia Jones vis-à-vis the circulation of texts and radical politics? See Walter Rodney, A. M. Babu, and Vincent Harding, *How Europe Underdeveloped Africa* (Washington, DC: Howard University Press, 1981); Abdias do Nascimiento, *Brazil, Mixture or Massacre? Essays in the Genocide of Black People* (Dover, MA: Majority Press, 1989; and Carole Boyce Davies, *Left of Karl Marx: The Political Life of Black Communist Claudia Jones* (Durham, NC: Duke University Press, 2007).Our citation politics have been selective and seem to avoid the (lesser-known?) more radical exponents of African diaspora theory.

7. The Caribbean, a particularly vigorous site for black/queer/diaspora work, has also been refocused in Faith Smith's new collection, *Sex and the Citizen: Interrogating the Caribbean* (Charlottesville, VA: University of Virginia Press, 2011). Unfortunately, this work is so new that I did not have time to fully consider it for this analysis. Omise'eke Natasha Tinsley, "Black Atlantic, Queer Atlantic: Queer Imaginings of the Middle Passage," *GLQ* 14, no. 2–3 (2008): 191–215; Paul Gilroy, *The Black Atlantic: Modernity and Double Consciousness* (Cambridge: Harvard University Press, 1993); Antonio Benítez Royo, *The Repeating Island: The Caribbean and the Postmodern Perspective* (Durham, NC: Duke University Press, 1992); Judith Butler, *Gender Trouble: Feminism and the Subversion of Identity* (New York: Routledge, 1990).

8. José Esteban Muñoz, *Cruising Utopia: The Then and There of Queer Futurity* (New York: New York University Press, 2009).

9. Hortense J. Spillers, *Black, White, and In Color: Essays on American Literature and Culture* (Chicago: University of Chicago Press, 2003), 168.

10. Moreover, scholars located in such professional arenas as education, public health, and law have been producing important work that can offer effective strategies. See especially Lance T. McCready, *Making Space for Diverse Masculinities: Difference, Intersectionality, and Engagement in an Urban High School* (New York: Peter Lang, 2010).

11. The newest works to join these include Carlos Ulisses Decena's marvelous *Tacit Subjects: Belonging and Same-Sex Desire among Dominican Immigrant Men* (Durham, NC: Duke University Press, 2001), Mignon Moore's sociological study *Invisible Fami-*

lies: Gay Identities, Relationships, and Motherhood among Black and Latino *Women* (Berkeley: University of California Press, 2011); and my own critical ethnography *¡Venceremos? The Erotics of Black Self-Making in Cuba* (Durham, NC: Duke University Press, 2011). Juan Battle, *Say It Loud, I'm Black and I'm Proud: Black Pride Survey 2000* (New York: Policy Institute of the National Gay and Lesbian Task Force, 2002); Wesley E. A. Crichlow, *Buller Men and Batty Bwoys: Hidden Men in Toronto and Halifax Black Communities* (Toronto: University of Toronto Press, 2004); Gloria Wekker, *The Politics of Passion: Women's Sexual Culture in the Afro-Surinamese Diaspora* (New York: Columbia University Press, 2006); David A. B. Murray, *Opacity: Gender, Sexuality, Rade, and the "Problem" of Identity in Martinique* (New York: Lang, 2002); Juan Battle, Social Justice Sexuality Initiative, 2010, socialjusticesexuality.com/about/.

12. Please see Bryant Keith Alexander, "Reflections, Riffs, and Remembrances: The Black Queer Studies in the Millennium Conference," *Callaloo* 23, no. 4 (2000): 1285–305; Jennifer DeVere Brody, "Theory in Motion: A Review of the Black Queer Studies in the Millennium Conference," *Callaloo* 23, no. 4 (2000): 1274–77; and Vincent Woodard, "Just as Quare as They Want to Be: A Review of the Black Queer Studies in the Millennium Conference," *Callaloo* 23, no. 4 (2000): 1278–84.

13. See Shari Frilot, *Black Nations/Queer Nations?* (Third World Newsreel, 1995). I must note the Black Nations/Queer Nations workshop session that I offered as a cofounder of the Aya Institute, "Building Community from the Inside Out." Thematically, it focused on starting with personal emotional and spiritual development as a first step toward community building, in keeping with Aya's work of weekly drop-in groups, board development, consultation, and therapeutic interventions for community-based organizations.

14. See especially Barbara Smith, Audre Lorde, and Joseph Beam. Much primary material, including personal papers and ephemera, can be found at the Black Gay and Lesbian Archive of the Schomburg Center for the Study of Black Culture in New York City.

15. See Black Gay Research Group, law.wustl.edu/centeris/pages.aspx?id=7848 and www.thebgrg.org/welcome-to-BGRG.html, respectively (accessed February 2011). "[The] Caribbean Region of the IRN is a clearinghouse . . . of information, research, and resources, to connect individuals from around the region and the world. . . . while the larger IRN is focused on academic scholarship, the Caribbean IRN promotes activism and creative work, as well as different kinds of engaged scholarship which seek to question, provoke and illuminate various ways of thinking around sexual minorities" (www.irnweb.org/en/about/region/caribbean). Herukhuti, *Conjuring Black Funk: Notes on Culture, Sexuality, and Spirituality* (New York: Vintage Entity, 2007).

16. Originally conceived of as a panel on comparative sexual rights, erotic autonomy, and "Archives and Politics 'For My Own Protection,'" my intention was to include in this issue a roundtable discussion featuring a few individuals whom I admire for the path-

breaking work they are doing to document/archive and improve black queer life and culture in a number of sites around the world (Steven G. Fullwood, Black Gay & Lesbian Archive, "Fire & Ink"; Zethu Matebani Forum for the Empowerment of Women; Colin Robinson, Coalition Advocating Inclusion of Sexual Orientation; Selly Thiam, None on Record; Ajamu X, Sharing Tongues; Rukus!) For a variety of reasons, this did not work out. These projects that propose to "save" culture, share tongues, and put on record provide a very differently configured and no less "political" politics, which the working group is committed to engaging. One of our immediate forthcoming projects, therefore, will be to reconvene, revise, and publish this important conversation.

17. My formulation owes a debt to the anthropologists Marshall Sahlins and Sherry B. Ortner as well as to Stuart Hall (previously cited). For Sahlins, the "structures of conjuncture" is the recursive engine of history. In structures of the conjuncture, interpellations or received meanings collide with audacious "acting out" impelled by the subjects' own will (which is not necessarily against or strategically "resistant" to those discourses, laws, traditions, etc.), creating new discourses and practices. Ortner has marked this as a key node of practice (which my brand of black queer ethnography follows). Marshall David Sahlins, *Historical Metaphors and Mythical Realities: Structure in the Early History of the Sandwich Island Kingdom* (Ann Arbor: University of Michigan Press, 1981); Sherry B. Ortner, *Making Gender: The Politics and Erotics of Culture* (Boston: Beacon, 1996).

18. Antonio Gramsci and Joseph A. Buttigieg. *Prison Notebooks* (New York: Columbia University Press, 1992), quoted in James Clifford, "Taking Identity Politics Seriously: The Contradictory, Stony Ground," in Stuart Hall, Paul Gilroy, Lawrence Grossberg, and Angela McRobbie, *Without Guarantees: In Honor of Stuart Hall* (London: Verso, 2000), 94.

19. From Audre Lorde, "The Transformation of Silence into Language and Action," in *Sister Outsider: Essays and Speeches* (San Francisco: Crossing Press, 1980), 42.

20. Quoted in Woodard, "Just as Quare."

21. Jasbir Puar, "Queer Times, Queer Assemblages," *Social Text*, nos. 84–85 (2005): 121.

22. Jacqueline Nassy Brown, *Dropping Anchor, Setting Sail: Geographies of Race in Black Liverpool* (Princeton: Princeton University Press, 2005).

23. Kamari Maxine Clarke and Deborah A. Thomas. *Globalization and Race: Transformations in the Cultural Production of Blackness* (Durham, NC: Duke University Press, 2006).

24. See, for example, *Stuart Hall: Critical Dialogues in Cultural Studies*, edited by David Morley and Kuan-Hsing Chen (London Routeledge, 1996); Paul Gilroy, "It Ain't Where You're From, It's Where You're At," *Third Text* 5, no. 13 (1991): 3–16; Paul Gilroy, *The Black Atlantic: Modernity and Double Consciousness* (Cambridge: Harvard University Press, 1993); Kobena Mercer, *Welcome to the Jungle: New Positions in Black Cultural Studies* (New York: Routledge, 1994); Hazel V. Carby, *Reconstruct-*

ing *Womanhood: The Emergence of the Afro-American Woman Novelist* (New York: Oxford University Press, 1987); Carby, *Cultures in Babylon: Black Britain and African America* (London: Verso, 1999). Ignoring or effacing this not only elides the realities of transnational black life but also attempts to erase a formidable body of creative literature that documents and imagines this. See, for example, Paule Marshall, *Brown Girl, Brownstones* (Old Westbury, NY: Feminist Press, 1981); Ana-Maurine Lara, *Erzulie's Skirt* (Washington, DC: RedBone, 2006); Dionne Brand, *At the Full and Change of the Moon: A Novel* (New York: Grove, 1999); and Thomas Glave, *The Torturer's Wife* (San Francisco: City Lights, 2008).

25. "Stroke" is another name — more common in British English usage — for what is often called a "(forward) slash" in the United States.

26. In feminism and queer theory, Sara Ahmed, *The Cultural Politics of Emotion* (New York: Routledge, 2004); Heather Love, *Feeling Backward: Loss and the Politics of Queer History* (Cambridge: Harvard University Press, 2007); Lauren Berlant, *Intimacy* (Chicago: University of Chicago Press, 2000), and Ann Cvetkovich, *An Archive of Feelings: Trauma, Sexuality, and Lesbian Public Culture* (Durham, NC: Duke University Press, 2003), among others, have produced beautiful and usable examples of this. We are also profoundly shaped and inspired — from the time we were children and young adults — by the prose and poetry of writers like Zora Neale Hurston, James Baldwin, Gwendolyn Brooks, Chinua Achebe, Derek Walcott, Dionne Brand, Toni Morrison, and others, who are of course masters of affective and performative writing. For many of us, therefore, black/queer/diaspora is as much about the writing — that is, not "writing up" data, reporting, or mimicking the prose style of French theory but attempting to convey feeling as supplement or complement to information — as (and articulated to) theory and methodology.

27. Critique need not be mean-spirited or biting to be incisive. Moreover, we find that reenacting the Battle Royal scene in Ralph Ellison's *Invisible Man*, where a group of young black men literally fight for the chance to win a college scholarship — until only one is left standing — while white men, drinking beer and slapping each other on the back, cheer, is no way to work an intellectual project. Ralph Ellison, *Invisible Man* (New York: Vintage, 1995), 17–21.

28. From Audre Lorde, "A Litany for Survival," in *The Black Unicorn* (New York: Norton, 1978), 31–32.

29. Tinsley offered this way of refocusing my attention to love, after reading an early draft of this introduction. I am very grateful for her encouragement to boldly proclaim love.

30. See Chela Sandoval, *Methodology of the Oppressed* (Minneapolis: University of Minnesota Press, 2000), 146.

31. One must not see this collection as a static "organization" or even a "collective" or formal group. We are cotravelers looking for kin. One key aspect of this project is to foster productive and enduring working relationships among the participants. We look

forward to a highly collaborative process and adherence to principles of peer mentorship and training of graduate and undergraduate students. Toward that end, advanced graduate students participate with junior, newly tenured, and senior faculty members. As the project progresses, we look forward to hosting a transnational consortium of scholars, artists, and activists, housed in part at Yale.

32. This is not to suggest that "male autogenesis" could not be one of many options in a queer future, but to acknowledge the effects this has had to date on scholarship and politics — including the project of silencing other (feminized) voices. For incisive and searing readings of this in black studies, see Hazel Carby, *Race Men* (Cambridge: Harvard University Press, 1998); and Joy James, *Transcending the Talented Tenth: Black Leaders and American Intellectuals* (New York: Routledge, 1997).

33. Hortense J. Spillers, "All the Things You Could Be by Now, If Sigmund Freud's Wife Was Your Mother: Psychoanalysis and Race," in *Black, White, and in Color: Essays on American Literature and Culture* (Chicago: University of Chicago Press, 2003). For me, this is also intimately related to Essex Hemphill's calling out of the psychoanalytic strand of Afrocentric thought that reproduces Eurocentric heterosexism: Hemphill, "If Freud Had Been a Neurotic Colored Woman: Reading Dr. Frances Cress Welsing," in *Ceremonies: Prose and Poetry* (San Francisco: Cleis Press, 1992). Like Nina Simone said of her composition "Mississippi Goddamn!": "This song is a show tune, but the show has not been written for it yet." That is, "All the things" is aspirational (we "could be") and urgently necessary ("now"), at once. I must thank Lisa Kahaleole Hall. After an especially frustrating queer studies symposium on transnationalism, in which people of color remained unthought of until scholars of color arrived in the room, she and I riffed, waxed, and played on her suggestion that Michel Foucault is not, in fact "the daddy" of all queer critique. Of course, there are a number of permutations of this genealogical puzzle.

34. Cathy J. Cohen, "Punks, Bulldaggers, and Welfare Queens: The Radical Potential of Queer Politics?," *GLQ* 3 (1997): 437–65. See also Cathy J. Cohen, *The Boundaries of Blackness: AIDS and the Breakdown of Black Politics* (Chicago: University of Chicago Press, 1999)

35. Cathy J. Cohen, "Deviance as Resistance: A New Research Agenda for the Study of Black Politics," *Du Bois Review* 1 (2004): 27–45.

36. M. Jacqui Alexander, "Not Just (Any)Body Can Be a Citizen: The Politics of Law, Sexuality, and Postcoloniality in Trinidad and Tobago and the Bahamas," *Feminist Review* 48 (1994): 5–23. See also Alexander, "Erotic Autonomy as a Politics of Decolonization: An Anatomy of Feminist and State Practice in the Bahamas Tourist Economy," in *Feminist Genealogies, Colonial Legacies, Democratic Futures*, ed. M. Jacqui Alexander and Chandra Talpade Mohanty (New York: Routledge, 1997), 63–100.

37. See Alexander, "Not Just (Any)Body," 5.

38. See, for example, Fredric Jameson, *Postmodernism, or, The Cultural Logic of Late Capitalism* (Durham, NC: Duke University Press, 1991).

39. Jafari Allen, "Looking Black at Revolutionary Cuba," *Latin American Perspectives* 36, no. 1 (2009): 53–62; Allen, *¡Venceremos?*

40. This formulization is inspired by James C. Scott's work. See Scott, *Seeing Like a State: How Certain Schemes to Improve the Human Condition Have Failed* (New Haven: Yale University Press, 1998).

41. This is not surprising when one follows the money. It simultaneously flowed from George W. Bush–era "faith based" neoliberal funding initiatives and organizations like Focus on the Family to black "megachurches" like that of Eddie Long's New Birth Missionary Baptist Church in Atlanta; to abstinence-only provisos in foreign aid to do HIV/AIDS work in various places in the world; and from fringe evangelical groups like that of "ex-gay" Pastor Phillip Lee from the US-based "His Way Out" ministry, which do homosexual "reparative therapy" in the United States, Africa, and Caribbean. See, for one small example, IGLHRC's "Uganda: The US Religious Right Exports Homophobia to Africa": www.iglhrc.org/cgibin/iowa/article/pressroom/pressrelease/868.html; and "Ugandans Oppose US Christian Right Interference in Africa's Sexual Politics," Public Eye, www.publiceye.org/christian_right/exporting.html (accessed May 30, 2011).

42. Jennifer Williams offered an incisive reading of this in her paper "The Audacity of 'Quare': The Practice and Politics of Black Queer Shamelessness" (presented at the States of Black Desire Conference, Paris, France, April 2011), which inspired my use of the concept of audacity.

43. M. Jacqui Alexander, "Danger and Desire: Crossings Are Never Undertaken All at Once or Once and for All," *Small Axe* 24 (2007): 154–66.

44. See E. Darick Johnson and Mae Henderson, *Black Queer Stories: A Cultural Anthology* (Durham, NC: Duke University Press, 2005).

45. Muñoz, *Cruising Utopia*), 1.

46. And what is it about race that both makes it so difficult to explicitly state this truth and compels me to explicitly state it, even at the risk of the usual "reverse racist" balderdash so often leveled against black and other people of color who call out mundane, routine features of our racialized lives?

47. Among these, see especially Juana María Rodríguez, "Queer Sociality and Other Sexual Fantasies," *GLQ* 17 (2011): 331–48; Jafari Sinclaire Allen, "For 'the Children' Dancing the Beloved Community," *Souls* 11, no. 3 (2009): 311–26; and the incisive and necessary critique of a person not of color on a closely related theme: Judith Halberstam, "Shame and White Gay Masculinity," *Social Text*, nos. 84–85 (2005): 219–33.

48. Cymene Howe, "Undressing the Universal Queer Subject: Nicaraguan Activism and Transnational Identity," *City and Society* 14, no. 2 (2002): 237–79.

49. See, for example, Combahee River Collective, *The Combahee River Collective Statement* (Albany, NY: Kitchen Table, 1986); Hortense J. Spillers, *Black, White, and in Color*; Joy James and T. Denean Sharpley-Whiting, eds, *The Black Feminist Reader* (New York: Wiley-Blackwell, 2000); Toni Cade Bambara, *The Black Woman: An Anthology* (New York: New American Library, 1970); and Patricia Hill Collins, *Black Feminist Thought: Knowledge, Consciousness, and the Politics of Empowerment* (New York, Routledge, 2000).

50. More than a few of the members of the working group have experienced editors, senior colleagues, peer reviewers, and others who espouse these views, implicitly and explicitly. This certainly reveals their ignorance of this important work, but may also expose an unreconstructed racism and/or misogyny.

51. Roderick A. Ferguson, *Aberrations in Black: Toward a Queer of Color Critique* (Minneapolis: University of Minnesota Press, 2004), 110.

52. See Cheryl Clarke, "The Failure to Transform: Homophobia in the Black Community," in *Home Girls: A Black Feminist Anthology*, ed. Barbara Smith (New Brunswick, NJ: Rutgers University Press, 2000): 197–208; and Ron Simmons, "Some Thoughts on the Challenges Facing Black Gay Intellectuals," in *Brother to Brother: New Writing by Black Gay Men*, ed. Essex Hemphill (Washington, DC: Redbone, 2007).

53. Joseph Beam, "Brother to Brother: Words from the Heart," in *In the Life*, ed. Joseph Beam (Freedom, CA: Crossing Press, 1984): 230–42.

54. Audre Lorde, "School Note," in *Black Unicorn*, 55.

55. Hemphill, introduction to *Brother to Brother*, xliii.

56. Johnson and Henderson, *Black Queer Studies*, 6.

57. Sharon Holland, foreword to Johnson and Henderson, *Black Queer Studies*, ix.

58. Sharon Holland, "Foreword: Home Is a Four-Letter Word" in *Black Queer Studies*, ix–xii.

59. "Quare" of course refers to Johnson's important intervention in black queer studies, "'Quare' Studies, or (Almost) Everything I Know about Queer Studies I Learned from My Grandmother," *Text and Performance Quarterly* 21 (2001): 1–25.

60. Holland, foreword, x. The oeuvre of Sharon Bridgforth and Marvin K. White, two of the most important contemporary black lesbian and gay writers, both continue in this tradition of parsing "home" constituted within collapsed time in their poetry, performance, and prose. This is powerfully expressed in White's newest work, *Our Name Be Witness* (Washington, DC: Redbone 2011) and Bridgforth's performance novel *Love Conjure/Blues* (Washington, DC: Redbone 2004).

61. See David L. Eng, "Queering the Black Atlantic, Queering the Brown Atlantic," *GLQ* 17 (2010): 203.

62. Rinaldo Walcott, "Outside in Black Studies: Memory from a Queer Place in Diaspora," in Johnson and Henderson, *Black Queer Studies*, 90–106.

63. Thomas Glave, *The Caribbean: A Gathering a Lesbian and Gay Writing from the Antilles* (Durham, NC: Duke University Press, 2008).

64. See, for example, Diane Brand, *In Another Place, Not Here* (New York: Grove Press, 1997).

65. Sylvia Tamale, *African Sexualities: A Reader* (Oxford, UK: Pambazuko Press, 2011); Mark Epprecht, *Heterosexual Africa? The History of an Idea from the Age of Exploitation to the Age of AIDS* (Athens: Ohio University Press, 2008); Neville Wallace Hoad, *African Intimacies: Race, Homosexuality, and Globalization* (Minneapolis: University of Minnesota Press, 2007); Neville Wallace Hoad, Karen Martin, and Gracie Reid, *Sex and Politics in South Africa* (Cape Town: Double Storey, 2005).

66. In her 2006 feature film, *Rag/Tag*, for example, the Nigerian/British filmmaker Adaora Nwandu masterfully tells a black gay love story, suffused with tensions between African and Caribbean people, middle class and poor, and between England and Nigeria as simultaneous homeplaces. The British director Ricki Beadle-Blair is also remarkable in terms of popular gay- and lesbian-themed theatrical productions portraying black queer protagonists: he went from his irreverent Channel 4 television program *Metrosexuality*, which portrayed a multiracial, multiethnic queer black British family of choice, to direct several episodes of the Logo cable network's Noah's Arc and the feature film sequel, as well as other projects including stage productions of *The Mangina Chronicles*.

67. Robert Reid-Pharr, *Black Gay Man: Essays* (New York: New York University Press, 2001).

68. I am using the term *classical era* to stand in for a more precise way to mark the longue durée of the 1980s: the moment in which conjunctures of black power, women's liberation and gay liberation, AIDS, Ronald Reagan and Margaret Thatcher, structural adjustment, and urban decay, for example, set the conditions for the emergence of black lesbian and gay cultural expression in sites worldwide.

69. Phillip Brian Harper, "The Evidence of Felt Intuition" in Johnson and Henderson, *Black Queer Studies*, 106, 118.

70. Harper, "The Evidence of Felt Intuition," 113.

71. Rinaldo Walcott, "Somewhere Out There: The New Black Queer Theory," in *Blackness and Sexualities*, ed. Michelle M. Wright and Antje Schuhmann (Berlin: Lit Verlag, 2007), 29–40.

72. Gayatri Gopinath, *Impossible Desires: Queer Diasporas and South Asian Public Cultures* (Durham, NC: Duke University Press, 2005), 11.

73. David L. Eng, "Queering the Black Atlantic," 11.

74. José Esteban Muñoz, *Disidentifications: Queers of Color and the Performance of Politics* (Minneapolis: University of Minnesota Press, 1999); Juana María Rodríguez, *Queer Latinidad: Identity Practices, Discursive Spaces* (New York: New York University Press, 2003); Lawrence M. La Fountain–Stokes, *Queer Ricans: Cultures and Sexualities in the Diaspora* (Minneapolis: Uniersity of Minnesota Press, 2009); Richard 999 Fung, "Looking for My Penis: The Eroticized Asian in Gay Video Porn," in David L. Eng and Alice Y. Hom, *Q&A: Queer in Asian America* (Philadelphia: Tem-

ple University Press, 1998): David L. Eng, *Racial Castration: Managing Masculinity in Asian America* (Durham, NC: Duke University Press, 2001).

75. Martin F. Manalansan, *Global Divas: Filipino Gay Men in the Diaspora* (Durham, NC: Duke University Press, 2003).
76. Decena, *Tacit Subjects*.
77. Urvashi Vaid, *Virtual Equality: The Mainstreaming of Gay and Lesbian Liberation* (New York: Anchor, 1995); Kenji Yoshino, *Covering: The Hidden Assault on Our Civil Rights* (New York: Random House, 2006).
78. I do not wish to overstate this. African Americanist scholarship has long contributed to this by jealously policing the boundaries of black studies against national, gender, sexual, and language difference, if not the boundaries of black identification itself. But at the same time, too often African Americanists are left to do the "dirty work" of calling out racism—which carries a heavy personal and political burden and vulnerability.
79. To be certain, US racial formation is particular, and the role that the nation-state plays on the international stage is unique. Still, it is not historically "exceptional" with respect to its transformation in the institution of transatlantic chattel slavery, which can be seen throughout the Americas, for example.
80. Roderick Ferguson and Grace Kyungwon Hong, *Strange Affinities: The Gender and Sexual Politics of Comparative Racialization* (Durham, NC: Duke University Press, 2011), 1.
81. Ferguson and Hong, *Strange Affinities*, 1.
82. Ferguson and Hong, *Strange Affinities*, 13.
83. Walcott, "Somewhere Out There," 32,
84. Despite our best efforts, logistics, language, limited networks, and disparate measures of "quality" and "appropriateness" across different types of borders, as well as limitations of space and time (of would-be participants and of this publication), all proved formidable. While the contributors are in fact diverse by dint of place of birth, ethnicity, national heritage, degrees of identification with black hybridity and "mixedness," gender expression, sex, religion and spiritual expression, and other measures; each of them, like me, has been trained and/or currently works in the "elite academy" of the United States. Most of the articles were researched in anglophone contexts.
85. Walcott, "Somewhere Out There," 33.
86. Holland, foreword, xii; italics are mine.
87. I have written about this elsewhere. See "One Way or Another: Erotic Subjectivity in Cuba" (forthcoming) and *¡Venceremos?* While "the erotic" has been theorized by several foundational thinkers, its political and intellectual genealogies vary. The important collection by Don Kulick and Margaret Willson, *Taboo: Sweet Identity and Erotic Subjectivity in Anthropological Fieldwork* (New York: Routledge, 1995), enlarged our understanding of sexuality and desire in the fieldwork encounter. However, my formulation of erotic subjectivity includes and goes well beyond associations with sexual

identity, including Kulick's use of the term to refer to "sexual life." Erotic subjectivities are not only realized by confrontations with extrinsic power or structures; more pointedly, these practices are made through, and form one part of a complex process constituted by, embodied experiences, which include gender, race and color, and nationality.

88. Audre Lorde, "Uses of the Erotic, " in *Sister Outsider: Essays and Speeches* (Freedom, CA: 1984), 57.
89. The brackets underscore the particularities of black citizenship that Livermon draws out in his essay, which make South Africa a unique case.
90. Combahee River Collective, *Combahee River Collective Statement*.
91. See, for example, Edward Wilmot Blyden and Ralph Lynch Hollis, *Black Spokesman: Selected Published Writings of Edward Wilmot Blyden* (New York: Humanities, 1971); and W. E. B. DuBois, *The World and Africa: An Inquiry into the Part Which Africa Has Played in World History* (New York: International Publishers, 1965).
92. Rinaldo Walcott, "Queer Returns: Human Rights, the Anglo Caribbean, and Diaspora Politics," *Caribbean Review of Gender Studies* 3 (2009): 1–19, 4, sta.uwi.edu/crgs/november2009/journals/Walcott.pdf (accessed January 23, 2010).
93. Saidiya Hartman, *Scenes of Subjection: Terror, Slavery, and Self-Making in Nineteenth-Century America* (New York: Oxford University Press, 1997); Hartman, "Venus in Two Acts," *Small Axe* 26, no. 3 (2008): 1–14. Frederick Douglass's *Narrative of the Life of Frederick Douglass, an American Slave* (Boston: St. Martin's, 1993), and Toni Morrison's *Beloved* (New York: Knopf, 1987) ("This is not a story to pass on") come to mind as important mediations on this methodological conundrum.
94. Personal communication with the author.
95. Cohen, "Punks, Bulldaggers, and Welfare Queens," 22.
96. Joy James, "Radicalizing Feminisms," in *The Black Feminist Reader*, ed. Joy James and T. Denean Sharpley-Whiting (New York: Wiley-Blackwell, 2000), 239–60.
97. See, for example, Faye V. Harrison, *Decolonizing Anthropology: Moving Further toward an Anthropology for Liberation* (Washington, DC: Association for Black Anthropologists, 1991); Linda Tuhiwai Smith, *Decolonizing Methodologies: Research and Indigenous Peoples* (New York: Zed Books, 1999); Carole Boyce Davies, Meredith Gadsby, Charles Peterson, and Henrietta Williams, *Decolonizing the Academy: African Diaspora Studies* (Trenton, NJ: Africa World Press, 2003); and M. Jacqui Alexander, *Pedagogies of Crossing: Meditations on Feminism, Sexual Politics, Memory, and the Sacred* (Durham, NC: Duke University Press, 2005).
98. Cohen, "Deviance as Resisteance," 27–45.
99. Liz Galst, "Saving Lives, Promoting Democracy, Alleviating Poverty, and Fighting AIDS: The Case for Funding Lesbian, Gay, Bisexual, and Transgender Populations," Arcus Operating Foundation, 2010, www.arcusfoundation.org/images/uploads/downloads/Saving_Lives_Report_Arcus_Galst_2010.pdf (accessed January 6, 2011).

Editorial Note

A CONVERSATION "OVERFLOWING WITH MEMORY"

On Omise'eke Natasha Tinsley's "Water, Shoulders, Into the Black Pacific"

Jafari S. Allen, with Omise'eke Natasha Tinsley

During the opening discussion of the Black/Queer/Diaspora Work(ing) Group symposium in 2009, the literary theorist Omise'eke Natasha Tinsley began her remarks on her *GLQ* essay "Black Atlantic, Queer Atlantic: Queer Imaginings of the Middle Passage" by invoking M. Jacqui Alexander's contention that "water overflows with memory . . . emotional memory, bodily memory, sacred memory."[1] This is one way to express the need to develop a black feminist epistemology to uncover submerged histories that traditional historiographies cannot, or will not, validate. In "Black Atlantic, Queer Atlantic," Tinsley frames the paucity of historical documentation and the need for creative responses as a legitimate way to represent black women's histories. Taking seriously Alexander's entreaty that "searchers must explore outside narrow conceptions of the 'factual' to get there . . . crossing several currents canalized in traditional scholarships, muddying divisions between documented and intuitive, material and metaphoric, past and present, so that 'who is remembered and how, is continually being transformed through a web of interpretive systems,'" Tinsley has contributed an excerpt from her historical novel, "Water, Shoulders, Into the Black Pacific," to this special issue. In doing so, she has also incited a rich and important debate among reviewers and editors, which was in some ways prefigured by the lively discussion members and friends of the Black/Queer/Diaspora Work(ing) Group engaged in during the initial conversation of the two-day symposium. Thus I invited Omise'eke to talk with me about the piece — her inspiration, methodology, process, and political choices.[2]

Jafari S. Allen: So, my love, in the interest of what some may think of as "disclosure" and others will correctly understand as another instantiation of the love ethic of black/queer/diaspora, I must say at the outset that you are someone whom I have gotten to know through the black/queer/diaspora conference circuit over the past few years.[3] I mention this because it speaks to the contentions that I made in the introduction (which your comments inspired me to amplify) about the distinct love ethic of black/queer/diaspora work and the erotic potential of these gatherings to bring people together in a way in which one can become, as you have become to me, *a friend of one's mind* and spirit. Your work in *Thiefing Sugar* has already made a significant impact on the way we read Caribbean literature (and life), and your previous *GLQ* essay, "Black Atlantic, Queer Atlantic," likewise breached the levees of black diaspora studies and queer studies.[4] The terrain is expanded and enriched in your wake. Nevertheless, we are *here*, in the ether of cyberspace, to talk about another aspect of your work — I almost said "a departure," but I do not think it is, really.

Would you talk about the methodological and theoretical provenance or genealogy of the excerpt from "Water, Shoulders, Into the Black Pacific" printed here, please? After reading it for the first time, my mind went to Saidiya Hartman's work, not only "Venus in Two Acts" but also the ways in which her *Scenes of Subjection* reads against the grain of existing archives, and in doing so reveals both what you can get from existing records — even very problematic ones — and incisively raises the question of the *impossibility* of knowing some of the particularities of historical experience and subjectivity.[5] Of course here, M. Nourbese Philips's *Zong!* comes to mind also, as does the notion of a spectral queer subjectivity haunting the archive and the literatures produced through it, for example, that our fierce departed brister Vincent [Woodard] theorized in his work on shape-shifting in African American literature and folklore.[6] "Water, Shoulders, Into the Black Pacific" seems to be one possible answer to all of this, and of course, to Hortense Spillers and Barbara Smith and Makeda Silvera, and even Evelynn Hammonds, for example, who called for representations of black women's sexuality — their erotic experiences.[7] And your teacher, Barbara Christian, whom I know you credit with inspiring this work. This is a great tribute to her, I think. Here I see you attempting to revindicate the theoretics of those who in Christian's words "have always been a race for theory."[8] One of the most important things you do here, alongside the warm embrace of your language, and the sort of *drylongso* quality of everyday life you illustrate in soft tones—it is so sweetly crafted and so like life—is its subtle provocation to look farther (and further), deeper, and elsewhere. I know that I have said a lot here, but I also know that you are sometimes shy or reticent about laying out the profundity of what you have done, so I thought I'd get the ball rolling! Yes, please talk a bit about the methodological and theoretical provenance or genealogy of "Water, Shoulders, Into the Black Pacific."

Omise'eke Natasha Tinsley: My self-questioning intensified as I read new scholarship exploring the particular importance of imaginative work in theorizing the intimacies that women of color participate in and contest. Recent black feminist criticism, including the beautiful new writing of M. Jacqui Alexander and Saidiya Hartman, argues persuasively that to tell meaningful stories of black womanhood—and particularly black women's sexuality—traditional scholarship, and especially academic work that relies on the archive, can never suffice.[9] While archives may be a point of departure, they posit, scholars must turn to creative methodologies to intuit and imagine narratives of black women's freedom: a freedom that has remained an impossibility in official discourses but that must be invented *even where it did not exist* in the past, in order that it might exist in the future. In the poignant article "Venus in Two Acts," Hartman writes of her own attempt to imagine relationships between female captives in the Middle Passage that the intent of such imaginative scholarly work is "to imagine what cannot be verified . . . to reckon with the precarious lives which are visible only in the moment of their disappearance. . . . It is a history of an unrecoverable past; it is a narrative of what might have been or could have been; it is a history written with and against the archive."[10] "Water, Shoulders, Into the Black Pacific" also dives into such a (counter)history. Taking seriously that there are things conventional historical or literary scholarship cannot accomplish in telling the complex, elided stories of gender, desire, and personhood in the African diaspora, my creative theorizing asks questions whose very value might be that they have no "real" answer. What else can black women desire besides what the archive documents? Where else can blackness imagine itself besides the Atlantic?

But of course, like these writers, I too began in formal archives. I pored through transcripts from the Regional Oral History Office at the University of California, Berkeley; made my way through records housed at the Richmond Museum, including private photos, newsletters, ship launching programs, and videotaped interviews; and scoured historiographies about the East Bay during World War II. I learned that between 1942 and 1945, Richmond became a hub of the black

Pacific as Henry Kaiser erected four shipyards in the once sleepy town and sent recruiters to the South to lure women to California. Arriving by trainloads, African Americans, Creoles, Pueblos, and Chinese swelled Richmond's population in a unique wave of female migration from Louisiana and the peri-Caribbean Gulf states that permanently changed the state's racial demographics and temporarily changed its gender dynamics, garnering women of color unprecedented earning power. In interview transcripts, I found stories about newly economically independent female shipbuilders leaving husbands, taking casual male lovers, or staying single because they now could.

The archives I consulted also included previous work by, for example, Gretchen Lemke Santangelo (*Abiding Courage: African American Migrant Women and the East Bay Community*); Shirley Ann Wilson Moore (*To Place Our Deeds: The African American Community in Richmond, California, 1910–1963*); and Marilynn S. Johnson (*The Second Gold Rush: Oakland and the East Bay in World War II*), following their leads to other sources.[11] My immediate, completely unfounded assumption after reading about relationships between women in the shipyards was that this shipboard sex was between female shipbuilders—those who returned to make the ships work for them in off-hours. So I excitedly set out in search of an interview transcript about same-sex shipboard erotics, hoping to find a story that I would then analyze as part of my emerging project on queering African diaspora oceanographies. This proved a fantasy. I never found the story of same-sex desire that I set out in search of—the story that I was sure must be part of this queer, ethnically messy, gender-troubling wave of migration. And because I couldn't find it in the archives, I finally decided that the most challenging academic project I could undertake would be to write that story myself: to write historical fiction that would draw from oral histories to imagine intersections of migration, work, and desire experienced by African and Caribbean American women who came from the Mississippi Delta to the San Francisco Bay to work in Kaiser's shipyards.

The novel, titled "Water, Shoulders, Into the Black Pacific," follows three female protagonists, Louisiana Creole, southern African American, and black Filipina shipbuilders who come through intersecting diasporas to work with, sleep with, compete with, dream of each other in strange ways that lace Atlantic, Caribbean, Mississippian, and Philippine Sea histories through their daily conflicts and desires. These are Serena, a woman of Haitian descent who moves to Richmond from New Orleans, where her mixed race renders her ambiguous to those around her; her lover Johnnie, an African American from Tennessee who, in a new state and profession, experiments with passing as a man; and Caridad, daughter of a Buffalo soldier and a Filipina, who finds herself attracted to Serena and her relationship with Johnnie. These characters move as part of different but overlapping diasporas—Caribbean, African, and Asian—and their interactions evoke common histories and tensions between these groups, whose members have both crossed paths and been set at odds in North American racial landscapes.

My focus on African American shipbuilders—women who spent their days together in ships' holds and on ships' decks not as captives but as workers and, who knows, perhaps did return there at night to drink, dance, and re-create—is not only an interest in a particular moment of black Pacific history. It is an inquiry into how this moment at once continues and rewrites earlier, painful histories of black women packed side by side on ships where they nevertheless forged community. How does the warship that women construct at once echo and figuratively dismantle the slave ship that constructed them as property? What are the historical and cultural implications for African diaspora studies when we record black women as shipbuilders rather than shipmates—or, more accurately, as shipbuilders and shipmates rather than cargo? How are the community-building structures elaborated during enslavement reconfigured to build new kinds of alliances and tensions between women arriving from differently situated (Creole, African American, Asian American, indigenous) experiences of a common continent?

But of course Kaiser's shipbuilders were not building slave ships but US Navy battleships, so-called victory and liberty ships, and this novel about their work is also a counternarrative to tropes of American empire. Perhaps even more tidally, though, the idea of imagining not only female shipbuilders but also black queer female shipbuilders captivated me in its potential to dramatically disrupt the gendered, racial, and sexual divisions of empire that the image of the battleship is supposed to solidify like iron. What would it mean not only to displace white male masculinity from the ship's helm but to choose as a new narrative focus neither the brown male masculinity nor the white female femininity. What if we envision black female masculinity, black queer femininity, and other nonnormative racialized genders building and boarding the battleship? Such envisioning would open space that resists easy gendered mappings which might automatically position blackness, queerness, and femininity on the side of resistance to power; after all, shipbuilders were literally in the belly of the imperial machine, and their mobility to the Pacific coast was both because of and despite the imperial mobility of US militarism during and after World War II. Here we see the ships from the point of view of black bulldaggers, Creole femmes, or black Filipinas as they climb scaffolding and weld the hold.

My decision to write fiction—a challenging one, which I've compared to jumping off a cliff—emerged out of a commitment to black feminist praxis: to black feminism not as an identity politics but as a critical lens, one that demands constant interrogation of how we (public intellectuals) constitute and communicate knowledge. As a graduate student, I was profoundly influenced by my teacher Barbara Christian's response to the elitism of hegemonic feminism and by her call to take black women's creative work as seriously as self-consciously theoretical texts. I long ago memorized the passage in "The Race for Theory" in which she asks:

> For people of color have always theorized. . . . And I am inclined to say that our theorizing (and I intentionally use the verb rather than the noun) is often in narrative forms, in the stories we create, in riddles and in proverbs, in the play with language, since dynamic rather than fixed ideas seem more to our liking. How else have we managed to survive with such spiritedness the assaults on our bodies, social institutions, countries, our very humanities?[12]

Following this call, my book, *Thiefing Sugar*, engages black women's literary productions as theoretical texts, reading Caribbean poetry and fiction—ranging from anonymous songs to plagiarized novels to prize-winning poetry collections—as narrative theorizing about race, colonialism, sexuality, and gender. But I began to wonder whether I was taking Christian's idea far enough, and whether there was not still an underpinning of elitism in my practice—which read narrative theorizing as work that other black women performed, but one in which I, as an academic, did not participate. In replicating this traditional literary-critical division of labor, was there still something lingering of that split between body (the feelingness, the messiness of fiction) and mind (the pseudo-objectivity, the "order" of criticism) that Christian showed to be so devastating to black women from slavery onward? What, really, was stopping me from becoming a narrative theorist?

JSA: Indeed. I find this fascinating, and inspirational, as I also attempt to take seriously Christian's foundational entreaty, in my ethnographic practice, but in a different way, of course. This seems to me to be so important to push forward, all at once: on the one hand, Spillers's notion of "first order naming," which happens through perhaps more traditional social science and history; and, on the other, frontally challenging this, which finds black queers and insurgent women "word poor" in the academic realm while we have so much word wealth (perhaps not invested well?) in our communities.[13] A number of related questions of methodology came up during the initial discussion at the symposium. After I made introductions, Natalie [Bennett] made this important intervention, which we returned to several times:

> I was thinking about the way that you introduced everybody in terms of our individual biographies, and it raised the question: what does interdisciplinarity mean in the production of Black queer theories? Or Black queer studies proper? I am thinking about all the stuff that I teach in "Genders and Sexualities in the Caribbean": although I trained as a sociologist, I have always used novels to do particular things. However, I am also finding that we seem to be moving very quickly toward novels and fictional works [in our teaching and theorizing], because it allows certain kinds of thinking and imagining. Part of what has been happening . . . in our individual work, is a *retreat*—or perhaps what I mean is more like a *fleeing to fiction*—a particular kind of imagining, and away from making the material conditions of Black queer lives more central to our thinking and theorizing.

I remember feeling some folks bristle a bit when Natalie offered this. *A retreat, or a fleeing.* Provocative, yes? Very evocative, too. And of course she is saying this as someone who, in her teaching, reaches outside sociology to literature to *do the work*—perhaps of revealing black queer subjectivities—that sociology does not, will not, or cannot do (it is interesting that ethnography does not do this for her—my hope for ethnographies of black queer experience is that it someday will). Like me, Natalie "wonder(s) if some of those questions, or what it is that we are using literature to do, cannot also be reproduced in other kinds of spaces." Other social scientists in the room—Natalie, Rinaldo [Walcott], who trained as a sociologist but really works interdisciplinarily as a critical cultural studies scholar, and I—wanting to push social scientists to join the work, since I don't see this as an either-or proposition—were likewise concerned that we not let social science off the hook, apropos of the unique gifts it could bring to the black/queer/diaspora project. You asked us to consider

> what sort of work does literature do in the academy? What does it mean to not only read literature as theory but to read sociology as literature—what kind of critique of knowledge production can happen there? But another question that I think it might be interesting to think more about while we are together is: what is the role of literature in particular and art in general in social justice movements?

Given this, and given all the work we depend on literature to do — and please let me know whether you think this question is not precise to this conversation, or to reframe it — what are the limits of literature?

ONT: My answer is quite simple: there are no limits to what literature can do. None. And I can say that because I consider that whenever creativity is expressed through writing of any kind, literature is produced. So then, yes, not only social sciences but physical and biological sciences, too, I think of as literature. Because how much phenomenal creativity does it take to research the human genome, for example, and then put that into language? And I say this not to be literature-centric in a naive way, not at all. I say this following Sylvia Wynter's critique of the divisions of academic disciplines, which split apart, colonize, and hierarchize knowledges that are in fact powerfully connected — knowledges of what Wynter calls *the human* that span art, biology, sociology, and on and on and on, but that the academy atomizes.[14] So for me it is with deep respect and an anticolonial political engagement that I consider physics and sociology to be a kind of literature . . . and yes, of course, if physicists were to call literature a science, I would find that beautiful, too.

JSA: I have to say this: while two of the reader reports for your excerpt (from important literary scholars) were as glowing as my own (gushing) assessment of your work, an objection we heard from one of the reviewers (another literary scholar) and from a historian was that *one cannot in fact supplement history with invented narratives*. The very question is fascinating and telling, in the context of an interdisciplinary journal, and in the context of a special issue like ours, which claims to propose something "new." For me, the question seems to reveal a less-than-critical dependence on "history" as an unproblematic and transparent endeavor, which is striking to me as an anthropologist, because of anthropology's by-now-elaborate self-critique (if not self-correction); it's at least a rhetorical gesture toward its kinship with, for example, travel writing, journalism, and fiction; and its making room for experimental modes of ethnography, within and outside anthropology. There seems to be some high-end policing of the borders of history. During our black/queer/diaspora symposium, Rosamond S. King commented that "I think it's very much about disciplinarity, because you can, in a comparative literature department, do a reading of lesbians and slavery. You can do a reading of nineteenth-century Trinidadian Jammettes, for instance [as she has brilliantly done], much more easily, I think, than you can do a dissertation in history on those things."[15] But the policing is not only by historians. These issues also came up, more generally, at our first roundtable discussion. I think that many of us feel very strongly, as Michelle [Wright] said during the roundtable, that "in many ways history is the most important discipline," so perhaps we all want to *protect it*? Is that it? One of the comments asserted:

> Most certainly, historians would have a problem with an argument that, even after some citations and analysis, can be read as suggesting black women should be free to create their histories as a replacement for documented narratives.

During the roundtable, you and Matt [Richardson] seemed to be presenting a much more nuanced argument about archives and history and imagination than this (supportive) critic allows. Of course, your comments above begin to show the complex theoretical-methodological nexus at work here. *How do you respond to this?*

ONT: I am very struck by this reviewer's language critiquing the idea of black women *being free to create their histories*. Well, why shouldn't we be? This takes me back to Sylvia Wynter again, and to other African diaspora scholars who have critiqued the idea that descendants of enslaved Africans have achieved freedom—and who, like the beloved Barbara Christian, have pointed to the fetters on *what we can even imagine* as a measure of this continued unfreedom. No one is talking about replacing documented narratives, but can we put other kinds of knowledges in conversation with these, and if not, *how very unfree are we???* If, as Barbara wrote, people of color have always theorized—and, I'd add, historicized—through narrative, why can't we count fiction, its meditations on history, the undocumentable voices that it hears, as another strand to add to our histories? If I know that it's true that women loved each other on those ships in Richmond but no documentation "proves" this, should I continue to pass over this fact in silence—as the love of black people and women for each other has always, always, violently been silenced? Or should I be free to create something where there has only been silence? If anyone told my daughter that she's unfree to re-create her history—to tell herself the stories that she needs to hear—I would be as angry as if they told her that she was unfree to create her future. Because, in effect, that's what they'd be telling her.

JSA: We were also fortunate to have my colleague, the gay and lesbian historian George Chauncey, join that first conversation at the symposium.[16] George has been very supportive of the black/queer/diaspora project as an important part of our work in lesbian, gay, bisexual, and transgender studies at Yale, and it was important to have his perspective as someone who does not explicitly do black diaspora work. During the discussion George was onboard with the points that you and Matt were making about the roles that fiction, literature, filmmaking, performance art, and so forth can play in suggesting new imaginative possibilities to us, and how communities can form and find themselves through this. But I think that the tougher epistemological question for him — and this is fair, I think — revolved around historical specificity and the responsibilities of historians and (other) social scientists. Matt had been talking about Cheryl Muhanji's *Her*, and the importance of that novel, after which George brought up the fact that there has been some archival research done on black Detroit and gay Detroit in the forties and fifties. George worried about how we can start adjudicating truth claims being made by various accounts of that scene. The question remains: (how) do we reimagine a historical narrative and framework through fiction?

ONT: Well, while I don't know exactly how to answer that question — because, really, there should be as many answers as there are works of historical fiction — I will say this. I think the idea that there's a single, "objective" truth that should or even could be represented in fiction is a very dangerous one. Of course, some people may want to write about things they know to have been true (in whatever way that truth works for them). And others may want to write about things that *could have been true* in the past — freedoms, loves, that *could have been* lived — in the hopes that this imagination will make it possible for them to become true in the future. Because, as you've so beautifully said, crying out for "no future" just isn't for people of African descent; we've been slated for no future since the door of no return. So we need alternatives to that painful, slaveheld past that colonial and plantation records so precisely and soul-crushingly document for us, in order to create alternatives to the living deaths that are supposed to be our future.

JSA: Michelle [Wright], in her comments on "disturbing dominant epistemologies in the academy," referenced, from her position as a literary scholar, the import of history and the problem, therefore, of black/queer/diaspora scholarship with reference to the larger academy and to established archives. She said:

> I always go back to a poster a good friend of mine had in college of Malcolm X, where he says that history is the most important of all disciplines. As a literature person I even agreed with that. And I think possibly that may be because I see history as so many different things. It is a narrative, it is a series of facts, it is a way of re-imagining. . . . African-American literature has to operate as a kind of social science even as it is an imagining, because you are aware that you are writing to a dominant group, and you have to negotiate these knowledges.

She talked about requiring her literature students to go to primary historical texts in libraries and archives to become immersed in the particularities of the context of the works of fiction she assigns, and through this articulation, pushing students to see the paradoxes in heteronormative bourgeois epistemologies—which she suggests is the work of queer studies.

Offering another perspective on disciplinary border-crossing, Rosamond S. King, who has traveled to places and interacted with folks whom ethnographers have yet to engage, offered:

> I know that for myself I would probably benefit more from the discipline of sociology because I come from places (comparative literature) where I did not have the opportunity to do things like that. I do not know how to do that. And how many other people are going to have the opportunity . . . to, for instance go to the Gambia. So if I had the opportunity, I should take advantage of it, and yet I don't want to do it badly, right? [at which point in the conversation Rinaldo and I interrupted her to say "Don't worry about that," and "Just get the stories documented"]. So I find myself find myself in this interdisciplinary role, and yet not quite sure of what I'm doing.

Of course, after directing social scientists to read more novels (and he could have said also see more performances, write more poetry, drink more homemade sangria, grow more okra . . .), Rinaldo helped bring together some of the streams that had been flowing in our discussion. And while this discussion was about methodology, it was always also—I think we all understood this—also about theory, and about ethics, as Rosamond averred. Rinaldo said that the kind of work that he wants to imagine he is doing, and the kinds of questions that he wants to ask, are in large part precisely material and embodied. We all agreed. He offered:

> And so . . . what is at stake in theory, what is at stake in conceptualizing this term, this word that way . . . seems to call for a range of different kinds of methods, and a range of different kinds of objects of study. In some of them we are going to sit down and talk to real live people and in some of them we are going to retreat to the novel, the poem, the play, music, and some of them we're going to retreat to spirituality.

And yes, m'dear Omi, in my thinking Rinaldo is one of the most devotedly secular of black diaspora theorists, so you and I may need to massage his sort of "agnosticism" [ha!] around the spiritual and the spectral. And there is that "retreat" again. Interesting. "But . . ." he said,

It seems to me that all of them have to be on the table in different kinds of ways at different kinds of times, and we have to be juggling with them. I always say to my students, if you are going to be an interdisciplinary scholar, it means you have given yourself the most difficult job in the academy to do. You have to do all of that. You have got to account for all of it.

Because I love Rinaldo and know that he will, at once, blush and roll his eyes when he sees this in print, I will add to his statement: Pranam/Ase/Axe/Amen!

ONT: Well, with his beautiful eyes rolling or not, I must say I completely, deeply agree with Rinaldo about the practice of interdisciplinarity. *And, but* — my agreement comes only if we're willing to expand our idea about "disciplines" of knowledge, and maybe even change that "d" word to something else. Instead, I like to think of deepening *currents* of knowledge and, then, creating crosscurrents between them. And to decolonize the epistemologies we're crosscurrenting, I think it's crucial to think of orisha stories and vèvès — of ring songs and shouts — of hair braiding and barbering — yes, of growing okra and working herbs — as currents of knowledge that need to be brought into the cross, in order to more fully articulate all the possible ways we (we, people of African descent, we, just plain people) have of knowing the world. To me, that's no retreat; and, since I can't deal in teleologies, it's no advance, either. To me, it's an ocean-blue circle coming back around, and fuller this time.

JSA: Pranam, sister. Thank you.

ONT: Thanks and love to you, Jafari. Ase, Ase, Ase o.

Notes

1. M. Jacqui Alexander, *Pedagogies of Crossing: Meditations on Feminism, Sexual Politics, Memory, and the Sacred* (Durham, NC: Duke University Press, 2005), 292; Omise'eke Natasha Tinsley, "Black Atlantic, Queer Atlantic: Queer Imaginings of the Middle Passage," *GLQ* 14, nos. 2–3 (2008): 191–215.
2. This dialogue is reconstituted from electronic correspondence between Tinsley and me, as well as transcription and notes from the public first session of the Black/Queer/Diaspora Work(ing) Group symposium (April 17–18, 2009). At that time, we sought to "warm up" our time together by bringing our individual interests, projects, and locations to the table. The "voices" and my own impression of the comments of Natalie Bennett, George Chauncey, Rosamond S. King, Rinaldo Walcott, and Michelle Wright were culled from this discussion.

3. We met at the "epic" Chicago conference on black and Latina/o sexualities in spring 2007, where I learned a lot from Omi—who was wearing the most beautiful thigh-high, soft leather stiletto boots—and from Lamonda H. Stallings, Marlon Bailey, Mireille Miller-Young, and a host of others during their papers, and at the bar, in hallways, and in hotel rooms where ad hoc workshops on black queer studies unfolded. Later, after the Yale symposium, Omi and I presented together, with Xavier and Matt, in London at Goldsmith's "Race and the Modern World" conference, April 2008; and I heard her paper on Erzulie poetics in everyday life of queer Haitian men, on a sterling panel with Dagmawi Woubshet and Jax Cuevas, at Syracuse University's conference "Transnationalizing LGBT Studies," LGBT Studies Program, September 2010; later, Omi, Matt, and I presented a panel at the Caribbean Studies Association meeting in Barbados, May 2010, where Natalie Bennett, Rosamond S. King, and Angelique 999 led the creation of a new Sexualities Interest Group of the international organization. All of this speaks to the myriad ways and means by which black/queer/diaspora work happens.
4. Omis'eke Natasha Tinsely, *Thiefing Sugar: Eroticism between Women in Caribbean Literature* (Durham, NC: Duke University Press, 2010).
5. Saidiya Hartman, "Venus in Two Acts," *Small Axe* 26 (June 2008): 1–14, and Saidiya Hartman, *Scenes of Subjection: Terror, Slavery, and Self-Making in Nineteenth-Century America* (New York: Oxford University Press, 1997).
6. M. Nourbese Philip, *Zong!* (Middletown, CT: Wesleyan University Press, 2008); Vincent Woodard, "The Shapeshifter Figure: A New Cartography of Sex and Gender Formation within Radical Black Antebellum Culture," PhD diss, University of Texas, Austin.
7. Hortense J. Spillers, *Black, White, and in Color: Essays on American Literature and Culture* (Chicago: University of Chicago Press, 2003); Barbara Smith, "Toward a Black Feminist Criticism," *Women's Studies International Quarterly* 2, no. 2 (1979): 183–94; Makeda Silvera, "May Royals and Sodomites: Some Thoughts on the Invisibility of Afro-Caribbean Lesbians," *Feminist Studies* 18, no. 3 (1992): 521–32; Evelynn Hammonds, "Black (W)holes and the Geometry of Black Female Sexuality," in *The Black Studies Reader*, ed. Jacqueline Bobo, Cynthia Hudley, and Claudine Michel (New York: Routledge, 2004).
8. Barbara Christian, "The Race for Theory," *Cultural Critique* 6 (Spring 1987): 52.
9. See Alexander, *Pedagogies of Crossing*; and Saidiya Hartman, *Lose Your Mother: A Journey along the Atlantic Slave Route* (New York: Farrar, Straus and Giroux, 2007).
10. Hartman, "Venus in Two Acts," 12.
11. Gretchen Lemke Santangelo, *Abiding Courage: African American Migrant Women and the East Bay Community* (Chapel Hill, NC: University of North Carolina Press, 1996); Shirley Ann Wilson Moore, *To Place Our Deeds: The African American Community in Richmond, California, 1910–1963* (Berkeley: University of California

Press, 2000); Marilynn S. Johnson, *The Second Gold Rush: Oakland and the East Bay in World War II* (Berkeley: University of California Press, 1993).
12. Barbara Christian, "The Race for Theory," in *Making Face, Making Soul: Haciendo Caras*, ed. Gloria Anzaldúa (San Francisco: Aunt Lute Press, 1990), 336.
13. Spillers, *Black, White, and in Color*, 154.
14. See, for example, Sylvia Winter, "On How We Mistook the Map for the Territory, and Reimprisoned Ourselves in Our Unbearable Wrongness of Being, of Desêtre: Black Studies Toward the Human Project" in Lewis R. Gordon and Jane Anna Gordon, *A Companion to African-American Studies* (Malden, MA: Blackwell, 2006).
15. Rosamond S. King, "Jamette Women's Double Cross: Creating an Archive," *Women and Performance* 11, no. 1, 203–10.
16. George's scholarship in fact has significantly pushed traditional twentieth-century American history to recognize lesbian and gay history.

EXTRACT FROM "WATER, SHOULDERS, INTO THE BLACK PACIFIC"

Omise'eke Natasha Tinsley

Every day is Ladies' Day at Richmond.
We love them and can't do without them. Now they do a big part of the job. Who are they? Our women.
—Headline from *Fore 'N' Aft*, Kaiser Shipyards Safety Magazine, June 2, 1944

There are many Negroes in the Richmond shipyards, and it would be hard to find more ardent workmen anywhere. For these men and women are filled with a spiritual fervor in this war . . . the sort of fervor that makes them sing as they work a ship's gun in rhythmic unison, or shout "Freedom!" as a ship goes down the ways.
—*Fore 'N' Aft*, May 1943

three: pearls

you, you walking past me on macdonald avenue with the slender fingers & uncompromising thighs & undaunted glints at hand or chest or wrist, you, if you're here working in the shipyards this wartime, you must want a lot. you don't have to tell me, we all do. you want so much, your want is like the color purple in the night sky or wind forcing its way through a closed window or a dancer spinning a hundred pirouettes, breathcutting & imperious. you want something impossibly possible only here, the wine colored cowboy boots you dreamed of in arkansas or the diamond ring bright as your glass doorknobs in minnesota, the bags of groceries you can't wait until you're out of your work soot to buy or the women who charge crisp paychecks to lay in the night bellies of boats, the curve of a brown boy's smile or the escape route from your airless house. the first ship launch i saw in richmond was the *ss george washington carver victory,* presided over by miss lena horne herself, & thousands of brown bodies ferried & trained & drove & walked from all over the bay to crowd the yard & watch her launch. when the ship slid into the may water a bright hatted, molasses brown woman ran forward like an ibis before a hurricane, her arms spread wide & her voice raised to the *carver* & the sky, she yelled, *freedom! freedom!* they wrote about her in the papers & *fore n aft,* the kaiser newsletter, & they praised her & the patriotism of the american negro. but i was there & what i heard wasn't a belief but a desire, like slaves' cries to mississippi river boats they dreamed of escaping on, something bottomless & ripe & older than one war. that cry, that, is what the wanting i feel on the streets of richmond is like, the wanting of boots & jewels & bodies that's wanting for something like freedom big enough to open the skies with a shout.

this saturday morning i'm downtown picking up the dress & hat i'm wearing to my birthday dinner with johnnie, & already all the wanting here is calling pearls of sweat to my hairline. i pass by the richmond café, its window advertising good coffee, quality food & a free war show in block letters, & notice a beautiful brown woman posing for a photograph. she has hair swept up to the skyline & wears a skirt tumbling with tropical flowers, night black stockings over thin calves, a long string of multicolored glass beads knotted between her breasts, & — even though it's july — a fur coat draped queenly over her shoulders. i see the shutter click & think, but, no picture will ever capture why you would want or even need to put so much color & wealth against your skin, & then smile with cheeks round as good luck.

when i open the apartment door johnnie is sitting bent over the *richmond independent,* the newspaper pinned to the kitchen table with her fist. *listen to this, serena, listen to this. there's a colored man riding a bus & he bumps up against a white sailor, of course, because you know how these buses full up. & six white sailors chase him off the bus, corner this one man by himself to beat him, & the independent says it's his fault for stepping on the sailor's toes in the first place!* johnnie always reads out these stories the papers run about negro crime & negro consumption & general negro dirtiness, always furious to make her veins throb, & i'm always touched, a little, by her earnestness in believing that newspapers are a place people tell the truth. in new orleans you know papers never print the truth, not about storms coming or coming elections or coming out balls or anything much. on spare scraps of paper johnnie writes down stories she thinks ought to be in newspapers & presses them together in an old leather sketch book. her favorite is one about frances albrier, a negro woman welder who threatened to sue the shipyard union when they refused to let her join then showed up in the yard in welder's regalia telling everyone, *well, i just happened to bust my way in!* i guess johnnie wanted to be a welder & other things that much, too, that she would have bust down anything that got in the way of her being who she already was in her mind.

oh, johnnie, you know the reporters for that paper would never forgive a negro for being uppity enough to own a nice pair of shoes to step on a sailor's toes with, i say, crossing to kiss her cheek & set my packages on the table. next door a muffled man's voice booms over us, *boy, give your sister's toy back, now!* & felix, the boy child, whimpers. the walls at harbor gate are white & new & crumbly when you pin a poster up, so thin when you lean on them you wonder if they can hold their own weight & so thin i think you could put a shoulder or a fist through them, never mind a voice. close as we're packed against our neighbors it must be a fire hazard, let alone a gossip hazard, johnnie grumbles every time we hear our neighbors' fights & dinners. (even though this project is supposed to be integrated we coloreds only live by other coloreds, so at least we don't have to know white folks' business.) bending now & draping my arm over her shoulder, i ask, *now baby, it's a beautiful morning, don't you want to read that paper outside? you know caridad is coming to do my hair & i don't want you to see, i want it to be a surprise.* & johnnie turns quickly like a waiting snake to bite my neck & laughs, answering, *well it's your birthday, girl, don't i get to surprise you?*

but it's true, i always loved reading the newspapers in new orleans; i always loved a good story. when i was sixteen the *times picayune* ran a serial called *kitty foyle* & afternoons i'd sit reading at my godmother's kitchen table with the western exposure, my fingers warm like passing over a candle as i held them to the newsprint. pretty kitty foyle was a career girl before i knew what that was, a poor girl who realized she needed *to be a complete woman with all a woman's satisfactions* & made her own way from the middle country to the coast always following her body & heart, falling for an improbable lover, making hard choices always the wrong choices, getting pregnant out of wedlock with a baby she throws away. *i feel lonely as a jew in germany,* kitty says when she's down. sometimes i imagined i was kitty & sometimes i imagined i was her best friend, that we'd share dresses & curl up together to tell secrets & give each other love advice.

that year was the first news of war, too, huge like hurricane warnings but less real. i remember the muddy gray movie theater light as i watched a newsreel of the evacuation at dunkirk, fire on choppy whitecaps & the british desperately piling out in sail boats & fishing boats & tug boats. & of course i remember the first sunday in december, 1941, when nénène & her niece nettie & i were working with two shirt buttons undone in the kitchen, getting ready for people coming for backyard supper & i was frosting a blood red velvet cake, white icing thick on the cake & my fingers too. we were listening to records, not the radio, so we were surprised when nettie's mother burst in, asking, *haven't you heard the news? japan just bombed pearl harbor! what? what's a pearl harbor, mama?* nettie asked & tantie fanned away the question, *no, girl, it's not a what it's a where, a place in hawai'i & hawai'i belongs to the united states, just like louisiana or those caribbean islands, so japan just bombed the states & that means war!* i never knew america was such a far reaching place, like france when it owned louisiana & haiti & canada; & when i finally learned it sounded like a woman's secret passed through alleys & kitchens, & i was stained red & white, & we were going to war.

happy birthday! caridad throws her arms around me when i open the door, & even though she's on her way to work she smells like rose water & coty face powder & the color pink. since she's working today & i'm not going in & it's my birthday, she suggested she come by my place to do my hair on the way to the yard & i said yes. we go to the kitchen to set up beauty shop, where she opens her bag & takes out mirrors & pins & irons & a book bound with three ribbons. *these are my best styles,* she says, smoothing the cover, *let's open it up & we'll look through & see which one you like, okay?* in the book are newspaper clippings of society girls & movie stars smiling from under elaborate curls but also other pictures, too, pictures of her mother & aunts, of her cousin playing the piano, of picnics at beaches & parks, of her & her sisters dressed in thin lacy dresses their mother had made for them in the philippines with pearls at their neck & hair in high waves. she explains all the pictures to me, who was where & when & why, what kind of fun they had.

& *look*, she says, retrieving a loose photo from the back of the book, *there's one more i want you to see, even though it's not a hairstyle. this is my old sweetheart.* she hands me a picture of a dark oval face, high cheekbones & thundering eyebrows, swirls of hair cropped close to the scalp. *oh, how handsome! what a prince, cari! what's his name? & what happened between you two? that,* she says slowly, smiling like a happy cat, *is* barbara. she pauses, waiting for the effect on me. *barbara's a tomboy, which is what we, what filipinos call people like your johnnie, we have a word for it. you see, you didn't think i knew but i always knew, & that's why i wanted to get to know you. that, & your beautiful spanish hair, miss serena.*

what? you have—& what's the word for girls like us, then? real women, caridad smiles wider & holds the mirror up to our faces together, our cheeks curving together at oblique angles. *now what do you think, the bouquet upsweep? & you see we have a lot to talk about while i curl.*

i don't have a book of my own, like johnnie or caridad, but i make up my own stories too. sometimes i imagine something like a movie where johnnie & i sail out across the pacific to hawai'i & there johnnie lives like a man, becomes a man, & he & i get married & spend a life of nights strolling on the beach with a flower behind my ear. but maybe i only make that story up because i don't have those words for johnnie & me, like caridad does, & if i did i could make up other kinds of stories that would take me other places. i imagine stories about my mother, too, i'm a grown woman i know but i imagine them still. i tell myself maybe she didn't die when i was born, maybe she just wasn't ready for a baby like kitty foyle wasn't & instead of throwing me away she let me be born then moved across the country to start a new life. & maybe her new life will take her here, one day, & i'll meet her in the yards, & she'll recognize me & be ready to know me; & all those years of wanting & not knowing will make sense.

there's a lot you wouldn't know about richmond & the shipyards if somebody didn't tell you, serena, caridad says over the iron's hiss. *like did you know right in downtown richmond there's a shop, a wig shop, where men come from oakland & san francisco & everywhere, doctors & lawyers & everything, to buy themselves women's wigs? at first they say it's for their girlfriend, maybe, but everybody who works there knows & likes to help them with accessories & everything.* she releases a curl from between her warm fingers to the nape of my neck. *& then there's a club in el cerrito just where cutting boulevard hits san pablo, you know, & that club is for men who dress like women. you go there, you know, everybody goes, men & women or women together or whatever, & there are these performers who are such good, beautiful women you can't tell them apart from real women. they have beautiful wigs & diamond & pearl necklaces & gowns & high heels & everything, so many costume changes & you can listen to them sing for hours because they have voices just like angels, they do!*

next door something topples loudly over & the boy twin yells *now look what you've done! daddy, daddy!* & the girl cries, *but daddy told you, felix, the doll is* mine! caridad laughs, *my goodness, do you think they're listening to us, too?* her hand brushes upward on my neck, following carefully with a bobby pin, setting another curl in place. *& this is the best, serena, just the best. you know how* *some people go back to the half built ships late at night to drink & party &, well, you know? what the men & women do? well there's a part of yard three where just women go, & you can go to the ships there & meet other women like johnnie or us & do whatever feels good . . . whatever, you know?*

i listen to caridad, liking the sound of her voice rising & falling at the secret parts, tutting & sucking in my breath because i know it tickles her to give me surprises like gifts to unwrap & because sharing this like a secret is making us friends. but of course i'm old enough to know about things like this in new orleans, even if i didn't go there like i haven't been here, & i'm not really surprised that all this is in richmond, too, since everything we want follows us here.

these stories about the ships make me think about other things, too, other things you heard about in louisiana. new orleans was a place where even after it was illegal to bring slaves over from other countries they were still sold downriver & auctioned at st. louis & chartres streets, & when i was little the old people remembered stories they heard from their people about what those boats were like when they finally anchored onto the end of the continent. on those river slaveships women all rode together in one part of the belly of the boat & men in another, & then were bathed & dressed & lined up & sold in the market women on one side, men on the other. & my godmother's mémère used to tell about women who, when they dragged them out of the cargo, had braided each other's hair in beautiful patterns & scratched designs on their scalp in glass; & about women who'd loved each other in the boats, & cried on the auction mornings when they were separated & sent messages up & downriver to each other for the rest of their lives. & even though that wasn't my story, even though my people were never slaves in america i never forgot that; because i was just a girl when i heard but i understood those ship memories were about wanting to be beauty & art & human & love when everything around you told you you couldn't be any of those things, but you were, you still were. & now here we were loving in other boats, boats we were building ourselves, & building to send out to another ocean that this country stretched into now, like a sun looking for a place to set; & everything is different, & nothing is, & it's my own time.

when i hear the apartment door open behind my back i'm still in the kitchen, still in my white cotton robe dusted in powder & rouge & only my silver rayon bra & panties underneath. *oh johnnie*, i say, *johnnie you're back so soon, i'm not ready!* i turn & johnnie's walking wolf-slow & copper-shiny toward me, her chest shielded behind a bouquet of twenty one red roses & her head cocked lightly to one side. *oh baby you look like a picture, just a picture, birthday girl. sit down, here, sit down, baby,* she puts the firelove red roses on the kitchen table & pulls a chair out to the middle of the floor, *sit right here & let me give you your birthday present.* she strokes my cheek, my neck, my shoulders that shiver through the cotton. *johnnie, i — my hair already, i . . .* she unties the sash & unrobes my left arm, whispering, *no, you sit still, just perfectly still, serena, you don't move til i tell you to & your hair & your beautiful will be just fine, just fine. now, close your eyes, let me surprise you.*

 the black & silver insides of my eyelids quiver to stay shut while she takes my hand between her thumb & forefinger & slides down to my floating knuckle. *okay, open, birthday girl* she says, & i open my eyes to a gold ring with three perfect pearls curving together in a triangle. *i know shipyard folks like to spend up on diamonds to show they can but you, i knew you'd want something different, something special like you. you like it, don't you, baby?*

 yes, oh yes, i love it. johnnie's fingers move to the button holding the rayon to my waist & her lips against my ear insist *don't move, now, remember, you just stay still.* & i want to move, so much, i want that so much & i want just as much not to be able to move, to feel the strain of muscling against the invisible ties johnnie presses me with & to be wrapped tight enough to struggle but never to float free, never, to float closer & closer into her storm & never float free of her hands. & i want this so desperately, moving against not moving, until the blood rushes in my ears & my wanting spirals like a tornado between earth & water & sky & thunder & johnnie presses my newly ringed hands together & i'm gone, violet & spinning & gone. this, this, *this* is what it feels like to be free today, it feels like surrender & melting & choosing what holds you down & lets you up & knowing this is only happening because you want it, you couldn't say it but you want it, you do. i am twenty one years old, today, & this is what it feels like.

four: homefront blues

welcome, everyone, to the monthly meeting of the richmond, california branch of the naacp. an undertone of blue in the white wall behind mrs. starks & mr. brown, picked up by the blue synthetic of the chairs we all sit on facing their welcome & bounced back by the july sky outside, suddenly closes the room in & makes me want to shut my eyes against its brightness. it's the third sunday of the month & i'm sitting as tall as i can at the back of our recreation center at harbor gate, where the naacp founded this chapter a few months ago because so many of us are unhappy with how, even though this warhousing project is supposed to be integrated, in front where blacks live are only blacks & in back where whites live are only whites. i'm on my blue seat between johnnie & cari & the room is packed, filled to the bluewhite walls with new-dressed shipyard negros and old-time richmond negros and even white folks, too. i know in a minute they'll read out the local & national naacp reports & then mrs. starks & mr. brown will talk about what we've all crowded in to hear, the resolution they've drafted to take to the richmond housing authority telling how they've reinvented segregation here even though the federal government says they can't. yes, i know the flow of these meetings, i've been here before.

    & no, i never, ever thought when i came to california that i'd end my every third sundays in a meeting like this. i just never thought, you understand, that i'd need to. that afternoon i got off the car with johnnie at ocean beach & saw everyone together at playland by the sea i thought this, this bay area was a different world, & here at this sheer-cliffed coast i'd arrived somewhere i could live so *colored only* would be my past, my childhood, & i could be a young woman & an old woman in another way. & even though i know different now & know why i'm here i'm suddenly surprised, like by that mix of blues that must have always been there but i didn't see it before, surprised by a flood of feeling that spills over my clavicle & onto my chest & brown eyes, suddenly. here i am undertowed by sadness, azure, clear-armed sadness at that thing i've traveled across rivers & lakes & countries with, that everyday & every year & every minute needing to prove that i deserve to take up space, too, & that i deserve to be a woman, too. mrs. starks stands to read the regional report, gracefully, & so no one notices how i fight to stop tears at my throat.

caridad, beautiful caridad has decided i'm her best friend. i've never had anyone choose me like that, so openly, or wear their love for me so very brightly, like floral print on a new summer dress. some shipyard women have started collecting scrap metal to make jewelry to sell & wear, & cari made a set of silver-like bracelets she gave me as a gift. lunchtimes she follows me to whatever beam i sit on, walking with her arm through mine, & leans in close to my ear & laughs & whispers when the singing shipbuilders come by. mostly, though, we tell each other stories about where we're from. she talks in a way that's its own kind of singing about her papa, his years in the philippines, the coastline her mother came from & the birds that chatter there & the people that died there, the officers' head shakings about negro soldiers loving filipinas but what could they do with two dark races side by side?, & her father's decision to go fight there in the first place not because he loved war so much but because, after fighting in cuba, he just didn't want to go back to not being able to get a cup of coffee at the same louisiana counters where white soldiers were being given free meals.

cuba? i ask, cuba, really? did you know my family came to new orleans from cuba, actually went from haiti to cuba then louisiana? what's it like, cuba, did he tell you? & she tells me his favorite memory, the one he made into a story over & over: how men on the ship did their own laundry & hung it to dry on the rails, dangling blue uniforms from all edges; & the morning they pulled into havana harbor, how he watched their one-toned blues blowing against the so many royal, turquoise, green, sky blues of the caribbean sea that that american cloth was just put to shame. at the end of that lunchtime i ask cari would she possibly be interested in coming to the naacp meeting next week? because we'd be talking about the segregation that wasn't supposed to be happening in richmond but, you know, was. yes, she said quickly & smoothing her pants as she stood up, oh yes she definitely wanted to come. she'd been angry enough to spit about the unions not wanting to let negroes in & making us form those colored auxiliaries, huh, & did you know those same unions wouldn't let filipinos in either? what is it they say, tarred with the same brush, or cut from the same cloth, or something?

because this morning johnnie & i woke up missing the mississippi river we took the f-train to berkeley to sit in bright, cotton-thin summer sun by a creek named for strawberries. not at all the same, no, but a small recollection of what johnnie calls homewaters. her mother was a transplant to the big river like i am to the bay; when she left her first husband she swore she'd never again be a farmer's wife, & after she moved to memphis & wore high heels every day & fell in love with the blues & married her next two husbands she never was. but johnnie's father's family is a century of river boat people, firemen who climbed levees & hauled coal & stoked boilers & flexed biceps & talked confidently. for johnnie the river is another country, a nearby, far away ancestors' land where women (who could only be chambermaids) had to stay separate from men, & colored men (the only firemen) had to stay separate from whites (the only deckhands), & ships' fire had to stay separate from riverwater (part of firemen's job). that big water was a country she could never live in but she'd always dream of, when she was a child like here in the shipyards.

but i'm from new orleans, & for me the river is something else again. i remember without anybody telling me how the mississippi built that city, how the sediment it washed from the middle of the continent to the gulf created new land around us from when i was a little girl until when i was a grown woman, how its current was so strong that houses there are built from keelboats they tore apart at the river's end rather than try to sail them back up; you see, i remember the ground we walk on is river, and the houses we live in are boats. so for me the mississippi is the place that everything americans will tell you is separate, just never was. i know that johnnie is right about her version of the river — but then again, i am too. when we talk about it by strawberry creek she accuses me of being a romantic about the father of waters, & laughingly i accuse her of the very same thing.

my dear serena,

i hope this letter finds you well, & every bit as beautiful as i left you. i really do wish i would hear from you sometimes, but maybe you're shy in letters like you were in person, or maybe yours are always in those planes that go down, i don't know. don't worry, though, i'm not mad about it, i know our marriage was a different kind. now me, you won't be surprised to hear, i'm still here in the middle of the pacific (don't worry, censor, i'm not going to tell her where!). by now most fellows in my unit are pretty well fed up with our situation, not the place so much but these white officers & how they think they can walk all over us, bust us down to private for no reason & keep us from going on leave EVER so we won't get in trouble with white women in CENSORED (which of course i would never do). & since we can't go off base all there is to do at night is go to church or gamble & talk about how we could organize back against those officers.

i agree with all those other fellows about that but i have to tell you something else, too. serena. the truth is, despite all that i'm really, truly happy here. let me see if i can explain to you why. well first, i really wish you could see the ocean here, it is just so beautiful like nothing i ever imagined. the waves are huge & blue & when all that water pulls back it lets you see the coral reefs spreading out & up like statues on the ocean floor. the waves are huge, like i said & the undertow is too, so some fellows think it's a kind of magic but i love the power of it. in the morning i wake up & have these tropical fruits for breakfast, fruits like you can't get anywhere & watch that water rise & fall, & then evenings before dinner i swim there. & i just love the feeling of my muscles against the force of that water, the power of my body meets the power of the pacific, & when i come back out i pick up shells & pieces of dead coral that i save from time to time. so even though i hate that uncle sam brought me here it's like this is the place i'm meant to be in the world, you know? like i was born in new orleans but i was born here, too.

the sun is shining harder into the recreation center & its light washing out the walls as mr. brown stands by mrs. starks to read out the resolution that they've drafted to the housing authority. in assigning housing units in such a way to separate negroes from whites, he tells us, the richmond housing authority *is violating the spirit and the letter of the regulations set forth by the federal public housing authority covering racial discrimination and segregation.* this document is something they'll take to the housing authority, to the city council, to state representatives, federal offices, & without fail to all the newspapers in the bay area to print word for word. & then if our demands aren't met, we'll call a rent strike here at harbor gate to make them pay attention to the almighty dollar if not the people's words. *what this means is, there are so many of us who are tired of being put last, right? real change is going to happen, & it'll take us working folks to make it happen.*

serena, from séraphine. when cari asks me where my name comes from i tell her from my many-great grandmother, marie séraphine, the wave-colored quadroon who was born outside daughter to an indigo planter in haiti, died outside woman to an indigo planter in louisiana, & colored our family's fingers blue for generations. when the slave war broke out on her father's plantation marie séraphine's mulâtresse mother smuggled the girl under her skirts to the border & sailed her to cuba, where she lived (doing no one remembers what) until the spanish drove haitians out & she landed in new orleans with an adopted daughter called annaïse. *serena, from séraphine.* louisiana had just become american then & was cut up into newer & newer sections, blocks for creoles & creoles of color & americans (americans of color were slaves) who crossed neighborhood lines to market & love & gamble but not to stay. marie séraphine settled back of town, lakeside & away from the river in faubourg tremé with other haitians who'd come by way of cuba or the carolinas or georgia or jamaica, & a century later my mother & i were born there.

serena, from séraphine. these are the stories i have about the woman i'm named for & in the end they add up to less than cari's one about cuba. the important things, the things that make a person a person, i don't know. did she like the divided city, did it feel familiar or did she hate being kept in a quartered-off space? did she miss haiti, & did she miss her mother's part or her father's or something else again? where did she meet annaïse & why did she bring her to new orleans, & what did people think of the quadroon with the adopted brown daughter? *serena, from séraphine.* here i am in california, like marie séraphine with my own new waters & my own new kind of household with spouses & lovers & friends & my own new colors & old ones too, & am i following in her footsteps or going somewhere she'd turn her back on? & after all those years and living by it & growing it, what did she really think of the color blue, & what do i think of it now?

somehow when i tell caridad about new orleans & my family stories it doesn't feel quite like home, anymore. but neither does this place where i live.

but if johnnie & i are being easy about the mississippi this morning, maybe that's because there are just some things you wouldn't talk about by a creek named for strawberries. in this cotton-dry summer you wouldn't talk about the spring that river became an ocean, the easter north to south flooded rainwater that collected in waves & carried houses & people & trees through the center of towns & took away johnnie's father & i guess mine, too, in another way. i'd been promised to live with papa when i got a little older & he found a new wife, but in 1927 he lost his tailor shop & left new orleans for chicago; so after the flood days when nénène stacked mattresses & family stories to the ceiling to keep me dry i became really her little girl. but johnnie's father never left the river — he drowned there. like all colored men they could round up at gunpoint in that part of the delta he was driven to haul sand bags to the top of levees, & walking under the shoulder weight of sand & rain his feet slipped in mud & he fell the wrong way, into the river, & no one was allowed to go after him or even break step to look. not that that was the river taking him, no, johnnie told me once, that was powerlessness & white men. (johnnie's uncles started calling her that name after her father, john, because she was looking & acting like him more every day after he was gone.) i know because of that building ships has another meaning for her, my johnnie, something beyond *we can do it* or *good work, sister* or *warriors without guns* or any slogan bright colored posters tell us. that every weld is done perfectly to maybe keep a colored man afloat, to maybe keep him from sinking into the pacific or atlantic in someone else's battle for the world.

but there's another part to my being so happy here, serena, let me see if i can put it in a way that will make sense to you. i wrote you before about how we're working alongside natives on this island, how uncle sam hires them to build roads & bridges & everything & pays just in meals even though they're the best workers of anyone. (officers spend so much time keeping us away from whites but they sure don't mind mixing us together with natives). well one of these men, he & i have become particular friends. he calls himself agu, which is short for something else i think, & if a man can be beautiful then i'd say that he's beautiful. did you know natives here are coloreds, or at least something that looks awful like us? agu has skin the color of nutmeg, hair as bushy as mine (if you remember), a jawline that comes down in a perfect slant & dark brown eyes & long lashes & eyebrows the shape of seashells, a mouth curved like a horn & a chest of muscles i wish i could claim. i'm learning to speak a little of his language & he knows some english, too, & when we're not working he takes me fishing & teaches me to use a spear like him. now we may come from a country of fishermen but you still can't imagine what you can catch that way, & even what you can just catch with your bare hands in these waters. one time when we were out together he found a baby octopus, just a little guy, & he picked him up & was letting him walk all over his legs & hands like a pet & so i asked, hey agu, can i try that too? he handed him over to me & the little octopus latched on & gee, it was the most incredible feeling, those eight curling legs & all those round cups on my arms sucking & releasing, sucking & releasing, just pushing jolts of electricity through me from head to toe. i don't know how else to explain what it feels like to be with him, but somehow it's always like that. now it's true, fellows are being court martialed here for sodomy all the time, but i want you to know i'm not talking about anything like that at all. i'm talking about just me & him, a true blue friendship, & a feeling that if i weren't a married man, you know, maybe i'd want to stay here & live like this, in something beautiful.

mrs. starks & mr. brown have finished presenting their resolution & abruptly as a thunderclap, moving frantically up from our blue seats, flustered chests & red restlessness scale the room like a hard blush. white folks are standing confidently to drone on how they support this plan, as if we asked their permission, & colored church folks are tall on their feet chiming in baritones that this isn't the way to get white richmondites on our side, no, they've been here a long time & know quiet is a better way to make a place for ourselves. & now itching across my shoulderblades & stomach & swaying me without warning something new is breaking me open, so open, a hot current of blood anger that magnifies everything & *everything* that should be different here but doesn't know how to be.

 i'm furious at all of it, the careless blues in the walls & the black & white of the papers & plans & words, i'm furious at everyone for not understanding the joke in all this: that *home* & *safe home* & *real home* have never been anything more than metaphors for something we never had, never will have & that never existed, & if we're fighting for it we have to know we're really fighting for something else in its name. oh yes some men may believe in home, maybe, because they think it's a woman's place closed in by her hands that continues to stay still like a picture while they run through war & work & death & exploration & technicolor imaginations that they've found a new world in whatever part of the pacific atlantic mississippi gulf governments & paychecks send them to or keep them in. but women, we workers supposed to be keeping that homefront that doesn't exist shouldn't we know better than to pretend that there can be anything like a real home, or another world, or a safe place for us and why do we — do i, does johnnie — why insist on fantasizing otherwise while we're fighting for space in projects that will be smashed to plaster at our feet after the war? why, why does there seem to be a limit like a front door to what we can even imagine, & why don't we want to say that all shades of blue is just where we live?

    caridad, next to me, says nothing but puts her hand over mine.

dear paul,

    thank you for your latest letter, & for your stories about this ocean you don't even know i live by, too. you really are a very sweet man, & your letters are lovely even if i do think you write them more for yourself than for me. i can say that, & i can say other things, too, because i know i'll never send this or probably any letter. if i did i'd need to explain what happened & i really don't know how to do that, yet. i guess when i married you i thought i wanted things, like a safe home & a good last name, but the more i tried living in those things the more it seemed like eating beignets every night for dinner — empty & sticky & a little sickly. now i'm living in temporary housing & things & loves i'm still looking for names for & this is so much more where i need to be to become me, serena. that june we were just such romantics, you & i, & i still am & want to be but about other stories, ones less predictable, more joyous & confusing than a wedding party. your letters tell me you're still a romantic too, paul, but i do hope you'll be more careful with your friend agu than you were with me. because i'm sure you get along, i'm sure everything you write is true, but under the little language you two have you can't tell how he really feels about americans when they've come run over his island & made people work in their own home for nothing but food; & even though you're creole, aren't you an american to him? just like under my quietness you couldn't tell how i really feel about men, which is not that they did anything to me like americans to agu but just that different people have different landmarks & loves in their lives than yours, dear. whatever happens, though, i really do hope that you'll be happy, husband, that you'll find a way of being in the world that's as beautiful as you hope for; and if that's a place of all men, well take it from me, that won't be such a bad thing at all.

CHATTING BACK AN EPIDEMIC

Caribbean Gay Men, HIV/AIDS,
and the Uses of Erotic Subjectivity

Lyndon K. Gill

In the popular imagination, the presumption of a particularly savage homophobia in the anglophone Caribbean has largely rendered homosexuality at worst implausible and at best impracticable for anyone living in the region.[1] Jamaica is the clichéd epicenter for this regionwide vilification, which rests on the delusion that deadly homophobic violence in Kingston is somehow categorically different from deadly homophobic violence in Washington, DC.[2] However, few islands of the anglophone Caribbean have escaped being painted with the same bloody homophobic brush daubed heavy-handedly across Jamrock. This is not to say that violence — wherever it takes place — is acceptable, but I do want to draw attention to the lives the presumption of impossibility snuffs out long before any attacker can raise a machete or the butt of a gun.

What is perhaps most unnerving about insisting on the recognition of same-sex desire in the anglophone Caribbean — especially among black men, a significant proportion of whom self-identify as "gay" — is that national, regional, and international public health officials have for some time now also been insisting on this very recognition.[3] In the public health discourses circulating through the region, the category of (Afro)Caribbean men who have sex with men (MSM) is disturbingly omnipresent even if these men remain for the most part invisible.[4] Haunting specters, these men are nearly always (over)represented by a subgrouping of openly gay Caribbean men.[5] Yet these self-identified gay men are the very population so many presume cannot exist and whom public health initiatives summarily overlook in an effort to find other "hidden" groups of MSM that serve as vectors from supposed disease-incubating gay communities into supposed disease-free heterosexual communities — a mythology that persists no less perniciously in the global North.[6]

The forbidding absence of Caribbean homosexuality in popular discourses and the dangerously (if dubiously) pervasive presence of Caribbean MSM in public health discourses both indicate a failure to recognize not only the existence of decidedly gay Afro-Caribbean men but also — and perhaps more important — the work these men have been doing for three decades to survive a scourge more devastating than banal homophobia: the HIV/AIDS pandemic. The following analysis sits with a group of these men to see how they go about surviving. By focusing on the Republic of Trinidad and Tobago (T&T), a central historical and contemporary site in the region's struggle against HIV/AIDS, I suggest that there may be lessons for us to learn by looking farther south than Jamaica.[7] Although much of the existing literature on HIV/AIDS in the Caribbean region has overlooked the substantial medical evidence proving that Trinidad (not Jamaica, as is commonly believed) was the earliest epicenter of the HIV/AIDS epidemic in the Caribbean's anglophone world, I still insist on looking to Trinidad as an important disseminating point for a particularly effective response to our three-decades-old pandemic.[8]

As instructive for the Caribbean region as it must be for other sites within the black (queer) diaspora, this particular response comes through Friends For Life (FFL) — a Trinidad-based HIV/AIDS nongovernmental organization (NGO) that is one of the only service provision organizations run principally by and for self-identified gay men in the Caribbean region — in the form of the organization's oldest and most resilient program, the Community Chatroom Experience (or simply the Chatroom). It is important to emphasize that the FFL Chatroom is not, in fact, a virtual space, even though its name might suggest as much to a generation weaned on the Internet. This chatroom is a fleshy actual space that bodies convene to share. What is most interesting about FFL's Chatroom for this engagement is its recognition that the interlinking of the political, the sensual, and the spiritual is vital not only for the efficacy and longevity of the program but also for the success of the organization itself. This interconnection of the political-sensual-spiritual forms the foundation of my articulation of "erotic subjectivity" as an epistemological proposition. I outline this theoretical intervention and then use it as a lens through which to read FFL's Chatroom as a praxis of survival. I end this analysis by gesturing briefly toward the wider potential of erotic subjectivity. I ask what lessons we, black queer folks (among others), might learn about combating the global HIV/AIDS pandemic from a grassroots black gay organization rooted in the very place where the epidemic started for the anglophone Caribbean. Erotic subjectivity points us toward one potential answer to that question.

Erotic Subjectivity: An Epistemological Proposition

The interrelation among politics, sensuality, and spirituality is central to my elaboration of what I conceive of as "erotic subjectivity."[9] I use erotic subjectivity as a decidedly epistemological proposition. I am curious about the potential of proposing a particular relationship between "the erotic" and subjectivity that challenges apolitical, passionless, and secular interpretations of how we come to know what we know about ourselves, each other, and our world. I propose this interlinked political-sensual-spiritual ("erotic") subjectivity in an effort not to replace one type of "universal" subjectivity with another but rather to expand the conceptualization of subjectivity so that its coherence is intelligible only through an assemblage of differences.

As an interpretive frame, erotic subjectivity is indebted to Audre Lorde's framing of the erotic in her 1978 speech "Uses of the Erotic: The Erotic as Power." In it, Lorde insists:

> The dichotomy between the spiritual and the political is . . . false, resulting from an incomplete attention to our erotic knowledge. For the bridge which connects them is formed by the erotic—the sensual—those physical, emotional, and psychic expressions of what is deepest and strongest and richest within each of us, being shared: the passion of love in its deepest meanings.[10]

Following from this reconceptualization and encouraged by Lorde to read the erotic through sensuality (even in its broadest sense as revelry in the senses) toward a wider range of interpretive possibilities, I propose that the meaning of "the erotic" can be stretched. Informed by Lorde, my articulation of the erotic expands beyond being mere euphemism for sexual desire and reaches simultaneously toward a political attentiveness and a spiritual consciousness. This tripartite political-sensual-spiritual awareness makes possible and desirable a more broadly and deeply conceived articulation of love. And it is this love that so often provides the motivation for political action, sensual intimacy, and spiritual hunger—together constitutive elements of an erotic subjecthood.

Erotic subjectivity is at once an interpretive perspective and a mode of consciousness; it is both a way of *reading* and a way of *being* in the world. This analytic frame encourages a recognition of the fact that systems of colonial (as well as neocolonial/imperial) domination depend partly on a tripartite strategy of coercion based on a politics of ontological racial difference, a hierarchy of spiritual rectitude, and a Victorian sense of (sexual) respectability—erotic *subjugation*, as it were. Erotic subjectivity is tasked with providing a postcolonial theoretical response to this mechanism of subjugation. This expanded political-sensual-spiritual perspective on the production of hierarchies of difference—the very alterity used to justify exploitation from the top down—begins to shed light on the incompleteness of official postcolonial movements (and their long-range ideological projects) in the Caribbean region, which largely continue to imagine the political, sensual, and spiritual as mutually exclusive realms of concern. The inability to think the political-sensual-spiritual together threatens to obscure even the clearest of postcolonial visions.

This particular attentiveness to—in their most abstract rendering—power hierarchies (the political), sensory intimacy (the sensual), and sacred metaphysics (the spiritual) provides the theoretical infrastructure of the analysis that follows. However, this analysis also recognizes the fundamental interconnectedness of theory and experience/practice. So an elaboration of erotic subjectivity must prove incomplete without attention not only to its theoretical moorings (even if Lorde's conceptualization of the erotic is saturated with the wisdom of personal experience and shared activism) but also to what it might be used to *do* in any given instance. Friends For Life—in its formation, in the consciousness of its leadership, and in its most successful program (the Chatroom)—demonstrates how to do work with an implicitly understood frame of erotic subjectivity. And it is through FFL that we are able to approach erotic subjectivity as necessary, life-saving praxis. We begin with the political.

A Politics of Voice: Grassroots Organizing and the Din of Survival

Founded on October 2, 1997, Friends For Life emerged between the two years in which T&T reported the highest numbers of AIDS-related deaths to date.[11] The simple—though formidable—directive that guided the founders of FFL pivots principally on the question of mortality. The perennially troubling dialectic between death and life—made even more ghastly by the ravages of an epidemic at its most ravenous—haunted FFL into existence. In other words, the organization's timely birth was the direct result of an unexpected death.

In 2003 and 2008 I conducted a series of interviews with FFL cofounder and longtime staff member Kerwyn L. Jordan. A thirty-seven-year-old Afro-Trinidadian gay man raised in Sangre Grande, Jordan described the painful loss that gave breath to the group's organizing imperative:

There was a group of us. I think seven . . . we became a clique, so that anywhere you see one of us, you see all of us. And then we somewhat missed one individual. [And Jordan casually inquired,] "But you know, it's a long time I haven't seen Reynaldo. Has anybody heard from [him]?" And there wasn't any genuine thought given to it until later on after like four months when Eswick [Padmore] and Cleveland [Gervais] and myself sat and we were thinking that something was wrong with him. . . . Because last time I saw him he really wasn't looking that good. But he did not tell me he was ill.

So, Eswick and Cleveland were considering whether to go and see him. . . . there was talk about it, but everybody had other commitments. So it never really came to fruition until the morning after the guy died. When Eswick went to visit him, he was told that he died the night before. We all were very distraught about that because here was a group of friends and we didn't even know our friend was dying. That was March of 1997.

We thought about doing something for these people who are afraid to even tell their own friends that they're sick, who might be discriminated against or ostracized even more by society—other than [for] being gay—now that they are HIV positive. [We wanted to] formulate something that we could do for them. We eventually called ourselves "Friends For Life."

. . . And of course the group is dedicated in the memory of Reynaldo Thomas.[12]

Thomas's passing would be only the first of many that this group of friends—the founding members of FFL—would have to endure. But the regret beneath their grief inspired a resolution to do for each other and for others all that they had not been able to do for Thomas.

Still reeling from this abrupt loss and discomforted by his own aching regret, Eswick Padmore—the forty-five-year-old Afro-Trinidadian gay man from Diego Martin who was FFL's principal founder—set out to form the nation's first gay-focused HIV/AIDS service provision organization.[13] Founded on a compassionate concern primarily for the well-being of gay Caribbean men, FFL was initially unconcerned with funding, legislation, infrastructure, or notoriety. Instead, FFL held as its core governing principle a commitment to the survival of the very gay men whose lives in some regard depended on it. Delano Thompson—a gay Afro-Trinidadian man in his midthirties and a longtime FFL member—reminisced about the organization's grassroots origins in an interview I conducted with him in Tobago in 2007:

> Friends For Life [he closes his eyes and smiles into a hard sigh]. This was an organization that when you talk about grassroots, it couldn't get any more grassroots than this. We were having meetings on the Promenade and in fast food outlets and they were throwing us out and so on because we didn't have a space . . . but we knew what we wanted to do. . . . Finally, we started doing hospital visits, visiting people, giving them that encouragement. . . . when you do this you encourage people to go on and then some people actually start recovering because part of recovery is a will to live. . . . We were doing that and people started taking notice.[14]

In fact, FFL was able to successfully convene and mobilize various networks of gay Trinbagonian men largely because the groundwork for this community building had already been laid by an earlier — though not well-documented — history of gay male organizing across the Caribbean region and especially in Trinidad.[15] In fact, FFL's longest-running program by far actually predates FFL.

The Chatroom began as a series of HIV/AIDS education and community-building workshops for gay men convened at least as early as 1994.[16] Ironically, it was precisely the informal resource-sharing fostered in the Chatroom that provided FFL with its first opportunity for official funding in May 2001 from UNAIDS — only three months before the Chatroom itself became the charge of FFL.[17] The Chatroom has for some time now kept breath in the body of FFL by serving as a mechanism for FFL to assess the particular needs of gay male communities, its capacity to meet those needs, and the nature of the relationship between it and those communities most in need.

Buttressed by the Chatroom, FFL has been remarkably successful at reaching working-class, underemployed, or unemployed urban Afro-Trinbagonian men who overwhelmingly self-identify as "gay" — and in many cases are quite vocal about being openly gay. It is precisely these populations who are inadequately attended to by the vast majority of the nation's HIV/AIDS-related initiatives. Given FFL's grassroots origin in a series of conversations among this very community of gay men, it is most appropriate that the organization is sustained by its inherited Chatroom — in essence, a space for discussion devoted to preserving life and defending a politics of overall well-being.

A weekly, two-hour open discussion forum, FFL's Chatroom remains to date a site for collective reflection and exchange that ultimately fosters community building — a vital activist gesture in its own right. Although HIV seroconversion is a likely motivating factor for a significant proportion of those who gravitate toward FFL, it is undoubtedly the case that a majority of gay men get involved in

FFL because it provides support services—both formal and informal—targeted specifically for and sensitive to the particular needs of gay men.

In a 2007 interview I conducted with FFL president and principal Chatroom facilitator Luke Sinnette, he explained the simple but crucial work of the Chatroom. Sinnette is a thirty-one-year-old Afro-Trinidadian gay man who was raised in Santa Cruz:

> I never anticipated that it [the Chatroom] would last, but the fact that it did last is a beautiful thing because it shows that people refuse to let go of liberation—*refuse* to let go of it. And [we at FFL] use that Chatroom as a place to bring persons in and just to have them yap and quarrel and talk. Because within every movement there's that space where talk happens. And that's all you do for a long time—just talk—even if you're arguing or disagreeing, just talk [and] talk. And somewhere in that talking, the tide starts to turn and it turns and turns until eventually it's pushing in the other direction.
>
> [I ask Sinnette to tell me what he thinks keeps people coming to the Chatroom.] It's the experience. It's the therapeutic value of the Chatroom. You can't deny that talking and venting about things helps. It's undeniable. Even persons who don't like to talk come to Chatrooms to watch other people talk. There's a way that just watching other people talk about things and hearing it— you don't have to say [anything]—can [encourage you to] reevaluate for yourself [from] hearing their experience and [thinking], "Um-hmm, I did that and maybe I should have done that [instead]." And that moves you; it's a growth. Human beings have this desire to be better tomorrow than they are today—they really do [he says with a spirited grace]. The Chatroom itself pushes it forward. I don't think I do anything remarkable other than ask questions at a Chatroom. But that power of the experience is what pushes it and keeps people coming back and coming back and coming back.
>
> . . . the most remarkable and most subtle things like just coming to a Chatroom and asking, "So, how does everybody feel tonight?" can [bring about] remarkable life-changing experiences for the person who answers, "I really don't feel good, but now that I'm here—phew!" . . . this is not *just* people coming together to talk—it's not, it's not just that!
>
> . . . And to not have this, to not have *this*?! When you think about it, if [the] Chatroom was missing, fifteen years down the line we would still be struggling to find out how do we get spaces to talk. But if we talk now,

fifteen years down the line we could be struggling to find how do we open a gay hospice for battered gay persons and to think about gay persons in a way that's not oppressive.[18]

A therapeutic space for exchange, assessment, and collective intervention, the Chatroom not only facilitates joint action but also provides a way to perpetually evaluate and improve those actions.

Even if this reflexive dialectic between conversation and action is not immediately recognizable or does not seem to follow an obvious teleology, it begins to come into view as part of a longer perspective on movement building. The simple act of "checking in" weekly with a fluctuating population of gay men has the potential to link individual experiences by fostering among its members a community of care in which each person begins to develop concern for the well-being of his fellow Chatroom participants. Not only is this shared sense of community a crucial political project in and of itself, but it also makes most other political activism possible.

The Sensuality of Activism: The Chatroom and the Uses of Desire

Intimacy has been central to FFL's activism from the very beginning, and a desire to sustain healthy intimate networks (between friends or sexual partners) has long sustained the Chatroom. Corporeal proximity in the Chatroom holds out the tender promise of various kinds of relationships that often provide the connective tissue for the organization's community-building initiatives. It would be naive to presume that sexual encounters and ongoing sexual relationships would not be included as part of the interpersonal contact facilitated by the Chatroom. In fact, FFL officially recognizes that one motivating factor behind the continued attendance of Chatroom participants has long been an interest in meeting potential partners.

Still, it would be a mistake to believe that the Chatroom—or any of FFL's programs, for that matter—has ever actively encouraged sexual intimacy between participants. The organization's forthright handling of sexuality ought not to be confused with promoting sex per se. Yet sex is central to FFL's HIV prevention work. If in T&T—as in the majority of the Caribbean region—sexual intercourse remains the primary route of HIV transmission, then HIV/AIDS activism in the region must attend to individual sexual practices and collective patterns of sexual behavior. Far from avoiding conversations about (safer) sexual practices and (improving) relationships, FFL has institutionalized these discussions and holds them at the center of the organization's work. The longevity of this intervention strategy is partly the result of the Chatroom's ability to hold open a sexually charged space devoted to conversations about sexual and social health concerns.

Although many of these conversations about sexual practices and intimate relationships are far from unrestrained, it is important to consider them in a context where most people still remain relatively tight-lipped about most forms of sexuality. Sinnette explained the irony of this context in our 2007 interview:

> You have the experience—and it's very close to my experience as well, so in that way, I'm indicative of a Trinidadian—where you like somebody, eventually you get close to them, and you might get intimate, but you don't really have a conversation about sex. But somewhere in this exploration you do things and figure it out. You get a touch that's not too nice and you don't want that one; you get a touch that's really good and you're ecstatic about it. But all of that in body language—in that nonverbal way of exploring and communicating. I think that's how Trinidadian sexuality is represented.
>
> I think in very many respects we're jarred by the nature of sex and how powerful it is. And so it's kind of scary. And so we try to bridle it in many instances, but bridle it without talk. So, like how you have that concept of being politically correct in the [United] States, you have in Trinidad more of a bridling of sexual words and descriptions by using words that are not so close to the sexual words like "butterfly" instead of "vagina."
>
> But at the same time [that you are] not speaking it . . . [you are nonetheless]—in quiet intimate spaces—doing that kind of exploring and touching. I don't mean touching with hands, but exploring and touching what is going on with yourself . . . not being sure about how far we should go and how deep. . . . But through it all, not that talking but that *doing* . . . doing it is allowable, but showing it or speaking it is too tough.[19]

Even though Sinnette eloquently echoes the overwhelming sentiment on the prohibitions and possibilities through which sexuality is negotiated by the various Trinbagonians (gay and not) whom I consulted—informally and formally—on the matter, articulating some "characteristically Trinbagonian" relationship to sexuality is perhaps less vital than recognizing the ambivalence that Sinnette brings to the fore.

The meticulously maintained gap between what is said about sex and what is done—though far from an exclusively Trinbagonian phenomenon—is readily recognized as a rather mundane practice among many Trinbagonians. If it is through touch—outwardly directed caress or inwardly directed contemplation—and not necessarily through talk that many gay Trinbagonian men (among others) explore their sexual desires, this may be—as Sinnette indicates—because the available language is presumed to outright refuse (or at least restrain) direct engagements with sex and sexuality in discourse.[20] However, a principally nonverbal, corporeal investigation of sexual permissibility poses a particular kind of challenge for HIV prevention initiatives among gay men for two reasons: (1) behavior change interventions are made exceedingly difficult if men are unwilling to have conversations about their actual sexual behavior patterns; and (2) successful interventions with individual men can be easily undermined if they are unwilling or unable to discuss necessary behavior changes—condom or water-based lubricant usage, for instance—with their sexual partners before or even during a sexual encounter.[21] However, it is certainly a mistake to presume that because these types of conversations are perhaps improbable that they are summarily impossible to cultivate. The Chatroom itself articulately contests any such presuppositions.

The Chatroom clears a space for open discussion about various topics—many directly or indirectly related to sexual practices, but just as many not primarily sexual at all—while serving as a perhaps undervalued assessment mechanism for (sexual) behavior patterns in gay communities. In Trinidad, the Chatroom sessions I recorded addressed not only (Internet) dating, commitment in relationships, and the meaning of love but also sexual assault, condom usage frequency, and the transmission, symptoms, and treatment of sexually transmitted infections—especially HIV. Although this range is far from comprehensive, it is certainly the case that sex, intimacy, and relationships are darling tropes of the Chatroom's perpetually extended conversation. These particular discussions provide both a model for the kind of open engagement necessary for condom-use negotiation and the discernibly alluring *frisson* of reveling in tabooed speech. Thus desire often determines both the thrust of the Chatroom conversation, even despite the facilitator's chosen topic in some instances, and the constitution of the Chatroom itself—a space that exists only as long as the longing for conversation lasts.

Clearing Sacred Space: HIV/AIDS Mortality and the Spiritual Impulse of the Chatroom

While they are a favorite topic and an understandable area of heightened concern for individual HIV-prevention interventions, sexual practices are far from the only recurring theme in the Chatroom. In fact, FFL's commitment to psycho-social holism as a fundamental part of its HIV/AIDS prevention care and support strategy compels a persistent framing of the Chatroom as a space of fellowship ultimately in the service of collective sociosexual and spiritual well-being. Implicitly addressed through group reflection on the sometimes metaphysical nature of that fellowship or explicitly considered in conversations about religious strictures—usually Christian—and agentive belief, spirituality is consistently summoned in the Chatroom partly because it is such a formidable presence in the lives of so many gay Trinbagonian men.

In the Chatroom—as in the vast majority of the seventy-five individual interviews I conducted with LGBT Trinbagonians on each of the sister isles—beliefs about the extent to which Christianity condemns or condones homosexuality (even for non-Christians) were perhaps less a matter of concern than individual spiritual communion with God. There can be little doubt that many Trinbagonian gay men struggle to resolve a presumed inconsistency between their sexuality and their religious beliefs; however, the majority of Chatroom participants have at least publicly found some means by which to reconcile their sexual desire and their spiritual foundation. It is often the case that FFL in general and the Chatroom in particular have inspired that reconciliation or at least served as a significant support structure for that reconciliatory process.

The commitment of FFL's leadership to a by-no-means-uncomplicated spiritual devotion undoubtedly determines the character of the organization and of the Chatroom with regard to faith. Padmore—FFL's principal founder, as mentioned previously—had the following to say about his spirituality:

> I don't know if to say, "I *am* religious." I don't know if to say I'm not. Now, of course, you have to understand also that—as far as I'm concerned—you don't have to go to church to pray. You can lie down in your bed, kneel down in your house, and God will answer your prayer. I believe that. You don't have to go to church. The church is just a place for the community to come together as one. But if you can't [go to church], you can't. Yes, you should; but if you can't, you can't.
>
> . . . We as gay people in growing up try to live to please people. Your mother says *x* and you're doing that. Your friends say *y* and you're trying that. We try to please everybody and in the end we don't please ourselves. I have reached the point where I realize that life is in me. And so, I'm going to live my life. I'm going to try in the process to please God because I don't think we can totally please Him. We are going to fall short, but it is a trying process. We keep trying and we keep praying and we keep

> asking for forgiveness. But for me it's a trying process and I'm going to keep trying.
>
> At the end of the journey, He's the only one who's going to judge me. Don't care what my friends say — what Luke says, what Kerwyn, Harry, Mary, Lyndon, or whoever — He is going to judge me according to how I live my life.
>
> And so, I'm going to try to do what I know I have to do and leave it up to Him in the end. . . . Not because you're gay God doesn't love you. He loves all people. . . . And at the end — anyhow you take it — He's going to judge you.[22]

Although he is raised in the Roman Catholic faith and still considers himself a devout Catholic — even if he is a bit errant in his churchgoing — Padmore emphasizes the quotidian intimacy of spirituality over and above any site-specific religious experience. He does not underestimate the importance of spiritual communion but realizes that it is the fellowship primarily that makes a space sacred and not the space that makes the fellowship something holy.

For Padmore, relationships — *inter*subjectivities — determine the domain of the sacred; one's personal relationship with a metaphysical presence *and* one's relationship with a community determine one's spiritual positioning. It may seem somewhat counterintuitive, but Padmore's life and work with FFL bear witness to the importance of personal spiritual struggle — a perpetual process — for providing a subject with clarity about the community in which to seek fellowship. Padmore's personal confidence about his own moral rectitude — the hard-fought result of constantly challenging himself to live up to his moral ideals — not only provided part of the push to birth FFL but also provides sustenance for his commitment to the organization.

If an intimate spiritual consciousness and a considered spiritual confidence form the soul of FFL, then the Chatroom clears a space for weekly reflection and reinforcement of that core in fellowship with a similarly oriented community. While it is certainly not the case that all participants in the Chatroom consistently share spiritual belief systems or even interpretations of a shared religion, it is their communion — even if they do not assemble for an explicitly religious purpose — that gives a spiritual quality to the experience. It is in this sense that the Chatroom comes to look like a church, temple, or mosque — not the structural home of a particular religion but a metaphorical clearing in which collective relationships (with the unseen and the seen) are fostered.

Just as conversations in the Chatroom need not always focus on HIV/AIDS to be a part of a holistic intervention strategy, so too can a spiritual intervention result from the very act of gathering for fellowship. In fact, the Chatroom's indirect—though no less persistent—emphasis on HIV/AIDS very likely encourages attention to spirituality as the result of a perhaps unwitting fear of mortality. If HIV/AIDS is central to FFL's organizing mandate and even the most casual reflection on this ostensibly fatal disease brings our inevitable mortality into especially sharp view, then spirituality—one of the principal means by which most of humanity attends to birth, death, and the "life" after each—effectively haunts considerations of HIV/AIDS and makes it nearly impossible to conceive of the pandemic without confronting death (as actuality or possibility) and turning to spiritual reassurances.

Nevertheless, it would be a mistake to presume that these spiritual considerations—often over and against any particular religious doctrine—are merely incidental for the Chatroom. Indeed, FFL and the Chatroom have both persevered in no small part because of their spiritually grounded participants and leadership. Although seldom defined as an explicitly spiritual space, the Chatroom has long served as one of the few ongoing—and certainly one of the oldest—forums within which gay Trinbagonian men collectively address issues of religion, spirituality, and sexuality in semipublic discussions. The Chatroom holds open a space for each individual to explore the possibility of an intimate and dynamic relationship with a spirituality not necessarily moored to any particular religious doctrine. But by collectively strengthening this spirituality, the Chatroom also encourages a sacred intimacy cultivated in community. The forum serves as an underrecognized site for collective spiritual fellowship.

Conclusion: On the Uses of Erotic Subjectivity

The various types of relationships—political alliances, sexual networks, and spiritual connections—that Friends For Life fosters through the Chatroom experience have been the organization's saving grace for a decade. And the uses to which FFL's leadership puts erotic subjectivity has in turn sustained a community of principally gay Afro-Trinidadian men for just as long. An elaboration of a praxis of survival inherited from the experience-based theorizing of Lorde and set down in Trinidad by a group of mourning friends at the height of a devastating epidemic, this analysis began by outlining erotic subjectivity as an epistemological intervention. I then turned to Trinidad—an important site for monitoring early responses to HIV/AIDS in the Caribbean's anglophone world—to introduce FFL and its Chatroom program. The organization and its most resilient program both model a gay male–initiated and gay male–focused strategy for survival rooted in an implicit respect for erotic subjectivity. This look at FFL is offered through the theoretical prism of erotic subjectivity both as interpretive lens and as the driving principle — even if not explicitly named as such — behind an imperative of collective fellowship. In fact, it was by exploring the uses of the political, the sensual, and the spiritual in the formation, the leadership, and the oldest program of FFL that I fleshed out my articulation of erotic subjectivity. In essence, we came to know what it *is* primarily through exploring what it *does* — or how the political-sensual-spiritual manifest and coexist in the psycho-social work that the FFL Chatroom does for gay Afro-Trinbagonian men.

It is the fertile intertangling of the political, sensual, and spiritual in the emergence, leadership, and primary program of FFL that holds pride of place in this analysis. This trinity is not incidental but central to the intervention FFL is making as a gay-centered, HIV/AIDS service-providing Caribbean NGO. Often an explicitly named activist organizing environment in which interpersonal connections are cultivated as a way to encourage the building of support networks, the FFL Chatroom channels collective concern for the health and well-being of fellow gay men into a political project. Yet because this grassroots-oriented, community-building work not only requires collective concern but also demands a consistent corporeal proximity, sensuality figures prominently in the survival project. The Chatroom is enhanced by its insistence on bodies in contact. And far from getting in the way of the important matter at hand, sensuality *is* the way to best attend — fingers outstretched — to an epidemic.[23] And if contagion inevitably reveals various routes of contact — in essence, the myriad places and means by which we (or any living species) touch — then HIV not only places a steady finger on our intersubjectivity but also pushes us toward an *intra*subjective confrontation with our own mortality.[24] If considerations of mortality tend to be the center pole in the hallowed ground of spirituality, then the metaphysical haunts any discussion of HIV/AIDS. So the absence of formal engagement with religion in the Chatroom cannot be misrecognized as a spiritual lack. In fact, I have made the case that the Chatroom serves as a figurative sacred space, providing weekly respite and fellowship. This analysis has highlighted the usefulness of recognizing an interlinked spiritual-sensual-political (erotic) subjectivity for a grassroots struggle to survive in the midst of a vicious pandemic.

In the hands of Friends For Life, the political, the sensual, and the spiritual become tools for building, holding, and transcendentalizing community. A not always deliberate frame and a not always explicitly determined method, erotic subjectivity persists nonetheless as one of the organization's most valuable resources, its most fixed capital. If it is true that AIDS in the anglophone Caribbean was first discovered among gay men in Trinidad, it might be wise to return to that self-same isle for one of the oldest HIV prevention and support models birthed by Afro-Trinbagonian gay men in an effort to save their own lives. Welcoming the viral spread of the FFL Chatroom model — across the Caribbean, throughout the black queer diaspora, and even beyond these sites — introduces into a host of spaces not only a way to think the political, spiritual, and sensual together but also a mechanism for *doing* community-based work informed — even if indirectly — by a contagious erotic subjectivity.

Notes

I must first thank Jafari Allen not only for inviting me to participate in the Black/Queer/Diaspora Work(ing) Group he convened in 2009 at Yale University but also for patiently encouraging and editing this article for publication. I am also most grateful to Vanessa Agard-Jones and Phanuel Antwi for their meticulous reviews of an earlier version of this essay. Rinaldo Walcott helped point me in the right direction, and I appreciate his gentle nudge. Finally, an anonymous reviewer's critique encouraged many of the text's improvements, and for that I am also thankful. Of course, any shortcomings in what follows are solely my own.

1. Of course the smoke-fire counterargument against this elision is seldom apparent to anyone quite confident that Caribbean-born homosexuals living and loving in the region where they were born simply cannot exist. As irritating as it is to admit, homophobic smoke is often a pretty good indication that the fire of homosexuality is raging on nearby.
2. For press coverage of a recent spate of violence against lesbians and trans women of color in Washington, DC, see Lou Chibbaro Jr., "D.C. Police Struggle over Disclosure of Transgender Murder," *Washington Blade*, July 21, 2011; and "5 Lesbians Attacked; Police Refuse to Take Report," *Washington Blade*, August 5, 2011. May Lashai Mclean rest in peace.
3. Although there exist significant self-identified lesbian, bisexual, and transgender communities in the Caribbean as well as individuals who embrace same-sex desire or gender nonconformity but reject LGBT identification or terminology (this latter group is still not very well documented in the available literature), these groups are not the focus of the present analysis. Similarly, although Trinidad's population is roughly split between populations of African and Indian descent (as a result of slavery and post-Emancipation indentureship), the organization on which this analysis focuses is overwhelmingly run by and for men of African descent, even if this is not explicitly intended or the participation of men (or women) from the various other racial/ethnic

groups found in Trinidad (including Native American, Chinese, Syrian, and white French Creole populations as well as mixes of these) is not discouraged.

4. For one of the most recent and nuanced treatments of "MSM" from its appearance in the medical literature in the late 1980s as a way to shift attention from identity categories (like "gay") toward behavioral categories, to its subtle "proleptic" movement toward an identity category in its own right, see Tom Boellstorff, "But Do Not Identify as Gay: A Proleptic Genealogy of the MSM Category," *Cultural Anthropology* 26, no. 2 (2011): 287–312. On the misuses of *MSM*, see also Ilan Meyer and Rebecca Young, "The Trouble with 'MSM' and 'WSW': Erasure of the Sexual Minority Person in Public Health Discourse," *American Journal of Public Health* 95, no. 7 (2005): 1144–49.

5. From the earliest MSM seroprevalence survey in the Caribbean region to one of the most recent—both conducted in Trinidad—recruitment bias has continually made it nearly impossible to accurately assess the scale of HIV infection outside the specific subpopulation of Caribbean MSM who identify as "gay" and frequent STI clinics or HIV/AIDS organizations. See Courtenay Bartholomew et al., "Transmission of HTLV-I and HIV among Homosexual Men in Trinidad," *Journal of the American Medical Association* 257, no. 19 (1987): 2604–8; and R. K. Lee, *Many Partnered Men: A Behavioural and HIV Seroprevalence Study of Men Who Have Sex with Men in Trinidad* (Port-of-Spain: Caribbean Epidemiology Centre, 2005). Although the alarmist statistics on Trinidadian populations of MSM that resulted from these studies provide a far-from-reliable glimpse of HIV prevalence within the general population of Trinbagonian MSM, they do reveal a history of frightfully high rates of HIV infection among gay-identified MSM who make use of STI prevention and management services. This portends danger for the wider population of MSM—but especially for gay men—regardless of whether the group's overall HIV prevalence rate is lower.

6. Since 1986 unprotected heterosexual intercourse has been the primary mode of HIV transmission in the majority of the Caribbean region (including T&T): see Bilali Camara, "An Overview of the AIDS/HIV/STD Situation in the Caribbean," in *The Caribbean AIDS Epidemic*, ed. Glenford Howe and Alan Cobley (Kingston: University of the West Indies Press, 2000), 2; Kamala Kempadoo, "Dying for Sex: HIV/AIDS and Other Dangers," in *Sex, Power, and Taboo: Gender and HIV in the Caribbean and Beyond*, ed. Dorothy Roberts et al. (Kingston: Ian Randle, 2009), 4; UNAIDS, *AIDS Epidemic Update* (Geneva: UNAIDS, 2010), 42. However, almost thirty years after the first cases of AIDS-related illness among homosexual men were reported in the medical literature, MSM are still identified in the Caribbean region (and across the globe) as one of the groups most at risk for HIV infection. But on what statistical evidence does such a claim rest? The overwhelming majority of the very same studies that attest to the disproportionate risk and elevated rates of HIV infection among MSM globally decry the absolute dearth of accurate statistical information on MSM

populations and call for much more systematic MSM surveillance systems in hopes of obtaining the very data necessary for making any confident statements about the risks MSM face in the HIV/AIDS pandemic. See C. F. Caceres, "MSM Populations in Low and Middle-Income Countries: Assessing Magnitude, Sexual Behaviour, and HIV Prevalence" (paper presented at the VXI International AIDS Conference, Toronto, August 13–18, 2006); Foundation for AIDS Research, *MSM, HIV, and the Road to Universal Access — How Far Have We Come?* (New York: amfAR, 2008); UNAIDS, *UNAIDS Action Framework: Universal Access for Men Who Have Sex with Men and Transgender People* (Geneva: UNAIDS, 2009); World Health Organization, *Prevention and Treatment of HIV and Other Sexually Transmitted Infections among Men Who Have Sex with Men and Transgender Populations* (Geneva: WHO, 2009); Stephen Baral, "Elevated Risk for HIV Infection among Men Who Have Sex with Men in Low and Middle-Income Countries, 2000–2006: A Systematic Review," *PLoS Medicine* 4, no. 12 (2007).

7. The Republic of Trinidad and Tobago is the southernmost archipelagic nation of the Caribbean, lying just outside the chain of islands known as the Lesser Antilles and just northeast of Venezuela. Although I have conducted ethnographic research on both of the two principle islands that lend their names to this archipelagic nation-state, the present analysis focuses on the island of Trinidad. Mindful of the significant historical, cultural, and political differences between the islands, I nevertheless acknowledge that Trinbagonian culture knows no particular geopolitical boundaries. It is also important to note that following naming practices on the island and in diaspora, Trinidadians of African descent will be referred to as "Afro-Trinidadians" (in contrast most notably to "Indo-Trinidadians" or Trinidadians of South Asian descent, who make up roughly half of the island's population).

8. There appears to be a consensus in the scholarly literature that the first cases of AIDS-related illness and death (recorded exclusively among gay and bisexual men) were reported in Jamaica as early as 1982. See Jai Narain et al., "Epidemiology of AIDS and HIV Infection in the Caribbean," *Pan American Health Organization Bulletin* 23, nos. 1–2 (1989): 43; Camara, "Overview," 2; Dorothy Roberts et al., eds., *Sex, Power, and Taboo: Gender and HIV in the Caribbean and Beyond* (Kingston: Ian Randle Publishers, 2009), xi. This literature rests that claim solely on Narain's assertion of this seeming fact; however, his 1989 article provides no official citation for this confirmatory case in the medical literature. Instead, there is unavoidable evidence gathered by the esteemed Trinidadian physician and University of the West Indies professor emeritus of medicine Courtenay Bartholomew and his team that refutes this claim. The available data — published in some of the most highly regarded, meticulously peer-reviewed, and widely circulated medical journals in the world — indicate that AIDS in the anglophone Caribbean was in fact first documented in Trinidad. See Courtney Bartholomew et al., "The Acquired Immune Defi-

ciency Syndrome in Trinidad: A Report on Two Cases," *West Indian Medical Journal* 32 (1983): 177–80, "AIDS on Trinidad," *Lancet* 1 (1984): 103, "Racial and Other Characteristics of Human T Cell Leukaemia/Lymphona (HTLV-I) and AIDS (HTLV-III) in Trinidad," *British Medical Journal* 290 (1985): 1243–46, and "Transmission of HTLV-I and HIV among Homosexual Men in Trinidad," *Journal of the American Medical Association* 257, no. 19 (1987): 2604–8.

9. Undoubtedly, libraries of scholarly texts have previously engaged Eros and subjectivity in one form or another. For one of the oldest written engagements with the subject, see Plato, *Symposium*, trans. Robin Waterfield (Oxford: Oxford University Press, 1994). However, a few more recent texts have made explicit use of the precise phrase "erotic subjectivity." See Don Kulick and Margaret Wilson, eds., *Taboo: Sex, Identity, and Erotic Subjectivity in Anthropological Fieldwork* (New York: Routledge, 1995); Jafari Allen, *¡Venceremos? The Erotics of Black Self-Making in Cuba* (Durham, NC: Duke University Press, 2011); and Mimi Sheller, *Citizenship from Below: Caribbean Agency and Embodied Freedom* (Durham, NC: Duke University Press, 2012). What distinguishes my particular usage of the phrase from these previous engagements is an investment in expanding an understanding of the erotic beyond intimacy/desire/love/sex toward a fuller conceptualization that holds on to this sensuality, but augments it with attention to broader registers of erotics.

10. The text of this speech delivered on August 25, 1978, has been most notably published in Audre Lorde, *Sister Outsider: Essays and Speeches* (Trumansburg, NY: Crossing Press, 1984), 53–59.

11. For statistics on AIDS-related deaths in T&T from 1996 to 1998, see the National AIDS Coordinating Committee of Trinidad and Tobago (NACC), *United Nations General Assembly Special Session on HIV/AIDS Country Report: Republic of Trinidad and Tobago* (Port-of-Spain: Republic of Trinidad and Tobago, 2006 and 2008), 6 and 9, respectively. For the most recent statistics on HIV/AIDS in T&T, see NACC, *United Nations General Assembly Special Session on HIV/AIDS Country Report: Republic of Trinidad and Tobago* (Port-of-Spain: Republic of Trinidad and Tobago, 2010).

12. Kerwyn Jordan, conversation with author, June 7, 2003, and July 7, 2008.

13. Despite the claim in FFL's official literature that its HIV/AIDS prevention, care, and support services include lesbians and MSM who do not necessarily self-identify as gay or bisexual, the organization has not yet been able to successfully execute programs geared specifically toward these populations. The most significant work FFL has done with lesbian or nongay/bisexual MSM populations has been the result of occasional one-on-one health education or referrals.

14. Delano Thompson, conversation with author, November 7, 2007.

15. The gay Jamaican American activist and author Thomas Glave suggests that gay and lesbian organizing in the Caribbean region may have begun as early as 1987 with Jamaica's Gay Freedom Movement (pers. comm., September 2010).

16. These workshops (or "Sex Talks" as they were called) were coordinated by the formidable Trinidadian dramatist, dancer, theater designer, and gay activist Geoffrey Stanforde. Stanforde was diagnosed HIV-positive in 1990 and died on October 25, 2001, at the age of forty-seven. See "Geoffrey Stanforde Dies after Illness," *Trinidad and Tobago Guardian* (Port-of-Spain), October 27, 2001.

17. Over four years after its founding, FFL received this first official funding commitment from an international HIV/AIDS organization. It was not until April 2008—over a decade after FFL's founding—that the organization received the first commitment of funding from the government of T&T. The NACC finally approved in 2008 a Chatroom maintenance and expansion pilot project that was submitted for approval in 2004. The ludicrousness of FFL's having been ignored for funding from the NACC for a full four years is made even more stark when one considers that the nation's 2003 *Five-Year National HIV/AIDS Strategic Plan* (NSP)—the document that effectively brings the NACC into existence as part of demonstrating a heightened prime minister–led response to the epidemic—*explicitly* mentions both FFL and the Chatroom as the key tools with which the nation will address HIV prevention among MSM populations. See Government of Trinidad and Tobago, *Five-Year National HIV/AIDS Strategic Plan: January 2004–December 2008* (Port-of-Spain: Republic of Trinidad and Tobago, 2003), 19, 22, 23, 47. Yet the Chatroom did not receive any funding whatsoever from the NACC until the final months of the final year of this five-year NSP—which has since been extended for an additional two years.

18. Luke Sinnette, conversation with author, July 9, 2007.

19. Sinnette, conversation.

20. Calypso music may seem to offer a centuries-old counterexample to this claim because of the persistence of sex and sexuality as tropes. However, the genre's sly facility with double entendre echoes the point I am making about Trinbagonians' strategic reliance on indirection when discussing sex and sexuality.

21. On the importance and the challenges of communication between Caribbean male sex partners, see Brader Brathwaite and Godfrey Sealy, *Gay Research Initiative on AIDS Prevention in the Caribbean* (phases 1 and 2) (Port-of-Spain: Caribbean Epidemiology Centre, 1996, 2000 [1998]).

22. Eswick Padmore, conversation with author, August 7, 2003, and May 14, 2008.

23. The word *epidemic* itself is derived from the Greek for "resting upon or touching people."

24. For an elegant articulation of this relationship between contagion and contact, see Priscilla Wald, *Contagious: Cultures, Carriers, and the Outbreak Narrative* (Durham, NC: Duke University Press, 2008).

QUEER(Y)ING FREEDOM

Black Queer Visibilities in Postapartheid South Africa

Xavier Livermon

On any given Thursday night, the residents of Soweto gather around their radios to listen to the salacious radio show *Cheaters*. Inspired partly by the US-based television show of the same name, and broadcast on Jozi FM, the radio show encourages disgruntled lovers who suspect their partners of infidelity to call in and have the radio station investigate.[1] The show asks, "Are you having a problem with your lover? Infidelity, *Uyajola?*"[2] If the answer is affirmative, the parties are asked to call a hotline number. Typically, the investigation takes several weeks, but at its conclusion the disgruntled lover, his or her partner, and the person he or she is being unfaithful with are invited to the radio station. The invitation often involves some form of deception, as the idea is generally to attract the unfaithful lover and his or her accomplice to the station unaware of exactly why they are there. What follows is a raucous exchange of words between the wronged party, his or her lover, and the person with whom he or she is cheating. Unlike the American version of the show, which is screened on television, the radio version in Soweto is broadcast live and encourages audiences to comment and participate. Thus the pleasure of listening to the show comes not only from hearing the battling parties reveal the most intimate details of their dysfunctional relationships in the most graphic detail but also from the commentary and questions from the listeners who call in. Furthering the public humiliation of the parties is the fact that a large crowd often gathers outside the radio station itself, to catch a glimpse of the players. The aggrieved party receives offers of support and encouragement, while those considered on the wrong side of this moral play are subjected to verbal, and in some cases physical, abuse.[3]

Predictably, this radio drama plays out in ways that are specifically gendered and heteronormative. Overwhelmingly, those who seek redress in the public forum are women who have been wronged by unfaithful male lovers. This often pits the "good" faithful woman against the "bad" wanton woman who is the man's paramour. Not surprisingly, the men in this scenario are not usually the target of commentary or public scorn. Men calling the show to investigate the infidelity of female lovers are far less common. This is partly because of a certain machismo constructed around South African masculine identity where it is assumed that a man can handle issues of infidelity on his own, without getting others involved. Furthermore, because of gendered hierarchies inherent in postapartheid South Africa, men whose female lovers cheat on them with other men are more likely to receive scorn than support, because accusers are made less masculine in this process. This is because it is assumed that these men either could not sexually satisfy their partners or could not exert appropriate masculine control over their women.

One important exception to the involvement of men as accusing parties is the number of gay-identified men who have called in to complain about unfaithful lovers.[4] On one particular night in 2005, a gay man confronted his "straight" male lover about his infidelity.[5] The lover was fairly unrepentant and even went so far as to laugh openly about his infidelity and to boast that he had played his partner for money. In essence, he explained to all who would listen that the basis of the relationship was purely financial, and now that he had milked the duped gay man dry, he was moving on to greener pastures (presumably the other man with whom he was cheating). Then he stated that other "straight" men should, like him, realize the financial possibilities of relationships with gay men and similarly take advantage of them. "Brothers, let's fuck these gay guys and take their money." Immediately a number of young male callers phoned in, offering to help the unfaithful man in his enterprise. They offered their services, suggesting that they too would be willing to play the game, assuming the price was right. The aggrieved gay man lashed out, "I have been screwing you; you bitch! Why don't you tell your homeboys that? I hope they are prepared to give up their ass as easily as you were, 'cuz that's the only way they're getting any money!" Whether or not his assertion was true, he certainly upset conventional wisdom on the nature of same-sex relationships in Soweto, and this particular episode of *Cheaters* caused quite a sensation, as it became fodder for the Friday morning taxi commute, which serves as a primary version of "water cooler" talk in Soweto. These conversations after the fact revealed a lively public debate, much of which centered on the appropriateness of the increasing visibility of queer relationships and queer people in the black public sphere.[6]

This example animates many of the central concerns of this essay on black queer visibilities and the creation of freedom in postapartheid South Africa. For black queers, equal, if not more, importance must be paid to a notion of freedom that rests on forms of cultural belonging (family, community, culture, nation, and race) that retain their salience in the postapartheid era and cannot be fully accounted for by the state. As such, black queer struggles for recognition and respect are less about a challenge to the state (although this is important, particularly when state actors invoke culture to exclude black queers) than about a challenge to how black subjectivity is performed and imagined as heteronormative in the public sphere. Black queers actively challenge how their bodies are marked as the constitutive outside of blackness.[7]

For the South African queer activist Mikki van Zyl, belonging is a crucial construct that reveals the limits of human rights discourse for the most vulnerable queer South Africans. As a concept, belonging exposes the differential power relations that are sometimes obscured in the language of universal citizenship. Van Zyl writes:

> Belonging is a thick concept which includes affective and cultural elements making visible the limitations of citizenship through contextualizing the politics and power dynamics in discourses of human rights. It [belonging] also allows us to focus on the everyday dynamics of oppression which form the bedrock of marginalization and Othering.[8]

Belonging neatly frames the main assertions central to my argument. First, I argue that while securing legal and political rights as encoded in the constitution is an important first step to creating the possibility of freedom for black queer subjects in postapartheid South Africa, definitions of freedom must expand beyond the legal, political, and the economic.[9] Second, black queers forge possibilities for belonging through deliberate destabilizations of heteronormative notions of black identity. Third, as a concept, belonging navigates the fraught relationship between forms of legal/constitutional freedoms and social and cultural freedoms, serving as an important reminder that the existence of the former does not guarantee the possibility of the latter.

The notion of freedom central to the arguments that I develop here is sociocultural and is engendered through particular forms of cultural labor that increase visibility and create possibilities of belonging for black queer people in black social milieus. Heretofore, freedom has been typically conceptualized within the realm of political economy, with insufficient attention to cultural politics. Therefore, what is typically understood as necessary to exercise freedom is limited to forms of political representation or redistributive economic policy. In what follows, I insist on the interplay between the sociocultural, the sociopolitical, and the socioeconomic, revealing cultural politics to be a fecund site for examining the processes of freedom, particularly as it relates to black queer subjectivities. Freedom must be understood not as a set of political, economic, and legal rights that exist a priori waiting to be conferred on an abject population but as a sociocultural construct that is given meaning and contested in communities through citizens' actions. Freedom in this context refers to the ability of black queer individuals to create forms of visibility that work to enable what Judith Butler calls "livable lives."[10] These livable lives are constructed through public naming and performance of gender and sexuality dissidence with the understanding that such public disclosures will not result in the curtailment of or loss of life.

Black queers create freedom through forms of what I term cultural labor. The cultural labor of visibility occurs when black queers bring dissident sexualities and gender nonconformity into the public arena. Visibility refers not only to the act of seeing and being seen but also to the process through which individuals make themselves known in the communities as queer subjects. Ultimately visibility is about recognition, since "it is only through the experience of recognition that any of us becomes constituted as socially viable beings."[11] How that recognition occurs varies and includes the range of sensory perceptions including sight, but also important for my argument, sound in the form of speech acts, public pronouncements, and the act of listening.

Black queers demonstrate that far from being a Western contaminant, queerness is embedded in black communities. The historian Marc Epprecht argues that forms of public dissident sexuality have the effect of "destabilizing invented nationalist fictions about African masculinity."[12] In this essay, I examine how black queer citizens rework the identities of apartheid South Africa and use the space created by legal changes to create new forms of visibility and belonging for themselves. However, in a departure from other recent work on black queer visibilities, I focus on the representational as a key battleground that cannot be separated from the material.[13] Even middle-class black queers struggle to access the rights enshrined in the constitution — not for lack of material resources but for lack of cultural ones — where blackness continues to cohere around heteronormativity.

Visibility for black queers in specifically black cultural spaces continues to be policed, and the cultural labor done by black queers to challenge the heteronormativity of blackness continues to be costly. Examples of the policing of black queers in specifically black cultural and political spaces are numerous. Recently, political figures such as Jacob Zuma and Lulu Xingwana have garnered controversy because of homophobic comments they made in the public sphere. Zuma stated that in his day, gays would not have dared to make themselves visible in front of him, for he would have inflicted bodily harm on such a person.[14] Xingwana walked out of a recent exhibit featuring work by the black lesbian photographer Zanele Muholi, remarking that her photographs were not only "pornographic" but a threat to the project of nation building.[15] The council for traditional leaders called homosexuality un-African in stating their opposition to same-sex marriage in South Africa, arguing vociferously for the incompatibility of same-sex practices with "African culture."[16] These remarks, and others, by political figures, both elected and unelected, work to create an environment whereby black queer bodies are subject to policing and violence. The recent high-profile cases of rapes, beatings, and murders of black lesbians combined with other forms of homophobic violence experienced by black township–based queers further archives the high level of resistance to black queer visibilities in specifically black cultural and political contexts.[17]

Queer visibility, then, is not only about finding acceptance for difference within black communities but also about a defiance and a subversion of blackness in ways that are potentially transformative, thus creating the very liberation promised by the constitution and giving freedom its substantive meaning. I highlight the cultural labor of black queerness to suggest how it destabilizes heteronormative notions of black identity formed through explicit forms of public desire and gender conformity. These destabilizations have the effect of creating additional possibilities for all South Africans to forge livable lives. In doing so, black queers reveal both the possibilities and the limits of the postapartheid state and the salient difference between citizenship and forms of belonging.

Freedom, Visibility, and Cultural Labor

In 1996 South Africa became the first country in the world to provide protection for its gay and lesbian citizens.[18] Hence it also became the first state with a majority black population to provide these protections. Based on the fundamental notion of equality outlined originally in the Freedom Charter, the pertinent clause relating to queer citizens states,

> The state may not unfairly discriminate directly or indirectly against anyone on one or more grounds, including race, gender, sex, pregnancy, marital status, ethnic or social origin, colour, sexual orientation, age, disability, religion, conscience, belief, culture, language and birth.[19]

Several scholars have noted, however, the disconnect between the lofty language of the constitution and the real lived experiences of black queers in postapartheid South Africa.[20] In fact, as the social geographer Natalie Oswin details, the movement for Gay and Lesbian Equality represented by the Equality Project was able to successfully challenge homophobic legislation by creating the figure of the "black, poor, gay and lesbian," who was imagined to be the putative beneficiary of the organization's lobbying efforts.[21] This figure would have neither the economic nor the cultural capital to fully access the constitution's protections. While much has been made of the lack of the economic capital central to accessing protections based on insurance, marriage, and inheritance, less attention has been paid to the lack of cultural capital for black queers. Furthermore, while black queers as a group can do little on their own to overturn centuries of capitalist exploitation, they can and do work to create spaces for themselves to be respected and accepted as black queers in their own communities. It is this discursive cultural work that is the primary focus of my argument.

The fact that these laws have yet to bear fruit for the majority of black queer South Africans seems to strike many scholars of sexuality in postapartheid South Africa as paradoxical. The cultural anthropologist Graeme Reid highlights this paradox when he argues that homosexuality occupies an intermediary space in postapartheid politics, serving as a "litmus test for the success of constitutional democracy—emblematic of a human rights based social order, [while being] cast as untraditional, as un-African, and as unchristian—a dangerous threat to the social fabric."[22] However, I argue that there is little paradoxical about this representation (formation) of homosexuality at all; in fact, its ability in the South African context to be both representative of what the literary scholar Brenna Munro calls "democratic modernity" and a "threat" rests on the racialization of the queer body as white and the sexualization of the black body as straight.[23] That is, adding a racial analysis to a queer analysis reveals how the white queer body is emblematic of human rights protections used to position South Africa as a progressive queer-friendly tourist destination (for white queer tourists), while the black queer body remains the threat to African culture and tradition. The policing of queer bodies in postapartheid South Africa falls disproportionately on black queer bodies.

In other black spaces, this split does not exist. For a postcolonial black state, the split does not exist because the queer body is not allowed to be part of the black nation and therefore is not part of the citizenry. Numerous examples from Jamaica to Zimbabwe demonstrate the impossibility of the black queer national citizen. In diaspora formations where blacks are the minority, their belonging to the nation is already always a vexed subject regardless of their sexual identity. One needs only to look at the riots in Paris or Hurricane Katrina to see this. South Africa, however, offers the possibility for the black queer subject to have a different kind of relationship to both national and cultural belonging. Unlike spaces in Europe and North America, South Africa is understood as an ostensibly black state. Yet, unlike Uganda or Jamaica, there is a sizable white minority presence that considers itself autochthonous to the nation. I suggest, perhaps provocatively, that the clause on sexual orientation in the South African constitution was not developed with black queers in mind. My statement is not meant to discount the important work done by such black queer pioneers as Bev Ditsie and Simon Nkoli. Yet despite their efforts, Jacklyn Cock reveals how the inclusion of the equality clause was in the main a negotiation between a rather conservative, white-male-led queer constituency and important black male leaders of the liberation movement.[24] For the black majority, queerness is racialized as white and blackness is heteronormative. Therefore, I contend that the equality clause as it relates to sexual orientation was part of a concerted effort to retain the white minority population in postapartheid South Africa by suggesting that even those most abjected under apartheid rule (white queers) would be safe in the postapartheid state.[25] Andrew Tucker shows how the apartheid state's prohibitions against "homosexuality" were directed almost entirely toward the white population, and in some instances the apartheid state encouraged or at least looked the other way when it came to same-sex sexuality among black South Africans.[26] To return briefly to Reid's formulation, it becomes clear that for black queers, it is white queer bodies that represent the litmus test for constitutional democracy while their own bodies represent the threat to social order in a postapartheid state that is the fear of a government led by the black majority.

On some fundamental level, black queer South Africans know and understand this fact. Thus for them belonging must occur simultaneously on two levels. First, black queers must be recognized and create visibility and belonging within their communities. The labor of creating this visibility then destabilizes the consistent representation of queerness as outside blackness and blackness as heteronormative. This visibility and belonging can effectively animate the equality provisions of the constitution. Unlike black queers elsewhere, who are subjected to exclusions of either their racialized or their queered bodies (or in some cases such as the United States their racialized queer bodies), black queer South Africans have the possibility of full recognition from the state because of their location in Africa and the protections of the constitution. Yet this recognition at the state level can be lived only through forms of black cultural belonging that are vital to black queers, such as customary marriage practices. This point should not be overlooked by scholars and activists who seek to provide equal forms of protections for black queer subjects living elsewhere on the continent (or in majority black Afrodiasporic spaces like the Caribbean) under the auspices of human rights. Thus black queer attempts to gain freedom operate within this dichotomy between the state and community and are necessarily sociocultural in nature. While the state can create rights through legislation, it is only within the spaces of black communities that real protection lies.

Black queerness is important because it occupies this contradictory space in postapartheid South Africa. In what follows, I necessarily focus on the creative ways that black queers undertake labor to challenge their exclusion from forms of black cultural belonging. The cultural historian Robin D. G. Kelley argues that scholars should take a more expansive look at what is considered labor, particularly with respect to black communities in which forms of creative expression are labor.[27] I borrow this idea here to think about how the discursive labor of black queers is a form of creative vernacular expression that creates the space for black queer belonging. In this case, the cultural labor that I focus on is primarily discursive and representational because it is in this realm that black queers face significant exclusion and where they are most empowered to enact change.[28] I recognize that the forms of cultural labor black queers participate in are diverse and expansive and include television, film, literary, and visual art representation. However, I look specifically at forms of "quotidian conversations," everyday discursive practices that work to create social spaces for black queer belonging as a less-examined archive for examining processes of black queer cultural labor.[29] These black queer challenges to exclusion are about a purposeful reworking of identity and refashioning of selves both individual and communal. Ossified identities, created and imposed by colonialism and apartheid, and variously contested and given meaning and significance by various different communities themselves, are under increasing pressures as people seek to (re)define themselves according to new sociopolitical realities. A significant part of this redefinition involves the appropriation and use of Western-origin identifications such as "straight" and "gay" and their relationship with local vernacular terms describing nonnormative sexual practices. This essay shows that these Western-derived terms do not simply obliterate local ways to describe gender and sexuality dissidence. Instead, the terms *straight* and *gay* come to take on additional meanings related to local understandings of gender and sexuality. Local vernacular terms coexist with and are at times used interchangeably with international and global terms. This practice fundamentally changes the meaning of Western sexual identity markers as they come to describe a variety of positionalities, including cross-dressing and transgender identities for gay men and lesbian women and explicit same-sex desire for "straight" men and women not typically accounted for under the Western rubric of "gay," "lesbian," or "straight." Likewise, the meanings of the local vernacular terms such as *injonga*, which often described sexual positioning, sexual acts, and public gender performance, are reworked into categories of sexual identity.[30]

"Economic Bisexuality" and Other Queer Notions: Who Is Penetrating Whom?

I return to the opening ethnographic vignette to delineate how black queers appropriate public space, in this case the space of the airwaves, to create visibility for themselves. In appropriating widely held beliefs about transactional sex, the gay-identified man's non-queer-identified lover attempted to buttress his own claims to heterosexuality by relying on forms of masculine gender performance such as suggesting that he was the insertive partner during sexual intercourse, as well as claims about explicit public desire such as insisting that he was not nonnormative in his sexual identity. Since neither party is visible to the general public, gender performance was enacted through language and vocal expression. In this instance, the gay-identified man spoke in a softer, more high-pitched voice. While his voice was not so high-pitched as to be confused with that of a biological woman, it did contrast with the low vocal tones, cadence, and township-inflected slang of his more masculine partner. Thus, although neither party was visible to the majority of the audience, members of the listening community could infer that the gay-identified man, based on his speech patterns and vocal inflections, was the more stereotypically "feminine" of the two men in public gender performance.

The gay-identified man in this partnership uses the public airwaves to create queer visibility. He insists that he is a "wronged" party who has been cheated on by an unfaithful lover, and he argues for the radical equivalence of his relationship with that of the numerous heterosexual relationships typically featured in the show. The gay-identified man invites the audience to identify with him and to have sympathy for him as a gay man involved in a same-sex relationship. This is important, since a strong component of the show is its moral impetus that suggests that cheating is always wrong and that the person being cheated on and deceived is worthy of community sympathy and support. In fact, the head of the radio station blunts criticism of the show's more salacious and tawdry aspects by arguing that the show performs an important community service. Ostensibly, the fear of unwittingly becoming a part of the drama of *Cheaters* serves as a possible deterrent to community infidelity.[31] The queer man, like his heterosexual counterparts, places his life on display for public consumption and possible ridicule. However, in the discursive terrain that has been preestablished, not only is he a sympathetic character, but the audience is expected to identify with him as the "good" guy as well. His cultural labor of calling in to the show because he experiences the same problem of infidelity as many of the women who make up the show's core audience also "works" to humanize gay men and the queer body. The possibility of humanizing and destigmatizing queer relationships, of course, does not completely overturn preexisting homophobia that casts queer bodies as outside blackness. Yet the very location of the queer body at the center of this public cultural event embedded in Sowetan culture creates the possibility for at least the momentary decentering of heteronormativity. This labor is important because it forms the basis of a necessary public dialogue about sexuality and queer bodies that is not contained in legal-juridical discourse. Whether this kind of labor has long-lasting tangible effects cannot be precisely known, yet one must presume that on some levels there is an expectation that it does. By insisting on inclusion in this particular public space, this queer man is breaking the silence around queer bodies and insisting on recognition.

Equally important is the labor done by the straight-identified masculine man in this scenario to discredit and pathologize the queer body while marking his own body as nonqueer. To do so, the straight-identified man relies on several important tropes that allow black heterosexuality to cohere around publicly expressed sexual desire and gender conformity. These very tropes are called into question both through the labor of the gay man on the radio station and through my own ethnographic work.

The straight-identified masculine man relies, in particular, on the trope of "economic bisexuality." In an article detailing the queer sexual milieu of Abidjan, Côte d'Ivoire, the anthropologist Vinh-Kim Nguyen encounters a class of men who are described by his gay-identified male informants as "economic bisexuals." As the term suggests, these men engage in sexual relationships with other men solely for economic gain. In the case of *Cheaters*, the straight-identified man argues that he falls into this category and delights and revels in the angst of his spurned lover, since in essence there was no actual "love" in the relationship — only material exchange. The category of economic bisexuality challenges the conceptual limitations of transactional sex as an analytic on the African continent. These men provide a counterpoint to the often-raced, heterosexist, gendered, and classed literature on transactional sex that posits black, poor, and working-class heterosexual women as the primary agents of transactional sexual relations. Left uninterrogated are the ways in which many sexual relationships (even those among the Western bourgeoisie) are enacted with materiality in mind, and the ways that men may participate as agentive actors in pursuing "transactional sex," whether with women or, in this case, with other men. However, Nguyen suggests that the term *economic bisexuality* is too simplistic a way to describe the complex technologies of the self that mark the motivations of these straight-identified men. He states:

> [The] dismissal of bisexuality as "economic," rational, and calculating was, I found, often inaccurate. For many youth, the acquisition of style was desired in terms of being "fashionable" or the pleasure of belonging to a secret community rather than being part of a conscious strategy for "getting" men. Homosexual relations could not be reduced to economic strategy, nor were they simply about experimenting with gender roles. Rather, as forms of self-fashioning they incorporated concerns that were simultaneously those of material and emotional satisfaction, pleasure and desire.[32]

It becomes impossible to reduce sexual relations of this nature to their transactional aspect. Nguyen's precaution is important for the study of sexuality in Africa generally, and South Africa particularly, because it accounts for the complexity of sexual relationships that destabilize the generally accepted notion of these interactions as primarily transactional.

Regarding the radio show *Cheaters*, I suggest that the supposed transactional nature of the sex between the gay-identified man and his straight-identified masculine partner becomes a way for the straight-identified man to remove his body from queerness.[33] He accomplishes this by trading on commonsense understandings of the motivations for these relationships and to deny the queer man the equivalence he sought within the black cultural sphere that is accrued through the shared wrong of infidelity. If the relationship becomes solely transactional, then of course there is no equivalence with heterosexuality. The queer man is no longer the wronged party; rather, he becomes a predator using his financial might to corrupt an otherwise straight man into behavior the latter might not otherwise pursue. Furthermore, as the predator, the gay-identified man in this scenario functions in a colonial relationship with the straight-identified man. Thus, while removing his own body from queerness, the straight-identified man also removes the black gay man from blackness and toward whiteness.[34] I am not arguing here that South Africans generally find queerness more palatable if it can be couched in the language of transaction. However, I insist that in a situation of decreased economic possibilities and astronomically high rates of youth unemployment, the body may be one of the few resources that a young person has that can significantly improve his or her life chances.[35] Ultimately, relationships with individuals who can provide forms of material sustenance become, if not acceptable, understandable given the socioeconomic realities.

On more than one occasion I was told by several friends of mine that I could have a relationship with any young man or woman that I desired in the township. My relative wealth as an American who had access to education and financial resources would make me a desirable partner even among men who ostensibly had no previous interest in queer sexuality. The veracity of this claim, which I confess went untested, is less important than the fact that numerous people would make it to me. What it highlights is the complicated nature of sexual desire and the materiality of sex that suggests that the two can never be completely separated. Rather, desires for upward mobility occur through attachments that are both emotional and erotic. Yet the straight-identified man accused of cheating sought to disaggregate the sexual desire from material desire. In the case of *Cheaters* it is necessary to interrogate statements made about the transactional nature of the sexual act, for to speak of desire, love, and affection for their gay partners would cost these straight men their claim to heterosexuality. The popular discourse of transaction allows straight identity to remain intact.

In this scenario, however, the gay-identified man did not allow the straight-identified man to have the last word in defining the relationship. In one final defiant move, he revealed that if in fact the purpose of the relationship was transactional, the straight-identified masculine man earned the money not through the assumed role of penetrator in the relationship but by being penetrated regularly by the gay-identified, more feminine man. As numerous scholars have opined, queer relationships, particularly those centered in township spaces in South Africa, have often operated based on a strong butch-femme aesthetic, with butch and femme articulated around both gender performance and sexual role (top or bottom).[36] Masculine men and feminine women who identify as straight form relationships with gay-identified feminine men and lesbian-identified masculine women.[37] As the anthropologist Amanda Swarr revealed during her discussion of queer sexuality, butch-femme relationships "render same sex sexuality intelligible within [black] communities. They make it easy for families to understand 'gay' relationships because they pair masculinity with femininity."[38] Swaar further states, "Gender and sex are produced . . . through sex acts themselves in which partners articulate their respective genders."[39] Queer relationships then become visible through the assumed conflation of straight identity with gender-conforming public performance and appropriately positioned sexual acts. Straight masculine men penetrate gay feminine men; lesbian masculine women "penetrate" straight feminine women in this scenario.

The gay man in the *Cheaters* scenario as well as my own research among gay-identified feminine men in Soweto presents a striking challenge to this commonsense notion of queer relationships. For instance, Monday evenings are a surprisingly popular party night in townships in the Johannesburg area including Soweto. On these nights various "Monday blues" and "stokvel" parties are held to ease people back into the week.[40] Several of these parties are known to be either gay or gay-friendly venues. During one particular party, several of my gay friends worked their magic on the dance floor as they enticed masculine straight-identified men with their dance moves. Later in the evening I learned that one of my friends, Thuso, had successfully hooked up with one of these masculine men as his partner for the evening. He shared a laugh with me later as he recounted his tale:

> When we got back to my place I was all ready to be ravished by this straight guy. I mean he was a real man and I was expecting a good fuck. Instead he looked me dead in the eye and said, "We are both men here so I will fuck you and then you'll fuck me." I almost died. Needless to say this ruined the mood for the evening.[41]

I found the idea of my thin, rather frail-looking, feminine gender–performing friend being considered a "man" by his butch masculine sexual partner and desiring penetration from him to be equally humorous.[42] In their 1994 essay on gay sexuality in Guateng, Hugh McLean and Linda Ngcobo called such men *imbubes*. Evidently these are "men who go 50–50" in sexual relations and are therefore sexually versatile.[43] Although my friend chose not to indulge his partner's request for sexual versatility, I learned that this was not always the case. While many of the feminine gender–performing gay men were reluctant to admit that they had penetrated some of their straight-identified partners, others boasted of their exploits. I was stunned as my feminine friend Mandla pointed to the numerous men in his neighborhood whom he had fucked. While he disavowed seeking out this kind of sexual practice, he ultimately stated that "if they ask me to do it, then I'll do it. . . . I get asked to do it a lot." Neo, another feminine gay man, had this to say:

> Well it's all about having fun right? I mean when I was younger I would never, that would just end the whole thing. But hey if they want some meat

I'll give him some meat. It's all about having a good time and pleasing each other.[44]

What my research shows is that in the Johannesburg townships, a high degree of sexual versatility occurs in a lot of these relationships, although both parties are often reluctant to admit it, precisely because of the destabilizing effect such admissions can potentially have on forms of queer belonging, particularly as it relates to what Swarr has identified as the ability of the community to understand and therefore possibly accept such relationships. In other words, butch/femme creates possibilities for black South African queer belonging. The gender/sex system of public gender-conforming performance buttressed by particular sex acts is placed in crisis by the possible inversion of presumed sexual roles. I suspect the more stereotypically feminine gay man would have likely kept quiet had he not been so thoroughly humiliated by his ex-lover. By bringing his philandering partner on the show, he reveals the power of black queerness. First, black queerness destabilizes the heteronormativity of blackness by presenting black queer relationships as equivalent to heterosexual ones. Second, in his performative utterance, the gay-identified man forces the audience to rethink his lover's motivations for the relationship. Public proclamations of desire, or in the case of his philandering lover, the lack of explicit queer desire, do not suffice to instantiate heterosexuality. Third, public gender performance does not reveal either sexual desire or sexual identity. That is, masculine gender performance does not guarantee exclusive heterosexuality or that the masculine partner is insertive and therefore dominant.[45] It is this explosive revelation that shows the danger of black queerness to destabilize black heterosexuality, since even the most masculine of men can be "fucked."

I'm a "Double Adaptor": Emergent "Bisexuality" and New Identities

Above I explored how relationships between gay-identified and straight-identified queer men rest on understandings of explicit public desire, transaction, and gender conformity. Yet these understandings when held to closer scrutiny were challenged by the cultural labor of gay-identified queer men who claim public queer identities. Here I explore what it means when many of these formerly straight-identified, gender-conforming partners begin to understand themselves as and openly identify as bisexual. Significantly, much of the literature on black queer identities in postapartheid South Africa has focused on the emergence of sexual identity in relation to gay and lesbian identities. Work by McLean and Ngcobo, Swarr, Donald Donham, Reid, and Tucker has heretofore focused on how black queer South Africans, when confronted with new social and political identities both nationally and internationally, came to understand themselves as "gay" or "lesbian."[46] Less attention has been paid to what these changes in forms of social identities might mean for the gender-conforming partners of many of those who have adopted the gay and lesbian terminology.[47] I argue that changes in queer identity, that is, the rise of explicit nonheteronormative identities of gay and lesbian in postapartheid South Africa, have also given rise to a class of people who have begun to think of themselves as bisexual. Significantly, this label has been adopted by both men and women who in previous years would not have adopted any kind of identity label to describe their sexual practices. Importantly, in black communities, these individuals have been able to maintain straight identities because of their gender-conforming behavior and the fact that they still continue to publicly have relationships with members of the opposite sex. In this section, I discuss the rise of bisexuality as descriptor in black communities as yet another way that black queerness both becomes visible and destabilizes forms of black identity based on heteronormativity. The fact that those whose gender performance and presumed sexual role would allow them to defer queer identity choose to adopt bisexuality challenges heterosexualized conceptualizations of queerness that are built on models of penetration.

The late *kwaito* star Lebo Mathosa came out as bisexual in 2004 after years of speculation about her sexuality. Mathosa, the dance diva who has been described by many as the *kwaito* generation's Brenda Fassie, has been one of the most controversial figures in black public culture for over a decade.[48] Initially members of the multiplatinum-selling *kwaito* group Boom Shaka, Mathosa and her female counterpart Thembi Seete were often criticized for the hypersexuality of their dance routines. Traditionalists and feminists alike were concerned that Mathosa's presentation of her exuberant sexuality and her brash onstage performance persona suggested both a degradation of "traditionally demure" female sexuality and the objectification of women as sex symbols. Mathosa was well aware of the constant commentary about her body as a hypersexualized figure and defended herself on two fronts: first, by suggesting that she was weaving together an aesthetics of the African diaspora by incorporating dances from West and Central Africa, Jamaican dancehall reggae, and "traditional" South African coming out/initiation dances; and second, by insisting that what she presented onstage was a performance that was not meant to be taken literally as a true reflection of her personal desires or wishes.[49] Mathosa was continuously dogged by rumors of drug use and outrageous sexual practices. She herself fueled much of the speculation by suggesting that her sexual persona was for the consumption of not just heterosexual men (the presumed target of her performances) but gay and lesbian fans as well.

Throughout her too brief life, Mathosa was coy about her own sexual preferences. Despite the fact that she often performed at gay and lesbian events, and socialized in black queer social spaces, she never confirmed what many people suspected, that she was a lesbian. In two separate interviews Mathosa denied she was a lesbian.[50] In both cases, the interviewers linked rumors of her drug use with rumors of her sexuality into a discourse of excess, the notion being that Mathosa presented a form of wild or uncontrolled femininity outside the normative roles of black women in South Africa. Commenting on whether her image was too forceful for a South African public, Mathosa states, "I could have changed my image and look to be more feminine and timid, but I wanted to continue with what I have already made of myself."[51] Commenting on rumors about her sexuality, she denied being a lesbian and argued that the rumors of lesbianism and drug abuse were part of the territory of being a celebrity. She suggested that the rumors might also be good for her, for if she were a boring person, no one would bother to speculate about her behavior. Yet what intrigues me in these numerous interviews is Mathosa's attempt to rehabilitate her image through denying lesbianism, and the pervasive attempts by the media to equate drug abuse with lesbianism. Once again, the queer body, in this case the queer body of a black woman, must enter the public discourse through pathology and social depravity. Even in denying that she was a lesbian, Mathosa suggested that there is something inherently "wrong" with same-sex practices by reinforcing the notion that the very rumor of same-sex preferences constitutes something that is negative and designed to bring her down.

Therefore, it was unexpected when during a live radio interview Mathosa admitted that she was bisexual. After telling her fans on air that she was an open book and that people should feel free to ask her anything, a female caller took Mathosa up on her offer and asked if she were a lesbian. After a slight pause, Mathosa revealed that she was "bisexual," a "double-adaptor" in her own words, who enjoyed the pleasures of men and women. The origin of the term *double-adaptor*, like much slang terminology in postapartheid South Africa, is unclear. According to the *S'camto Dictionary*, *double-adaptor* is translated as "bisexual."[52] The double-adaptor slang terminology may come from the popular pin plugs that most South Africans use that plug into electrical sockets and then can take differently shaped plugs. In one sense, the notion of being a double-adaptor emerges from commonsense notions of penetration, since this particular plug fits into an electric socket and can also be plugged into. But the fact that *double-adaptor* appears in the *S'camto Dictionary* speaks to the widespread use of the term in specifically black township–based youth public culture as a term for a queer-identified individual who is separate from "gay" or "lesbian" and describes both identity and behavior that are considered separate from gay and lesbian.[53] Interestingly, the media seemed less fascinated by this explanation of Mathosa's identity; her coming out as bisexual elicited little response from both the mainstream and tabloid media. The only image that caught my eye in the weeks after the coming out was a picture of her in the *Sowetan* promoting an upcoming performance in which she was identified in the caption as having recently come out as bisexual. I would like to offer another anecdote through which to explore the notion of bisexual identity. At a 2003 party held in Meadowlands Soweto, four friends and I (who were all openly identified as black gay men) were enjoying ourselves at a party when we decided to leave early because of some damage our car had received. I was involved in a conversation with one of the young men at the party, and when I told him that we were leaving, he insisted that we stay. Confused as to why our presence at the party would make any difference to him, I asked him quite bluntly what it was to him if we remained or left. He shocked me by saying, "Well to tell you the truth, I'm bi." I assume that left unsaid in this declarative statement might have been the phrase "and I am interested in/attracted to one of you guys." When I told my friends about the revelation, they were surprised. However, their surprise was not that the person might be interested in one or more of us romantically; rather, it was that he would couch his interest in the sexual identity of bisexuality. Marco, one of my friends, explains, "Things are changing in South Africa. I mean ten years ago, you would never have heard a boy, especially a township guy like him, say he was bi."[54] My friends suggested that other norms of behavior were also changing because of the shifting discourse of sexuality and the increased salience and visibility of gay and lesbian identity in black spaces. "Guys used to hold hands and be very physically affectionate with one another. You see that less often these days as such behavior seems to be considered gay."[55] While I would like to leave aside for the purposes of this essay the interrogation of the second claim, I would like to explore further the first, which is that bisexuality as a descriptor of sexual behavior as well as sexual identity is a possibly new construct in the constitution of black queer publics, and to ask what work bisexuality does in shifting understandings of black queer sexuality and making it more visible.

Consider Mathosa, on the one hand, and the unnamed young man, on the other, as both enabling the creation of bisexual identity within black queer publics. Increasing visibility of a particular kind of queerness, that of gay and lesbian identity, with its associated commonsense markers of feminine gender for men and masculine gender for women has had a direct effect on their gender-conforming partner's sense of identity. Just as many of these same people may not have previously identified their sexual practices as sexual identity and now deploy the terminology of *gay* and *lesbian* for political strategy and self-fashioning, their formerly straight partners similarly have begun to access bisexuality. Part of this is the effect of the South African constitution, which cannot in its very nature define rights on the basis of unnamed queerness. Yet part of the rise in bisexuality as an identity for black queers must also rest on forms of self-fashioning and an increasing awareness of what bisexuality allows these individuals to achieve: the ability to attract potential partners and demand visibility and respect for themselves outside heteronormativity. Again, bisexuality might be called an emergent form of belonging in black Sowetan culture.

The fact that a gender-conforming individual, in this case either Mathosa or the young man whom I met at the party, would publicly queer his or her identity when he or she does not have to speaks to a shifting terrain of identity made possible precisely by the rise of gay and lesbian identity in postapartheid South Africa. These individuals shift some paradigms in the discussion of sexuality in many non-Western contexts, which tends to be overly theorized on the basis of active-passive relations that rely on the notion of penetration and gender performance enacted through sexual roles. Many of these bisexuals may enjoy a fluidity of roles in their sexual practices, including "top," "bottom," and "versatile" sexual roles. With this definition of bisexuality, it then becomes possible for a gender-conforming man or woman who performs conventional gender practices publicly and takes on the assumed sexual role appropriate to that gender performance to be queer by adopting bisexuality as an identity. Furthermore, such individuals, if they do not have sexual desire or sexual relations with the opposite sex, can even adopt *gay* or *lesbian* as identity markers. Both sets of individuals, the gender-conforming gay or lesbian and the gender-conforming bisexual, work to destabilize heterosexuality, since neither gender conformity nor sexual role signifies heterosexuality as it may once have been assumed to do so.

Conclusion

I have argued that black queer South Africans are not able to enjoy fully the privileges encoded in the South African constitution as *black* and *queer*. I suggest that this is because cultural politics consistently mark the black queer body as the constitutive outside of blackness and the queer body is subsequently racialized as white. This creates a conundrum for black queers, who are caught outside both the representational and the material realities of queerness. Lacking both the economic capital to benefit from provisions related to marriage, insurance, and inheritance, and the cultural capital to be inclusive of blackness, they enact different forms of discursive labor to shift the cultural politics of blackness and argue for their inclusion into black communities as explicitly black queer subjects. As of now, while black queers may enjoy the protection of the state, such provisions cannot guarantee that these protections will have any real meaning in their lives. The current regimes of representation do not allow black queers to experience their lives wholly. To experience freedom in postapartheid South Africa, the black queer body must enter either a deracinated queerness or a blackness divorced from sexuality. Realizing this, black queers struggle against definitions of blackness that are inherently exclusionary and heteronormative. These exclusive definitions of blackness mean that freedom for most black queers remains elusive. To create possibilities for freedom, black queer South Africans enter the discursive realm and enact forms of cultural labor, even forms of belonging, to destabilize the heteronormative construction of blackness. By claiming discursive visibility in the public sphere, black queers work to create the possibilities for freedom.

This possibility for freedom as an explicitly queer subject has implications for black queers worldwide. Black queer South Africans are not estranged from the state by their blackness, nor are they estranged from the state by their queerness. They are, however, estranged from realizing the freedoms enabled by the postapartheid South African constitution by their black queerness. This estrangement is one that cannot be resolved at the state level but must occur in communities that ultimately can provide safety and security to black queers and thus make the rights of the constitution meaningful. If black queers could get to a point in South Africa where they were accepted and respected in their communities, then they could take the first steps toward creating radically different forms of black cultural and national belonging that do resist heteronormativity. For now, however, this remains only a possibility and not a full realization. This essay is an exploration of one way that black queers will continue to labor within the means they have available to push past the limits of blackness and make the promises of the constitution a reality.

Notes

1. Jozi FM is a Soweto-based station. Formerly a community-based radio station, it is now being run for profit.
2. *Uyajola*, in this particular case, might translate loosely as "Is he or she fooling around?"
3. A strong part of the show's appeal is the ethical element, where there are clear "good" and "bad" people. In this sense, like all "reality" television, the various parties have a strong incentive to play to type. Furthermore, while the premise of *Cheaters* is loosely based on the American television show of the same name, there exists a vibrant and antecedent storytelling tradition of radio dramas in South Africa that often follow the soap opera tradition of melodrama. These shows are presented on state-owned African-language radio stations and often play out with clear villains and heroes. While *Cheaters* is "reality," it is clearly scripted by the hosts in a similar genre.
4. During the time that I listened to the show in the fall of 2005, I never once heard a lesbian couple call in to the show.
5. An abundance of literature on queer identities in South Africa speaks about gender-conforming men who identify as "straight" having sex with gender-nonconforming men (often, but not always, gay identified) and retaining their identity as straight. For more discussion of this phenomenon, see Hugh McLean and Linda Ngcobo, "Abangibhamayo bathi ngimnandi (Those who fuck me say I'm tasty): Gay Sexuality in Reef Townships," in *Defiant Desire: Gay and Lesbian Lives in South Africa*, ed. Mark Gevisser and Edwin Cameron (New York: Routledge, 1995), 158–85; Donald Donham, "Freeing South Africa: The 'Modernization' of Male-Male Sexuality in Soweto," *Cultural Anthropology* 13, no. 1 (1998): 8; Amanda Lock Swarr, "Moffies, Artists, and Queens," *Journal of Homosexuality* 46, no. 3 (2004): 76–77; Graeme Reid, "How to Become a 'Real Gay': Identity and Terminology in Ermelo, Mpumalanga," *Agenda* 67 (2006): 137–45; Reid, "'A Man Is a Man Completely and a Wife Is a Wife Completely': Gender Classification and Performance amongst 'Ladies' and 'Gents' in Ermelo, Mpumalanga," in *Men Behaving Differently: South African Men since 1994*, ed. Graeme Reid and Liz Walker (Cape Town: Double Storey Books, 2005), 205–29; Andrew Tucker, *Queer Visibilities: Space, Identity, and Interaction in Cape Town* (Malden, MA: Wiley-Blackwell, 2009); and Tucker, "Shifting Boundaries of Sexual Identities in Cape Town: The Appropriation and Malleability of 'Gay' in Township Spaces," *Urban Forum* 21 (2010): 107–22.
6. *Queer* is used in this essay primarily as an analytic. Following the earlier work of Marc Epprecht, *queer* refers not to a sexual identity but to a way to think through how "nonnormative [genders] and sexualities infiltrate dominant discourses to loosen their political [and cultural] stronghold." Marc Epprecht, *Hungochani: The History of Dissident Sexuality in Southern Africa* (Montreal: McGill-Queens University Press,

2004), 15. In his later work, Epprecht suggests that *queer* functions as "an antiessentialist approach to researching gender and sexuality that is open to the whole range of human sexual diversity." Marc Epprecht, *Heterosexual Africa? The History of an Idea from the Age of Exploration to the Age of AIDS* (Athens: Ohio University Press, 2008), 13. For more on the use of *queer* analytically in South(ern) Africa, see Epprecht, *Hungochani*, 11–16, and *Heterosexual Africa*, 15–20.

7. The concept of a constitutive outside is indebted to Judith Butler's use of this term to describe how the normative is constituted by what is excluded or its constitutive outside. Butler used this formulation to discuss how same-sex desire relates to heterosexuality. In this case, I am suggesting that for black communities, queerness represents a similar constitutive outside. For more discussion of Butler's concept, see Judith Butler, *Bodies That Matter: On the Discursive Limits of "Sex"* (New York: Routledge, 1993).

8. Mikki van Zyl, "Beyond the Constitution: From Sexual Rights to Belonging," in *The Prize and the Price: Shaping Sexualities in South Africa*, ed. Melissa Steyn and Mikki van Zyl (Cape Town: HSRC, 2009), 367.

9. During apartheid, there were four designated racial categories: white/European, Coloured, Indian/Asian, and black/African. Blackness took on a political dimension during the fight against apartheid. This political blackness, perhaps akin to the US terminology "people of color," developed out of the black consciousness movement and encompassed Coloured and Indian identities. For the purposes of the present essay, I use the term *black* as it is generally used popularly in South Africa and in the communities where I did research. Therefore, when I use *black*, I am not referring to Indian and Coloured South Africans.

10. For more discussion of the concept of livability, see Judith Butler, *Undoing Gender* (New York: Routledge, 2004).

11. Butler, *Undoing Gender*, 2.

12. Epprecht, *Hungochani*, 22.

13. See Tucker, *Queer Visibilities*, 13. Tucker seems to identify a danger in "focusing at the level of representation and limiting an understanding as to how materialities that surround, limit and give opportunity to different communities can go to affect representations." While I am sympathetic to this danger, I argue for the importance of examining representation qua representation and make the assertion that questions of culture and representation are already always constitutive of materiality. See also Stuart Hall, "Subjects in History: Making Diasporic Identities," in *The House That Race Built: Original Essays by Toni Morrison, Angela Y. Davis, Cornel West, and Others on Black Americans and Politics in America Today*, ed. Wahneema Lubiano (New York: Vintage Books, 1998), 289–99.

14. The exact quote from Zuma was as follows: "Same-sex marriages are a disgrace to the nation and God. . . . In my day an *ungqingili* [considered by many Zulu-speaking

black queers as a derogatory term for a gay person] would not have stood in front of me. I would knock him out." For more information, see "Zuma Earns Wrath of Gays and Lesbians," *Mail and Guardian*, www.mg.co.za/article/2006–09–26–zuma-earns-wrath-of-gays-and-lesbians (accessed December 3, 2010).

15. Lulu Xingwana was quoted as saying that the pictures were "immoral, offensive and going against nation building." For more discussion, see Hlengiwe Mnguni, "Minister Snubs 'Porn' Exhibition," *news24.com*, www.news24.com/SouthAfrica/News/Minister-snubs-porn-exhibition-20100302 (accessed December 3, 2010). For more commentary on the controversy, see Gabeba Baderoon, "On Looking and Not Looking," *Mail and Guardian*, www.mg.co.za/article/2010–03–09–on-looking-and-not (accessed December 4, 2010).

16. For a larger discussion of the House of Traditional Leaders and Their Opposition to Same-Sex Marriage, see Graeme Reid, "The Canary in the Constitution: Same Sex Equality in the Public Sphere," *Social Dynamics* 36, no. 1 (2010): 38–51.

17. For a discussion of homophobic violence in Johannesburg that precedes the media attention given to lesbian rapes and murders, see Graeme Reid and Teresa Dirsuweit, "Understanding Systemic Violence: Homophobic Attacks in Johannesburg and Its Surrounds," *Urban Forum* 13, no. 3 (2002): 99–126. To address the situation, black lesbians have organized a group named the Forum for the Empowerment of Women. Their website is www.few.org.za. In October 2010 black queers in Vosloorus, a township in the East Rand near Boksburg, staged a protest against police-sanctioned and perpetuated homophobia. For more information, see Karabo Keepile, "Call for Probe into Alleged Homophobia in Vosloorus," *Mail and Guardian*, www.mg.co.za/article/2010–11–04–call-for-probe-into-alleged-homophobia-in-vosloorus (accessed December 4, 2010).

18. The equality clause is unclear in how it refers to transgender and intersex individuals. According to Thamar Klein, "In 1996 South Africa was the first and is still the only country worldwide to enshrine the rights of trans persons in the Constitution." See Thamar Klein, "Intersex and Transgender Activism in South Africa," *Liminalis: Journal for Sex/Gender Emancipation and Resistance* (2009): 26, no. 3. Her article suggests that the rights of intersex and transgendered persons were secured through activism that resulted in the interpretation of the equality clause to expand the definition of "sex" to include intersex individuals (accomplished in 2006) and a broader interpretation of "gender" and "sexual orientation" to include transgendered persons. Part of the cultural labor enacted along with this activism was for individuals to increasingly take on public transgendered, and less often intersex, identities.

19. The Freedom Charter was a manifesto of ten core principles that guided a coalition of representative political organizations from South Africa's major racial groups. The ANC (African National Congress), South African Indian Congress, Coloured People's Congress, and the South African Congress of Democrats came together to draft the

document based on the fundamental equality of all of South Africa's racial groups. It was signed in Kliptown, Soweto, in June 1955. The material quoted is from the South African constitution.

20. For more discussion of this disconnect, see Jacklyn Cock, "Engendering Gay and Lesbian Rights: The Equality Clause in the South African Constitution," *Women's Studies International Forum* 26, no. 1 (2003): 35–45; Natalie Oswin, "Producing Homonormativity in Neoliberal South Africa: Recognition, Redistribution, and the Equality Project," *Signs: Journal of Women in Culture and Society* 32, no. 3 (2007): 649–69; Tucker, *Queer Visibilities*; Zanele Muholi, "Mapping Our Histories: A Visual History of Black Lesbians in Post-Apartheid South Africa," www.zanelemuholi.com (accessed July 1, 2010); and Reid, "Canary in the Constitution."

21. Oswin, "Producing Homonormativity," 666.

22. Reid, "Canary in the Constitution," 38.

23. I am aware that postapartheid South Africa contains a complex array of racialized bodies including the four-race categorization of apartheid and more complex definitions of blackness and African identity created by increased immigration from elsewhere on the African continent and the desire to deracinate the category of African. However, equally noteworthy is how queer sexuality is presented in binary terms, particularly by those in black communities who police black gender and sexual nonconformity. Those who are concerned with policing black sexuality limit their critique to black South African communities, rarely extending their pronouncements to new immigrant communities or South Africans of other racial backgrounds. Their concern about the contaminant that is queer sexuality is limited to a concern about the effects of dissident sexualities on black South African communities. Furthermore, the discursive production of black queer South Africans as outside South African and African blackness rests on the constant production of these black queer bodies as somehow aligned with all that is white, Western, and foreign. For more on this construction of queer sexuality as a "white man's disease," see Neville Hoad, *African Intimacies: Race, Homosexuality, and Globalization* (Minneapolis: University of Minnesota Press, 2006), 68–89; Epprecht, *Hungochani*; Epprecht, *Heterosexual Africa?*; Margaret Aarmo, "How Homosexuality Became 'Un-African': The Case of Zimbabwe," in *Female Desires: Same Sex Relations and Transgender Practices across Cultures*, ed. Evelyn Blackwood and Saskia E. Wieringa (New York: Columbia University Press, 1999), 255–80. The quotes are from Brenna M. Munro, "Queer Family Romance: Writing the 'New' South Africa in the 1990s," *GLQ* 15 (2009): 398.

24. See Cock, "Engendering Gay and Lesbian Rights." The behind-the-scenes negotiations between gay and lesbian rights activists and the black leadership seemed to bypass many of the black queer activists "on the ground." For a detailed discussion of the creation of the equality clause and its racialized and gendered exclusions, see Neville Hoad, Karen Martin, and Graeme Reid, eds., *Sex and Politics in South*

Africa: The Equality Clause/Gay and Lesbian Movement/the Anti-Apartheid Struggle (Cape Town: Double Storey Books, 2005).

25. For an insightful discussion of the importance of the white body to postapartheid South Africa, see Lewis Gordon, foreword to *I Write What I Like: Selected Writings*, by Steve Biko (Chicago: University of Chicago Press, 2002), xii.

26. Tucker, *Queer Visibilities*, 109–10.

27. Robin D. G. Kelley, *Yo' Mama's Disfunktional! Fighting the Culture Wars in Urban America* (Boston: Beacon, 1997), 45.

28. This does not mean, however, that the economic exclusions faced by black queers are unimportant or that the discursive and representational exists in a sphere completely separate from the material.

29. I thank Marlon M. Bailey for pointing out that this study is informed by everyday vernacular conversations.

30. On the reclamation of local vernacular terms to assert sexual identity, see Epprecht, *Hungochani*. On the malleability of Western-based sexual identity terminology, see Tucker, "Appropriation and Malleability."

31. In a country with the highest number of adult HIV cases in the world (approximately 5.7 million, according to UNAIDS 2010), the idea that personal infidelity is a community concern definitely has some merit. See UNAIDS Report on the Global AIDS Epidemic (Geneva: Joint United Nations Program on HIV/AIDS, 2010).

32. Vinh-Kim Nguyen, "Uses and Pleasures: Sexual Modernity, HIV/AIDS, and Confessional Technologies in a West African Metropolis," in *Sex in Development: Science, Sexuality, and Morality in Global Perspective*, ed. Vincanne Adams and Stacy Leigh Pigg (Durham, NC: Duke University Press, 2005), 253.

33. Writing in a different context, Mark Hunter describes a situation where a young man constructs his sexual identity as "not gay" and is able to maintain heteromasculinity *because* his relationship with a queer man was purely transactional. It is accepted by his peers and his community because it is seen as purely for money and not for love. See Mark Hunter, *Love in the Time of AIDS: Inequality, Gender, and Rights in South Africa* (Bloomington: Indiana University Press, 2010), 175.

34. In so-called transactional relationships involving heterosexuals, neither the "sugar-daddy" nor the "sugar-mummy," if they are black, is represented in this colonial trope. This may be due to the historical and contemporary experience of wealthy white men in relationships with poor black men that may in fact be "colonial" in nature, yet interestingly such relationships, when they are heterosexual, lack the colonializing stigma.

35. Black unemployment is high, having increased from 23 percent in 1991 to 48 percent in 2002. For more, see Naomi Klein, *The Shock Doctrine: The Rise of Disaster Capitalism* (New York: Picador, 2007), 272. Youth unemployment is particularly high, at 72 percent for women ages fifteen to twenty-four and 58 percent for men ages

fifteen to twenty-four. See Republic of South Africa, Department of Labour, *Women in the South African Labour Market* (Pretoria: South African Department of Labor, 1995–2005), 18. More recent statistics suggest that black youth unemployment is 53 percent, more than four times that of white youth. See "Youth Unemployment Is a Ticking Time Bomb," TimesLive, www.timeslive.co.za/local/article625827.ece/Youth-unemployment-is-a-ticking-time-bomb—Mdladlana (accessed December 4, 2010).

36. See McLean and Ngcobo, "Abangibhamayo bathi ngimnandi"; Donham, "Freeing South Africa"; Swarr, "Moffies, Artists, and Queens"; and Amanda Lock Swarr and Richa Nagar, "Dismantling Assumptions: Interrogating 'Lesbian' Struggles for Identity and Survival in India and South Africa," *Signs: Journal of Women in Culture and Society* 29, no. 2 (2003): 491–516.

37. See Swarr, "Moffies, Artists, and Queens"; Reid, "Man Is a Man"; and Tucker, *Queer Visibilities*.

38. Swarr, "Moffies, Artists, and Queens," 84.

39. Swarr, "Moffies, Artists, and Queens," 85.

40. At such parties, *mogodu*, a type of tripe typically made from sheep intestines and believed to help cure and stave off hangovers, is often served. *Stokvels* are savings societies where members pool their money to be distributed at particular times of the year or used in times of emergency. Some *stokvels* throw parties to raise funds.

41. Thuso, conversation with author, January 2004.

42. Thuso's feminine gender performance was enacted through forms of androgyny including wearing lip gloss and having a light dusting of foundation on his face. Similarly, his wild and abandoned style of dancing while at the party, including flirtatious gestures, gyrations of the hips, and limber fluid dance movements involving the hands and arms, is associated with feminine gender performance.

43. See Ngcobo and McLean, "Abangibhamayo bathi ngimnandi." Reid, in his discussion of "ladies" (gay-identified feminine men) and "gents" (straight-identified masculine men) in rural Ermelo, also provides an example of a masculine "gent" who on spending more time in Johannesburg comes to identify as gay. More disconcerting for the "ladies" of Ermelo is his insistence that he can have sex with another "gent" named Mandla. See Reid, "Man Is a Man."

44. Mandla, conversation with author, July 2009.

45. While I understand that being the insertive partner does not necessarily make one the dominant individual in a sexual relationship, I am interested in investigating how commonsense interpretations center on the equivalence of masculinity with penetration and dominance.

46. Donham, "Freeing South Africa"; Reid, "Man Is a Man"; Tucker "Queer Visibilities" and "Shifting Boundaries of Sexual Identities in Cape Town"; Swarr and Nagar, "Dismantling Assumptions"; and McLean and Ngcobo "Abangibhamayo bathi ngimnandi."

47. The gay and lesbian terminology is animated by legal protections on the basis of sexual orientation. Thus to access rights enshrined in the constitution on many levels requires the strategic and political adoption of gay identities. For more of a discussion on the relationship between rights and identity, see Cock, "Engendering Gay and Lesbian Rights"; and Tucker, *Queer Visibilities*.

48. Brenda Fassie was a major pop icon who emerged in 1980s South Africa and was noted as much for her controversial personal life, which included public professions of lesbianism and battles with drug abuse, as she was for her onstage charisma and performance style. For more on Fassie, see Pumla Dineo Gqola, "When a Good Black Woman Is Your Weekend Special: Brenda Fassie, Sexuality and Performance," in *Under Construction: "Race" and Identity in South Africa Today*, eds. Natasha Distiller and Melissa Steyn (Sandton: Heinemann, 2004), 139–48. See also Desa Philadelphia, "Brenda Fassie: Africa—The Madonna of the Townships," *Time*, September 15, 2001, www.time.com/time/magazine/article/0,9171,1000782,00.html (accessed November 26, 2011).

49. Many commentators were quite resistant to the idea that what Mathosa was putting forth onstage bore any resemblance to traditional dances done by young women throughout South Africa. The fact of the matter is that the interpretation of "traditional" dances is an open field, but I would suggest that what many may have been resisting was Mathosa's right to label the aesthetic "traditional" while divorcing it from its functional context. For example, some of the aesthetic may have occurred in female-only spaces, where sexuality could be celebrated outside the gaze of men; by bringing these performances into the public light and presenting them to mixed-sex audiences, Mathosa (and her partner in crime, Seete) were contravening social conditions. In addition, some of these dances may have been associated with particular cultural contexts or even initiation ceremonies and as such were considered inappropriately contextualized.

50. Madala Thepa, "Up Close and Personal with Lebo Mathosa," *Sowetan Sunday World*, December 5, 2004, 4; Amanda Ngudle, "Lebo Mathosa Speaks Out: Drugs, Lesbians, and Lies," *Drum Magazine*, September 23, 2004, 15–16.

51. Thepa, "Up Close and Personal."

52. Lebo Motshegoa, *Township Talk, the Language, the Culture, the People: The A–Z Dictionary of South Africa's Township Lingo* (Cape Town: Double Storey Books, 2005); Tom Dalzell and Terry Victor, eds., *The Concise New Partridge Dictionary of Slang and Unconventional English* (New York: Routledge, 2008), 215.

53. According to www.speaksouthafrican.com, "Scamto is the township-speak that is a mixture of words and derivations of words from all 11 languages and includes many words from the traditional tsotsitaal that was the language of the township gangster element" (accessed July 1, 2010). According to *Ethnologue*, Scamto is a mixed language used mainly by youth and developed in the 1980s from the original Tsotsitaal.

Ethnologue also suggests that Scamto is "basically Zulu or Sotho language with heavy codeswitching and many English and Afrikaans content morphemes." See Paul M. Lewis, ed., *Ethnologue: Languages of the World*, 16th ed. (Dallas: SIL International, 2009).

54. Conversation with author, December 2003.
55. Conversation with author, December 2003.

WHAT THE SANDS REMEMBER

Vanessa Agard-Jones

environment:
all that surrounds our bodies:
what exists along/be/side us and what we have created:
what surrounds us because of what we surround
. . . . .requires an examination of the distinctions between the human
and nonhuman . . . . . world
implies location, shelter, belonging, not belonging
. . . . ..asks how we are both inside and outside, there because here,
interconnected
. . . . .and therefore a center
becomes place and placeholder, repository of guilt and outrage, a
saturated, empty syllable
—Tamiko Beyer, "Notes Towards a queer::eco::poetics"

Drawing this poem's evocation of "environment" into the Caribbean's landscape, might we imagine Tamiko Beyer's "saturated, empty syllable" as something akin to a grain of sand? In the region, sand is ubiquitous; it is, as Beyer puts it, both place (beach) and placeholder (landscape marker). Here, on these islands, it "exists along" and "be/side us"; it "surrounds us." For Beyer, the syllable is a repository of feeling (of "guilt and outrage"), and in this essay I ask that we consider sand as a repository both of feeling and of experience, of affect and of history, in the Caribbean region. Here sand links us unswervingly to place, to a particular landscape that bears traces of both connection and loss. I imagine it to be "saturated" with the presence of people who have walked on and carried it, but simultaneously "empty" of the archaeological and forensic traces that would testify to that presence. If water is the romantic metaphor that has irredeemably made its place in Caribbean and African diasporic studies, sand is the less embraced referent that returns us to the body's messy realities. Water washes, makes clean.[1] Sand gets inside our bodies, our things, in ways at once inconvenient and intrusive. It smoothes rough edges but also irritates, sticking to our bodies' folds and fissures. In this essay I ask what it might mean to pay close attention to sand, this object that exists at the point of nature's hesitation between land and sea. Heeding a call by Natasha Omise'eke Tinsley that in black queer studies our "metaphors be materially informed; [that] they be internally discontinuous, allowing for differences and inequalities between situated subjects," I propose that we experiment with sand in addition to water as a tool for that metaphorical thinking, to track fleeting references to same-sex desire and gender transgression in Martinique.[2]

This essay's aim is to bring together two strands of inquiry, first, into the meaning of what Makeda Silvera once (in)famously called the "invisibility of (Afro-) Caribbean lesbians [and gays]" and the endurance of narratives about their relationship to a presumably "silent" archive, and second, into the rapport between tropes of invisibility and the physical landscapes that people who might be called "queer" inhabit in the Caribbean region.[3] One of my concerns is the persistent bias toward what is imagined to be diaspora's radical potential both in academic figurations of "queer" lives in the Caribbean and in activist narratives about what it might take to make those lives qualitatively "better." While queer of color theorists have been doing quite a lot of powerful thinking about Caribbean queerness in relation to diaspora, in this essay I want to insist on a deeply local framing of these questions and to argue for a fine-pointed scholarly interest not particularly in movement, but in place and emplacement.[4]

Sand emerges as a compelling metaphor here, as a repository from which we might read traces of gender and sexual alterity on the landscape.[5] Ever in motion, yet connected to particular places, sand both holds geological memories in its elemental structure and calls forth referential memories through its color, feel between the fingers, and quality of grain. Today's sands are yesterday's mountains, coral reefs, and outcroppings of stone. Each grain possesses a geological lineage that links sand to a place and to its history, and each grain also carries a symbolic association that indexes that history as well. In her groundbreaking essay on the politics of erotic autonomy and decolonization in the Bahamas, M. Jacqui Alexander asks "how . . . sexuality and geography collide," and as diaspora continues to be idealized as the Caribbean's cutting edge, the fate of those who do not or cannot move in this vaunted age of mobility—people attached to local geographies—often drops out of analytic purview.[6] I think with sand here to understand that collision, to both question and document how people with access to only limited forms of mobility, like those of the shifting sands, live their genders and sexualities within the region.

This essay asks what it might mean to refute the idea that queerness does not and cannot exist, or must somehow remain invisible, in the Caribbean, and that it is only through diasporic movement that people gain their capacity to be legible, visible, and politically viable subjects. Rather than reject studies of movement and migration as both analytic frames and material experiences for Caribbean subjects, I ask what it can mean to pay equal attention to the rooted, to those Caribbean people who build lives for themselves right where they are, under conditions of both intense contradiction and sometimes, too, intense joy.[7] Spatial stabilities often profoundly mark the lives of same-sex desiring and gender-transgressing subjects in the region, and this essay demonstrates that considering genders and sexualities in quotidian, place-specific terms can function as a critical dimension of how we join Caribbean to queer analyses.

The events that inform this work take place in Martinique, a territory where centuries-long debates about the ideal nature and extent of its autonomy from the French state continue to be struggled over and illuminated by sexual politics. Because the island is not independent, it operates under a legal regime unique to the Caribbean vis-à-vis sexual rights. As just one example, in many countries in the region homosexuality is criminalized and "homosexual acts" are punishable by law, but these practices clash with France's legal code, which both affords protections and extends certain rights, like access to civil unions, to same-sex couples.[8] In the face of policies like these, local figures have argued that homosexual practices are unacceptable to 95 percent of the Martinican population because this population is said to hold "Christian" values different from those of French metropolitans.[9] This argument runs in tandem with a familiar narrative that displaces all same-sex desire onto the colonizer and onto depraved, decadent white bodies. Sited within the racialized politics of citizenship in France, these questions about community ethics and cultural sovereignty retain tremendous everyday importance for Martinican residents.

Like their heterosexual and cisgendered counterparts, same-sex desiring and gender-transgressing Martinicans are forced to grapple with an intersection of epistemological violences as they navigate various social worlds. Throughout the region Martinicans continue to be understood as products of a kind of modernist failure, having not followed the standard postcolonial teleology to independence as did the majority of the other territories of the global South. Locally, same-sex desiring and gender-transgressing people become subject to a culturalist agenda that rationalizes homophobia as an expression of cultural sovereignty and as a way to defend Martinican "local values" against those of the French state. These same people are also interpellated by a French universalist agenda proffered by metropolitan LGBT activists that requires the revindication of a particular type of (out, loud, and "proud") queer subject—an agenda that also, undoubtedly, violates.[10] This essay revisits tropes of queer invisibility and frames its analysis around a conscious attention to place in this particular (and somewhat peculiar) context, bearing in mind the complicated ways that this putatively (post)colonial situation affects the lives of my interlocutors on the island, both contemporary and long past.

So what, then, does or can it mean to think about queerness on France's Caribbean periphery? This essay seeks to unite a scattered archive of same-sex desire in Martinique, and, following José Muñoz's work in performance theory, it focuses on ephemera, on the traces left behind from moments of queer relation.[11] I use both popular literature and ethnography to track fleeting references to same-sex desire and gender transgression on the island, drawing a through-line between nonnormative practices across both space and time. Queer studies has largely had to define its archive through this kind of trace and absent-presence, searching for ways to both document and describe nonnormative modes of living and loving. Such theorists as Judith Jack Halberstam have compellingly described the assembly of archives, particularly those that unsettle normative interpretive regimes, as a process of scavenge; Mathias Danbolt has named the project of "touching [queer] history" as one shot through with ambiguities; Kara Keeling has written about the dual process of seeing a queer black past and producing it within the interstices; and Heather Love has urged that we understand why genealogies of this sort are at once ambivalent (as reminders of secrecy, violence, and shame) and urgent (as the groundings for future political projects).[12] Bearing in mind these structuring concerns, this essay thinks through the sexual politics of simultaneously memory and place, linking queer presence to the sands of two particular beaches on Martinique's coasts.

Saint-Pierre

In September 1635 Saint-Pierre became the colony of Martinique's first permanent settlement, established at the foot of Mount Pelée by French representatives of the Compagnie des Îles de l'Amérique. Seated on the island's western coast and opening out onto the Caribbean Sea, Saint-Pierre's port was Martinique's administrative and financial center for nearly 260 years. During the nineteenth century the city became known in colonial circuits as the Paris of the Antilles, as a cosmopolitan place where liberal sexual mores and a laxity about church membership were at the heart of the city's culture.[13] It housed the largest population of European migrants in the Caribbean region, and for that reason too it was a place of major social division. In a census taken in July 1901, Martinique's entire population was counted at 203,781 people, 36,011 of whom lived in Saint-Pierre. In the half century between emancipation (which came to French colonies in 1848) and Saint-Pierre's demise at the beginning of the twentieth century, fierce battles were fought in the public sphere among members of *béké* (white colonist) families, white functionaries from the metropole, members of the growing *métisse* and *mulâtre* (mixed-race and fair-skinned) middle class, and the overwhelmingly black servant/worker majority. Saint-Pierre was also a city of contradiction, for while violent struggles for power were endemic to the city's workings, so too was a type of social mixture that was most evident in the private and, above all, sexual sphere. The city's theater, brothels, and carnival celebrations were legendary, attracting wealthy joy-seekers from all over the island and from other islands, too, all throughout the year. While a spirit of *libertinage* had come to characterize French landholdings in the Americas from New Orleans to Saint-Domingue, Saint-Pierre emerged as a central site in France's eighteenth- and nineteenth-century economic, political, and sexual conquest of the region.[14] As the Martinican author and cultural critic Raphaël Confiant has argued, "Saint-Pierre was the city of all excesses."[15]

But on the morning of May 8, 1902, Mount Pelée, the volcano that sits just above the city, erupted—killing nearly everyone in Saint-Pierre within five seconds. It was the kind of volcanic eruption that inspired divine interpretation: a boiling, three-hundred-degree cloud of gas, steam, dust, ash, and pumice formed within the mountain and then burst forth. Hugging the earth and moving laterally at five hundred kilometers per hour, the cloud engulfed the city before anyone had time to react. This feat of nature was later named a *nuée ardente*, or a pyroclastic cloud. It was a phenomenon that had never been seen or analyzed before by the era's geologists and volcanologists. While Plinian eruptions (eruptions that shoot straight up into the air and end in lava flows) were familiar to the scientists of the day, this "new" type, which came to be known as a Peléan eruption, seemed to have come out of nowhere.[16] The Caribs, the indigenous inhabitants of Martinique, surely knew of the dangers of this volcano—they called it "Fire Mountain"—but that knowledge was lost in the genocidal campaign that the French waged in the name of imperial expansion. By 1902 Pierrotins (as the residents were called) had grown accustomed to living at the foot of a volcano and had taken to enjoying the warm sulphurous waters at its base for their curative practices. While there had been minor eruptions at the mountaintop in 1792 and again in 1851, these had been judged insignificant final gasps of a volcano on the decline. No one suspected that by the end of 1902 a local priest would have published a memoir called *Funeral Pilgrimage in the Ruins of Saint-Pierre*, or that a children's book comparing Saint-Pierre to Sodom and Gomorrah would claim to illustrate the wages of sin(s) gone too long unpunished.[17] Nor could residents anticipate that a year later, marking the first anniversary of the eruption, the island's newspaper would bear the headline: "Only Sodom is the analogy that we can make to the disaster at Saint-Pierre."[18]

The equation of Saint-Pierre with Sodom is of most interest for the present essay, particularly because the image of that doomed city is a recurrent one in Caribbean cultural imaginaries.[19] Alexander, commenting on the problems of invoking Sodom in the Caribbean, asserts that "Sodom requires no point of reference other than itself; it can assert authority without comparison, evidence, or parallel. Its power lies in the ability to distort, usurp, or foreclose other interpretative frameworks, other plausible explanations for its destruction, or other experiential dimensions of homosexuality [nonnormative practices] that oppose and refuse [dominant] constructions."[20] Here Alexander makes a compelling case for the metaphor's uselessness, for its power to obscure. But looked at differently, what might this repeated evocation of Sodom help us understand about the lives of Saint-Pierre's residents at the turn of the century? How might the image of Sodom have stood in for a range of things that could not be said or that could not have been spoken directly into the archive? Looked at differently, what traces might this image help us reveal?

When after the eruption Clémence Cassius de Linval, a longtime *béké* resident of Saint-Pierre and author of *Coeurs martiniquais*, wrote that "Sodom will sink because the volcano has vomited on the imprudent," or when a local priest criticized the city by calling it "the sad testimony to the impiety and immorality of this country: it is a real Sodom that God has punished," what did these writers communicate to their broader reading publics?[21] Rather than dismiss these writing strategies as reductive sleights of hand employed by chroniclers seeking the moral authority conveyed by biblical allusion, we might see these invocations of Sodom as a mode of indexing knowledge not only about same-sex desire but also about other modes of nonnormative relation and gender transgression, in pre-eruption Saint-Pierre. In an era when writing directly about these "queer" practices was taboo, calling Saint-Pierre the Sodom of the Antilles might have functioned as a privileged gesture — as a nod toward a mountain of things that could not be referenced directly.

Beyond these allusions, though, there remains at least one textual trace of Saint-Pierre's queerness: an erotic novel from the nineteenth century. While the relationship of fictional narrative to social analysis is not uncomplicated, it is clear that fiction captures something that social science often cannot. It moves beyond what can be readily observed, measured, and tabulated to more ephemeral phenomena that empirical methods often fail to capture. The novelist Samuel Delany warns about "generaliz[ing] from our fictions," but in this essay I ask that we consider them spaces for sustained inquiry and that we approach this work of pulp fiction as the location for an unstable, atomized archive of queer relation.[22]

Originally published in 1892 and rereleased in 1901, then recuperated and reprinted in 1992 and 1996, *Une nuit d'orgies à Saint-Pierre, Martinique* (*A Night of Orgies in Saint-Pierre, Martinique*) captures the social and linguistic registers of life in the city at the end of the nineteenth century.[23] Written in both French and Créole under the playful pseudonym Effe Géache (the initials F. G. H. in French), it is the story of three men who have long been running buddies, and in a classically French formula for narrative diversity, one is white (Philippe), one *mulâtre* (Jules), and one black (Hubert).[24] The erotic novel is the story of just one night, when after the friends have reunited they reminisce around a dinner table about old sexual liaisons and then head to a party in town. Confiant, in his preface to the 1992 edition, reminds readers that Géache's work is critical because it centers on experiences of misery, violence, and, of course, sex—experiences that, he maintains, were some of the most important dimensions of everyday life for residents of Saint-Pierre. Unlike the work of de Linval, who narrates life in Saint-Pierre as if it were a town populated only by *békés* and French metropolitans, Géache's story attempts a more realistic vision of the era's social context.[25] According to the historian Liliane Chauleau, after France's Third Republic was established in 1870, life in the capital took on a significantly more racially mixed character.[26] While misery and violence were undoubtedly an important part of that "mixed" life in the city, the representation of sex in *A Night of Orgies* is the narrative's most striking aspect. There Géache describes a range of sex acts for his readers, both consensual and not, sexual encounters enacted often in public: group sex, play with sex roles, female ejaculation, more cunnilingus and fellatio than can be counted on two hands, loads of anal play and penetration, and doggie-style sex (that, it seems, was fairly transgressive for the time). But Géache also offers two moments in the novel that give readers indirect access to same-sex desire and gender transgression in pre-eruption Saint-Pierre.

Early on in the narrative, Hubert (the dandy of the bunch) is on his way to the port to meet Jules, who is arriving on a boat from Fort-de-France, when he happens on a group of five women on a street corner. With little fanfare, these women are said to be "comparing and poking at each others' pussies."[27] It is a striking, but still oblique image, and is quickly passed over when Hubert throws up one of the women's skirts and forces her into a brief and violent sex act in front of her friends. This becomes a scene of base sexual violence, but what kind of trace of queer relationality might that one moment, just as Hubert arrived, have given us access to? Who were these women and what were they doing when Hubert approached? These women are later referred to as a group of whores (*catins*), but it is never clear whether that is their profession or a moniker ascribed to them as a result of their practices. Almost all of the women in the novel are called whores at one time or another, no matter what their social position. Hubert has clearly had a relationship with one of the women in the group, Jeanne, who jealously pulls his penis out of the woman he is raping just as he is about to ejaculate. But long before Hubert's arrival, when the women were alone and connecting with each other, what allowed this group's intimate touching, particularly in public, to be narrated in such a fashion? The language makes it seem commonplace, as if they were admiring each other's hair. So what does it mean that they were "comparing" pussies? And "poking" them?

Theorists of women's same-sex desire have made important use of these kinds of fleeting presences. They have challenged conventional disciplines' privileging of visible, empirical evidence, interpreting those stances as indictments of women-desiring-women's practices and forms of identification as either "impossible" or unmentionable.[28] The anthropologist Serena Owusua Dankwa, for example, writes compellingly about everyday intimacies between women in Ghana and about "modes of sexual sociality . . . [that exist] beyond the subcultural language of sexual identity politics."[29] In her analysis, norms of discretion and indirection structure relationships between women, with codes legible only to and between them. This, she argues, is not silence nor absence but a kind of tacit engagement that well reflects the kind of "queer" presence that has long been a legible part of life in Martinique: present yet not particularly remarked on, and represented only fleetingly.[30] These are the kinds of engagements that, as Jafari S. Allen has so elegantly described them, "require no parade and no declarations outside of [their] own cocoons of recognition."[31]

The second moment in the narrative that draws our queer attention comes midway through the novel, when the friends decide to leave the conviviality of their dinner table to attend a party at a place called Chez Babette, a bar and dancehall that actually existed before the volcano struck. Géache writes that Philippe helps his companions to "se travestir" before heading out into the night.[32]

Se travestir is an ambiguous, polysemic term, meaning simultaneously to disguise oneself and to cross-dress, and would also have been so in nineteenth-century Martinique. In this instance, the fact of the companions' work to change their physical appearances may be an important one. Martinique is known throughout the Caribbean for its "unusual" Carnival practices. Whereas Carnival is a time of sexual excess nearly everywhere in the region, in Martinique it is also a moment when men—from all walks of life and with varying attachments to masculine identities—*se travestissent en femme*, dress as women.[33] This practice was said to have begun in Saint-Pierre, the center of the first Carnival celebrations on the island.[34]

By 1892, the date of the novel's publication, cross-dressing had been firmly anchored in the social life of Pierrotins. When just under ten years later Pelée erupted and many of the city's former residents were dispersed throughout the French Caribbean, they brought the practice elsewhere, most notably to French Guyana, where the familiar figure of *touloulous solidaires* are often men dressed as women in the prototypical head-to-toe Carnival disguise.[35] The anthropologist Thierry L'Étang, in his oral histories with descendants of Pierrotins, has explored popular reinterpretations of the disaster that focus on *malédiction*, or divine retribution, as the genesis of the eruption. While the logics that he elicits are largely confined to stories of residents' disrespect of religious figures, he also documents stories that suggest that magically related gender transgression may have been a part of the city's maligned reputation. His interlocutor Antoinette, for example, talks of hearing about "young boys who turned themselves into dogs. They transformed into *diablesses* at noon, and *zombis* in the evening."[36] And his interlocutor George talks about a couple who always made their appearances in town "dressed as women . . . [who] frightened the young."[37]

Given this context of gender play and *travestissement*, Géache's mention of the men's redressing on their way to the dance could be read not simply as their dressing *up* but also as their assumption of nonnormative gender presentations. When Jules first arrives at the dock and Philippe proposes that they go out to this party, Jules laments that he has brought nothing to wear. That problem is easily solved later on, when Philippe presumably loans both men the necessary "disguises." Just as he had described the women on the corner, Géache writes this moment with little fanfare, yet both of these scenes highlight the indirect ways that moments of queer relation show up in Martinique's textual archive.

Like these moments unremarked upon yet inescapably present, when one drives the island's western coast today from the town of Carbet, up through Saint-Pierre, and on to the northernmost cove at Anse Couleuvre, it is impossible to miss the fact that the beaches' sands range from a light charcoal gray to deep, deep black.[38] Like the fleeting references to same-sex desire and gender transgression in *A Night of Orgies*, the sands in the area that surround Saint-Pierre are today a visual reminder of Mount Pelée's eruption. Like people, like places, like objects or ideas, sand has a history, a genealogy. The composition of sand varies, yet that variation is deeply dependent on its environment. Sand always carries a local imprint. In this area the beaches are black because particles in the sand are made up of basalt, which comes from volcanic ash. There the sands remember — or at least they reference — the eruption, and in doing so they call up all of the associations we might have with the city that once was. Those sands carry the imprint of the world that Mount Pelée both dispersed and destroyed on that day in 1902.

Sainte-Anne

Far to the south and east of Saint-Pierre, in an area that sits at the tip of a small outcropping on Martinique's other shore, lies a commune called Sainte-Anne. While pre-eruption Saint-Pierre was often imagined as a space of hedonistic racial mixture, Sainte-Anne has long held a far different reputation. During the 1950s the out-of-the-way commune was known as a refuge for rebels, for people who contested the continued dominance of *béké* and *mulâtre* elites in the lives of ordinary (mostly black) Martinicans, and was the center of the island's small cultural nationalist movement.[39] In the 1970s community members protested the building of the island's only Club Méditeranée and have since worked concertedly to thwart the development of a tourist industry in the commune.[40] After the local activist Garcin Malsa was elected mayor in 1989, he launched a campaign to remove all of the *tricolores* (the blue, white, and red French flags) from their official perches and to replace them with a red, black, and green flag, meant to declare Martinican independence from France. Today, when you drive into Sainte-Anne from the island's major highway, the first thing you see as you cross the boundary is a roundabout where the red, black, and green waves. But Sainte-Anne is known for another reason, too: it is home to one of the island's few meeting spaces for same-sex desiring men, a secluded cove called Anse Moustique on the least visited part of its largest beach, Les Salines.

On my first visit to the island, I hiked out to Anse Moustique at midmorning. Not only was it long before noon, but it was also the middle of the week, and I found myself alone on the beach, wondering how this empty place squared with the stories that I had heard men tell about their liaisons there. It was just a cove flanked by trees and low-hanging brush, opening onto a shallow stretch of the sea. The waves there were gentle, and the sand freshly flattened by the high tide. I was beset by two questions that have remained with me since. The first: why make this cruising spot all the way out here, in Sainte-Anne? On a good traffic-free day, Anse Moustique is over an hour's drive from the island's urban center. While the capital seems to always have one operational cruising strip, alternating between the central waterfront, La Savane (a city park), and the port, this beach is the only drag that has remained constant for more than two decades. Distance is one good reason, but there are other beaches on the island, themselves equally difficult to access. That Anse Moustique sits in one of Martinique's two nationalist communes reminds us of the omnipresence of queer relation. Rather than restrict the archive of these presences to the decadent city that Saint-Pierre once was, often read as European, Anse Moustique takes us into the hinterlands, often read as the site for black authenticity, to a context far different from the one described in Géache's novel. While Saint-Pierre was the embodiment of the island's cosmopolitanism, Sainte-Anne is a sleepy backwater. There unemployment rates sit at nearly 35 percent, and people remember vividly a not-so-distant time when many made their living by doing the tedious work of salt-collecting out on the flats.[41] People who live in the island's contemporary urban spaces often speak of places like Sainte-Anne, pejoratively, as being *en commune*. Said with a frown of the face and a roll of the eyes, they imagine the people in these places incapable of acquiring the sophistication assigned to the residents of more urban grounds.

As we sipped espresso in a café in Fort-de-France, I asked thirty-two-year-old Guillaume to describe Anse Moustique for someone who had never been there.[42] He and I had been talking about our experiences of the place, and most particularly about his first journey there, when a friend whom he had met online (through the website Adam 4 Adam) gave him a ride to the beach.[43] It was there that he first had oral sex with another man. This is what he said:

Guillaume: Listen, it's not like it's on anyone's way anywhere else. Anse Moustique? Whew [he sucks his teeth]. You have to drive all the way out to Sainte-Anne first (And with the traffic here? That can take over an hour!) and then you have to continue, continue, continue . . . all along that smaller road to Les Salines. And then you still have to get to Anse Moustique — now that there's that new access road — you know the one I mean. That you took for the party? — no, I don't remember when they opened it . . . my memory's bad . . . but you know the road, with all of the rocks and potholes, and it gets flooded, too, every time it rains (and you know it rains all the time here!). And then even after you park, you have to put on your boots and hike! [he laughs] But when you get there, you know. You know that the guys who are there are in the same spirit as you.

Vanessa Agard-Jones: How does that feel?

Guillaume: *C'est magique, chérie. Tout à fait. C'est magique.* [It's magic, my dear. Completely. It's magic.]

What makes Anse Moustique magic for Guillaume is the kind of shared space that it offers to the people who go there. This kind of experience is a critical dimension of what might be called "queer" culture on the island. The beach is so far out of the way that those who find themselves on its sands are a self-selecting bunch. The men there do not usually call themselves gay — instead of embracing an identity, they identify with an affective state — they often say they are *chaud* (hot) — in a hot period, needing release. In addition to the space, this is the "spirit" (*esprit*) that they share, a shifting terrain of desire much like the sands that heat and cool throughout the day. Many, like Guillaume, have girlfriends and wives on other parts of the island and are able to make the long journey out to the beach only a few times a month. As Lionel, another of my interlocutors, said to me, *On vient pour koker — c'est ça le but.* (We come to fuck — that's the goal.) But other things happen, too, at Anse Moustique. Men come to know and recognize each other, an important, but also potentially risky process on an island as small as Martinique, where propinquity feeds the gossip mill. Men who have come by bus and on foot often leave with others who have cars. Drinks and joints are brought and shared. Men play and bathe and rest in the sea. The magic is sexual but also social, equally about what Guillaume described as the "best blow job of [his] life" as about the kinds of connections, however tenuous, that the space offers for its users.

I think of Anse Moustique as another example of what Delany describes in his powerful set of essays *Times Square Red, Times Square Blue*, where he recounts the kinds of relationships that men built in Manhattan's porn theaters in the 1970s and 1980s. Refusing an easy nostalgia, Delany writes, "Were the porn theaters romantic? Not at all. But because of the people who used them, they were humane and functional, fulfilling needs that most of our society does not yet know how to acknowledge."[44] For Delany, these were places that fulfilled sexual needs, but also social ones — allowing for a kind of cross-class contact that was otherwise rare in his daily life. In Martinique, this kind of contact is even more rarified, as the island's class stratification is exacerbated by disparities in access to transportation and by the fact that living without a car limits access to a wide range of places on the island. This is not Delany's New York City, where, however cynically we might think about it, even the mayor rides public transportation. In Martinique, public buses run only in the capital, and they operate only Monday through Friday from 5 a.m. to 6 p.m. and on Saturdays until noon. Collective taxis get people without cars from town to town, but they are unscheduled and unreliable, and only go to the town centers rather than to more out-of-the-way places, like Anse Moustique.

Through Guillaume I met Bruno, an HIV-positive man in his forties who lives on social assistance in a small apartment in Fort-de-France. He scrapes to get by most months, supplementing his state income with a variety of hustles.[45] While he does not have access to a car, he travels to Anse Moustique fairly regularly, either by bus or hitchhiking to make his way to that other shore. When I asked him to describe a particularly memorable moment at Anse Moustique, he said this:

> *Bruno*: It was a Sunday a couple of years back, and I met a young man, a *béké*, who was seventeen years old. . . . I saw him walking with a piece of wood, swinging it like this, and he had on hiker shorts—and I asked him, "Are you lost?" He said "No, no, no. I'm just taking a walk." I asked, "Do you know where you are?" And he said, "I know this route." So I did a U-turn and came back to him and said, "Do you know there are a lot of homos here?" And he said, "Oh yes? I didn't know." And I said, "You didn't know?" "(You know when they say they don't know, they really know.)" And he said, "And you, are you homo?" And I said, "Yes, I'm homo—but don't be afraid." And he said, "I'm not afraid!" But he was scared to be penetrated, you know, because I had on a cap and baggy jeans, I was looking very BadBoy, and he had this idea about what was going to happen to him—but when I offered to suck him off he said—*tout de suite!*—*On va où?* (Where can we go?) *Tout de suite!* (Right away!) So we walked across the mangrove, and laid down a towel, and we made love there . . . but that young man he was seventeen—and he was a *béké*! And we talked for a long time afterward—he told me that he was a *béké*, and that he was in high school at the rich people's school, the private one in Fort-de-France. That's a story that I would love to see happen again—no, I haven't seen him again yet, but when we see each other . . . that would be something nice.

Bruno's story about his encounter with the young *béké* highlights the function of the beach as a space of both cross-class and interracial connection. In Martinique, *békés* are the descendants of the white colonial elite, the planter class that continues to dominate the island economically, though no longer politically. *Békés* are notorious for their remove from the rest of the island, for their enclosed communities on the east coast in and around Le François, and for their continued staunch refusal to "mix" with the rest of the island's population.[46] For Bruno, having this liaison — and, particularly, this postcoital conversation with a *béké* — remained in his memory as a singularly significant moment in his nearly twenty years of frequenting Anse Moustique. The conventional racial scripts that would have made their connection unlikely are disrupted here by the prospect of a blow job, by the potential for a moment of shared pleasure. Like Guillaume, who thinks of the beach in magical terms, Bruno appreciates it not just for the sex but also for the other kinds of social connection that the place makes possible.

While most evenings Anse Moustique is a cruising space for men alone, a few times a year a promoter named Jean-Marc throws large parties on the beach, trucking in a generator, DJ equipment, tiki torches, and party lights to welcome nearly two hundred people to dance and connect. Everyone brings a bottle to contribute to the bar (a requirement for admission), and after drinking and dancing most of the night away there is time for sea baths at dawn.

I arrive at 2 a.m., just as the party is getting under way. The sandy dance floor is already marked by the footprints of ecstatic dancers, moved by the DJ's facility with diasporic music — he moves seamlessly from soca to zouk, through calypso and dancehall, back to hip hop and R&B, and then again to something close to, though not quite, Chicago house. Women come to these parties in striking numbers, setting up their towels in a cove slightly separate from the men's side of the beach. Like their male counterparts, they drink and dance, often leading the more raucous line-dancing interludes orchestrated by the DJ. They too are the first to the sandy dance floor when the selector plays a slow zouk, and their grinding and twirling entices the male couples to join, swaying to the syncopated beats, forehead to forehead, crotches intertwined. There is a good deal of semipublic sex on these evenings among both men and women, who use the cover of night's darkness and the privacy of the surrounding brush to consummate their unions, however tenuous.

The day after one such party I called a woman in her forties named Karine to talk about the night's events. Karine works as a security guard and identifies herself by the French term *garçon manqué*, or "missed boy" (tomboy). In the years that I have known her, she has never had a serious relationship, but at these beach parties she is quite popular and is usually surrounded by a group of women of varying gender identifications. I had seen Karine head off down a path with a younger woman just as I was getting ready to leave the party. On the phone, I asked her what it was that she remembered most about the evening. In response, she said this: *Seigneur* (God), I woke up this afternoon with sand in my ass and all I could think about was that hot little *chabine* that I had on the beach.[47] Powerfully mediated through her experience of sand lodged in an uncomfortable place, Karine's corporeal association of the beach with her lovemaking made me wonder anew what the sand might offer us as a repository for queer memory.

Beyond the stories that Guillaume, Bruno, and Karine are able to recount, what remains of the vibrant sexual encounters that they have had at Anse Moustique? After the parties are over, and the blankets, empty bottles, and sound system cleared away, what reminds us of the importance of this site, for so many people? On that beach, the sand that people dance and lie down on holds something of those experiences—perhaps not materially, but metaphysically. Thinking about how we might understand this phenomenon, the second question that has beset me since my first solitary visit to that cove is this: what could an empty place tell me, an ethnographer, about same-sex desire on the island? Perhaps it is in the sands that I have my answer. The sand tracks this presence in a place where the archive is shallow, and where the ravages of the plantation, then later of the colony, and even worse still, of the salinated air, has meant the slow erosion of all things putatively concrete. Sand is born of, and speaks of, that erosion. On a beach where people live and love and dance together, there can be no definitive record. But far from V. S. Naipaul's condemnation of the Caribbean as a site of "ruination," the sand, even in its erosion, has its own integrity and retains its own history. The sand's memory is "a resolute commitment to those with whom . . . we are still dancing," a diffuse and oblique archive of movement in place, of loving on a local scale.[48]

Sand Is History

In his magisterial and now-iconic poem, St. Lucian writer and Nobel laureate Derek Walcott contends that, for the Caribbean region, "sea is history."[49] Invoked time and again as the ideal metaphor to index the complicated calculus of presence, loss, and absence that attends the history of the African diaspora in the Americas, Walcott's articulation of the sea is much like those of a cadre of literary workers and cultural critics who employ watery metaphors to help us better grasp and understand this history.

Working from a different angle, in my attempt to pay close attention to place, this essay invokes the most fine-grained element—quite literally—of the place where I work: the sand. From the sand on the beaches of Saint-Pierre, to the morning-after sand in Karine's ass, sand is everywhere in Martinique (as it is throughout the region). It is, of course, on the beaches, but it is also carried on the wind and on our bodies. It ends up on the kitchen floor, in the backseat of the car, in the bottom of my handbag, and in all manner of bodily orifices. While we have work that inspires and elucidates using metaphors of the mangrove and of the sea in Caribbean cultural studies, the sand has received no such attention. But what can the sand tell us?

Nearly everywhere on earth, sand is principally made up of one element — in some places silica, in others limestone. Ninety percent of a grain is almost always just one of those two elements. But the other 10 percent is the percentage with a difference — the percentage that, in its difference, matters — the percentage that can tell us something about the history of a place. In Saint-Pierre and its surroundings, that variable 10 percent is made up of the basalt that makes the sands black.[50] In Sainte-Anne, there is no geological marker in those grains, but they hold something all the same. While the sand's referents are far from concrete, they provide a model for one way to understand the memory of same-sex desire and gender transgression on the island — as diffuse yet somehow omnipresent. "Queerness," then, retains a kind of oblique permanence in Martinique that has resonance both in the structure of the sand and in the connections made on the island's shores. Rather than invoke ideas about absence and invisibility as the condition of same-sex desiring and gender-transgressing people, turning to sand as a metaphor for the repository of memory may help our analyses engage with more fine-grained and ephemeral presences than our usual archives would allow.

Notes

I would like to thank Jafari S. Allen, Alex Bell, Mathias Danbolt, Dána-Ain Davis, A. Naomi Jackson, and Ram Natarajan for their ongoing engagement with this work and for their astute feedback as it moved from talk to essay. My arguments were also productively honed through presentations at the 2010 "Queer Again? Power, Politics, Ethics" conference in Berlin, hosted by the generous and engaging members of the Gender as a Category of Knowledge Research Group, in a 2011 iteration of Simone Leigh's "Be Black Baby" art and performance event at Recess Art Gallery, and at the 2011 Caribbean Studies Association's annual conference in Curaçao, where discussions with my copanelists Lyndon K. Gill and Omise'eke N. Tinsley were beyond my imaginings and proved truly priceless. I am particularly grateful for Deborah A. Thomas, who has supported this work in all ways — (very!) big and small. My colleagues at Linköping University's Tema Genus and in Stockholm's broader gender/

queer/feminist studies networks were extraordinarily helpful as I made my way through the revision process, even at the height of Swedish summer. Finally, I thank *GLQ*'s three anonymous reviewers for their insightful and incisive readings, and hope to continue to engage their feedback as the broader project that includes this work develops. During the time that I developed this essay, my research was generously supported by a National Science Foundation Graduate Research Fellowship (and its Nordic Research Opportunity) under grant number DGE-0813964, as well as by the Bourse Chateaubriand of the Embassy of France in the United States.

1. This is not to discount the deep associations of water with both physical and emotional pain, with death and drowning, or of specific bodies of water (and their boundaries) with militarism. My point is also not to set sand in brutal opposition to water but to highlight the different kind of work that it might do given its material constraints, in its moderation of ideas about fluidity and motion. For important discussions of water, pain, and black historical memory, see Omise'eke Natasha Tinsley, *Thiefing Sugar: Eroticism between Women in Caribbean Literature* (Durham, NC: Duke University Press, 2010); and Marcus Wood, *Blind Memory: Visual Representations of Slavery in England and America, 1780–1865* (Manchester: Manchester University Press, 2000).

2. Omise'eke Natasha Tinsley, "Black Atlantic, Queer Atlantic: Queer Imaginings of the Middle Passage," *GLQ* 14 (2008): 204.

3. Makeda Silvera, "Man Royals and Sodomites: Some Thoughts on the Invisibility of Afro-Caribbean Lesbians," *Feminist Studies* 18, no. 3 (1992): 521–32. While Silvera's argument is pegged specifically to *lesbian* invisibility, and the particular silences/erasure that she argues condition our lives, I believe her broader critique would extend to same-sex desiring Afro-Caribbean people more generally. I use the words *queer* and *queerness* here as a shorthand, fully cognizant of the fact that they are not words that appear in the lexicon of same-sex-desiring and gender-transgressing subjects in Martinique. For a masterful analysis of the challenges of fitting language to our interlocutors' form/s and practice/s in black queer studies, see Tinsley, *Thiefing Sugar*, 5–15.

4. For work on queer Caribbean diasporas, see, for example, Ronald Cummings, "(Trans)nationalisms, Marronage, and Queer Caribbean Subjectivities," *Transforming Anthropology* 18, no. 2 (2010): 169–80; Lawrence La Fountain-Stokes, *Queer Ricans: Cultures and Sexualities in the Diaspora* (Minneapolis: University of Minnesota Press, 2009); Rinaldo Walcott, "Queer Returns: Human Rights, the Anglo-Caribbean, and Diaspora Politics," *Caribbean Review of Gender Studies*, no. 3 (2009); Timothy Chin, "The Novels of Patricia Powell: Negotiating Gender and Sexuality across the Disjunctures of the Caribbean Diaspora," *Callaloo* 30, no. 2 (2007): 533–45.

5. I am inspired here by feminist technoscience studies and by efforts to theorize a "posthumanities" that breaks down boundaries both between academic disciplines

and between bodies and their surroundings. For example, Anneke Smelik and Nina Lykke argue that "the human body can no longer be figured either as a bounded entity or as a naturally given and distinct part of an unquestioned whole that is itself conceived as the 'environment.' The boundaries between bodies and their components are being blurred, together with those between bodies and larger ecosystems (x)." This essay's use of sand as both material and metaphor resonates with Smelik and Lykke's concept "bits of life" (page xxi) and their theorization of people simultaneously with the biological/geological/chemical environments in which they live. Similarly, in her bid for complex systems thinking across disciplinary divides, Elizabeth Wilson calls for "some middle ground of conceptual advocacy in which the metaphoricity of depression and the neurobiology of depression cohabit, entwine and are inherently shaped by one another" (page 292). Like Smelik and Lykke, she works productively between metaphor and science, across the literary and the empirical, in ways that this essay also seeks to situate its work. See Anneke Smelik and Nina Lykke, "Bits of Life: An Introduction," in *Bits of Life: Feminism at the Intersections of Media, Bioscience, and Technology*, ed. Anneke Smelik and Nina Lykke (Seattle: University of Washington Press, 2008), x, xxi; and Elizabeth Wilson, "Neurological Entanglements: The Case of Paediatric Depressions, SSRIs, and Suicidal Ideation," *Subjectivity* 4, no. 3 (2011): 277–97; quotation on 292.

6. M. Jacqui Alexander, *Pedagogies of Crossing: Meditations on Feminism, Sexual Politics, Memory, and the Sacred* (Durham, NC: Duke University Press, 2006).

7. The anthropologist Gloria Wekker has long done this work in Suriname, and her *Politics of Passion: Women's Sexual Culture in the Afro-Surinamese Diaspora* (New York: Columbia University Press, 2006) is a compelling examination of many of the concerns with which I am preoccupied here.

8. N.B.: "homosexual acts" often serves as a gloss for anal penetration, a practice engaged in by people across sexual spectra, yet used to single out and penalize male same-sex couples for their lovemaking.

9. See, for example, an interview with Vauclin's mayor Raymond Occolier from 2007, just before the French national election campaign: www.dailymotion.com/video/x1i17o_occo-bondamanjak_news. Beginning at 3:20 he describes his stance as an "élu chrétien" (itself an oxymoron to the French state) as one that requires that he take a position against marriage, adoption, and other legal reforms for LGBT people. In the interview he purports to speak for the great majority of Martiniquai(se)s when he declares himself to be against sexual acts he calls "against nature," yet emphasizes that his positions on these issues do not, in his view, make him homophobic.

10. Vanessa Agard-Jones, "Le Jeu de Qui? Sexual Politics at Play in the French Caribbean," in *Sex and the Citizen: Interrogating the Caribbean*, ed. Faith Smith (Charlottesville: University of Virginia Press, 2011).

11. José Esteban Muñoz, "Gesture, Ephemera, Queer Feeling," in *Dancing Desires: Choreographing Sexualities on and off the Stage*, ed. Jane Desmond (Madison: University of Wisconsin Press, 2001).

12. Judith Halberstam, *In a Queer Time and Place: Transgender Bodies, Subcultural Lives* (New York: New York University Press, 2005); Mathias Danbolt, "Touching History: Archival Relations in Queer Art and Theory," in *Lost and Found: Queerying the Archive*, ed. Jane Rowley, Louise Wolthers, and Mathias Danbolt (Copenhagen: Nikolaj, Copenhagen Center of Contemporary Art and Bildmuseet Umeå University, 2010); Kara Keeling, "Looking for M—: Queer Temporality, Black Political Possibility, and Poetry from the Future," *GLQ* 15 (2009): 565–82; Heather Love, *Feeling Backward: Loss and the Politics of Queer History* (Cambridge, MA: Harvard University Press, 2007).

13. Claude Rives and Frédéric Denhez, *Les épaves du volcan* (Grenoble: Editions Glénat, 1997).

14. Doris Garraway, *The Libertine Colony: Creolization in the Early French Caribbean* (Durham, NC: Duke University Press, 2005).

15. Raphaël Confiant, "Libertinage à la Créole," in *Une nuit d'orgies à Saint-Pierre, Martinique*, by Effe Géache (Paris: Arléa, 1992). Unless stated otherwise, all translations from French and Martinican Créole are my own.

16. Alwyn Scarth, *La Catastrophe: The Eruption of Mount Pélee, the Worst Volcanic Eruption of the Twentieth Century* (Oxford: Oxford University Press, 2002).

17. U. Moerens, *Pèlerinage funèbre aux ruines de Saint-Pierre, Martinique* (Lille: Société Saint-Augustin, 1903).

18. Patrice Louis, *L'enfer à Saint-Pierre: Dictionnaire de la catastrophe de 1902* (Martinique: Ibis Rouge, 2002), 151.

19. This also holds true for sexual politics in other regions, wherever the influence of the biblical tale retains cultural meaning. For an analysis of the threat of Sodom-like destruction in early New England, see Jonathan Ned Katz, "The Age of Sodomitical Sin, 1607–1740," in *Reclaiming Sodom*, ed. Jonathan Goldberg (New York: Routledge, 1994).

20. M. Jacqui Alexander, "Erotic Autonomy as a Politics of Decolonization," in *Pedagogies of Crossing*, 51.

21. Louis, *L'enfer à Saint-Pierre*; Scarth, *La Catastrophe*.

22. Samuel R. Delany, *Times Square Red, Times Square Blue* (New York: New York University Press, 2001), 147.

23. Effe Géache, *Une nuit d'orgies à Saint-Pierre, Martinique* (Paris: Calivran, 1978).

24. This formula, echoed in more contemporary film and fiction as a black/blanc/beur triad, activates tropes of cross-racial friendship and common French citizenship while eliding both historical and contemporary structures of racial violence. For master-

ful analyses of antiblack racism within French multiculturalist imaginaries, see Pap Ndiaye, "Pour une histoire des populations noires en France: Préalables théoriques," *Le mouvement social* 213, no. 4 (2005); Ndiaye, *La condition noire: Essai sur une minorité française* (Paris: Calmann-Lévy, 2008); and Tricia D. Keaton, "The Politics of Race-Blindness: (Anti)blackness and Category-Blindness in Contemporary France," *Du Bois Review: Social Science Research on Race* 7, no. 1 (2010): 103–31.

25. For a searing critique of de Linval's whitewashed representations of the city, see Alain Yacou, *Les catastrophes naturelles aux Antilles: D'une soufrière à une autre* (Paris: Karthala Editions, 1999).

26. The archivist and historian Liliane Chauleau has chronicled these everyday conditions in two separate publications: *Le Saint-Pierre d'antan: Quelques aspects de la vie des Pierrotins d'autrefois: Conférence faite au Rotary à l'occasion de son 5e anniversaire, le 9 mai 1975* (Fort-de-France: Les Archives départementales de la Martinique, 1975), and *Pierrotins et Saint-Pierrais: La vie quotidienne dans la ville de Saint-Pierre avant l'éruption de la montagne Pelée de 1902* (Paris: Editions L'Harmattan, 2002).

27. Géache, *Une nuit*, 8.

28. Gayatri Gopinath, *Impossible Desires: Queer Diasporas and South Asian Public Cultures* (Durham, NC: Duke University Press, 2005).

29. Serena Owusua Dankwa, "'It's a Silent Trade': Female Same-Sex Intimacies in Post-Colonial Ghana," *Nora-Nordic Journal of Feminist and Gender Research* 17, no. 3 (2009): 193.

30. I take my naming of "tacit" forms and unremarked upon presences from Carlos U. Decena, "Tacit Subjects," *GLQ* 14 (2008): 339.

31. Jafari Sinclaire Allen, "For 'the Children': Dancing the Beloved Community," *Souls: A Critical Journal of Black Politics, Culture, and Society* 11, no. 3 (2009): 315.

32. Géache, *Une nuit*, 108.

33. On Carnival and sexuality more generally in the Caribbean, see Kamala Kempadoo, "Theorizing Sexual Relations in the Caribbean," in *Confronting Power, Theorizing Gender: Interdisciplinary Perspectives in the Caribbean*, ed. Eudine Barriteau (Mona: University of the West Indies Press, 2003); and Linden Lewis, *The Culture of Gender and Sexuality in the Caribbean* (Gainesville: University Press of Florida, 2003). On the francophone Caribbean, see Thomas Spear, "Carnivalesque Jouissance: Representation of Sexuality in the Francophone West Indian Novel," *Jouvert: A Journal of Postcolonial Studies* 2, no. 1 (1998); on Martinique in particular, David A. B. Murray, "Defiance or Defilement? Undressing Cross-Dressing in Martinique's Carnival," *Sexualities* 1, no. 3 (1998): 343–54; also see Patrick Bruneteaux and Véronique Rochais, *Le Carnaval des travestis: Les travestis makoumè* (Case Pilote: Éditions Lafontaine, 2006), which in calling attention to wide-ranging participation in the practice, insists that the phenomenon of *travestissement* was (and remains) "transclassiste."

34. While cross-dressing is also part of celebrations in Brazil, it is rarer in the insular Caribbean and does not hold the kind of traditional permanence that the spectacle of *travestis makoumè* holds in Martinique.
35. Isabelle Hidair, *Anthropologie du Carnaval cayennais: Une représentation en réduction de la société créole cayennaise* (Paris: Editions Publibook, 2005), 43.
36. The *diablesse* (*guiablesse, djablès*) is a popular folk figure, a female consort of the devil whose beauty is reputed to seduce men to their deaths. See also Lafcadio Hearn, "Martinique Sketches: La Guiablesse," for a nineteenth-century rendering in *Two Years in the French West Indies* (New York: Harper and Brothers, 1903).
37. Thierry L'Étang, "Saint-Pierre, Martinique: Mémoire orale d'une ville martyre et eschatologie de la catastrophe," in *Saint-Pierre: Mythes et réalités de la cité créole disparue*, ed. Léo Ursulet (Guyane: Ibis Rouge Editions, 2004), 25–26.
38. Édouard Glissant has written extensively about Martinique's black sands, most notably in "La Plage Noir" ("The Black Beach"), where he uses the beach's mutations (in this case, the one at Diamant) to think through both relationality and disorder in Martinican politics. See Édouard Glissant, *Poétique de la Relation* (Paris: Messageries du Livre, 1990).
39. See Sainte-Anne's longtime mayor Garcin Malsa's memoir for one perspective on this history: *L'écologie ou la passion du vivant: Quarante ans d'écrits écologiques* (Paris: L'Harmattan, 2008).
40. Éric Coppet, "L'avenir, Sainte-Anne et le marin," *Politiques publiques*, October 5, 2010.
41. For employment rates, see Institut National de la Statistique et des Études Économiques statistics, 2010 (www.insee.fr).
42. All names are pseudonyms.
43. Adam 4 Adam (www.adam4adam.com/) is an online dating and chat site for men who have sex with men, used often in Martinique by men seeking casual sexual partners, as well as friends.
44. Delany, *Times Square Red, Times Square Blue*, 90.
45. The anthropologist Katherine Browne, in *Creole Economics: Caribbean Cunning under the French Flag* (Houston: University of Texas Press, 2004), provides an important analysis of the ways that people make ends meet on the island, through a combination of legal and extralegal economic pursuits.
46. Emily Vogt's unpublished doctoral dissertation is one important source for this history, "Ghosts of the Plantation: Historical Representations and Cultural Difference among Martinique's White Elite" (University of Chicago, 2005), as is Édith Kováts Beaudoux, *Les blancs créoles de la Martinique: Une minorité dominante* (Paris: L'Harmattan, 2002), the belated publication from her field research on the island in the 1960s.
47. In Martinique, as in other parts of the French Caribbean, a *chabin/e* designates a per-

son of African descent with light (often very light) skin, but "African" features. These distinctions are well documented in Jean Luc Bonniol, *La couleur comme maléfice: Une illustration créole de la généalogie des "blancs" et des "noirs"* (Paris: Albin Michel, 1992) as well as in the anthropologist Stéphanie Mulot's doctoral dissertation, "'Je suis la mère, je suis le père!' L'énigme matrifocale. Relations familiales et rapports de sexe en Guadeloupe" (École des Haute Études en Sciences Sociales, 2000).

48. Allen, "For 'the Children,'" 320.
49. Derek Walcott, "The Sea Is History," in *Collected Poems, 1948–1984* (New York: Farrar, Straus and Giroux, 1986).
50. My understandings of sand's composition are drawn from Michael Helland, *Sand: The Neverending Story* (Berkeley: University of California Press, 2009); Bernard W. Pipkin, D. D. Trent, Richard Hazlett, and Paul Bierman, *Geology and the Environment* (New York: Cengage, 2007); and F. Michel and H. Conge's film *Histoire d'un grain de sable* (2004).

OF UNEXPLAINED PRESENCES, FLYING IFE HEADS, VAMPIRES, SWEAT, ZOMBIES, AND LEGBAS

A Meditation on Black Queer Aesthetics

Ana-Maurine Lara

The numerous absences and silences within formal archives, reflected in scholarship on black queer cultural productions and the contributions by black queer artists, impel us to parse the characteristics and genealogy of black queer aesthetics and art.[1] At the same time, however, there is a lack of language to define what is, ultimately, a vast and various field of practices and influences that cannot be pinned down to essential identities. Here I understand "black" and "queer" as nonstatic, strategic identities that mark community and erotic practices. For the purposes of this meditation, the work I discuss is marked by (1) its presence in defined black queer spaces and/or (2) the claiming of questions of the body and queer states of being by the artists. This meditation is a review of two temporally bound art events—*DASH: Metaphor and Connection* and the Ghetto Biennale—that took place in two disparate locations in 2009. In discussing these events, I am also meditating on questions of black queer aesthetics.

Discussions of black queer aesthetics are often grounded in analyses of historiographical methods—in other words, what artists *do* with history in the making/remaking/performance/reperformance of the self; discursive analysis, where all modes of artistic production are rendered as text and can include written language, visual language, or the body in performance; and an expansion and refashioning of the parameters of what is queer and black through examinations of the identity politics and practices.[2] However frustrated by the dangers of essentialism inherent to them, these modes of theorizing black queer aesthetics can also prove a useful and fertile ground for uncovering how artists intentionally perform and transform the meanings of identities for social critique and social change. The artists — and the art spaces — I discuss here are not directly engaged in questions of identity politics in their work. Rather, they take identity as a given background to their questions of how memory functions in consideration of what it means to be human.

I have also chosen to read these two events and some of the presented works within a larger framework of what I call Vodoun aesthetics. Within Vodoun, resurrections are the conceptual mapping of time and space onto material bodies for the reperformance of history, in the present, as the present. In Vodoun ritual, the lwas (the term given to the life force when represented anthropomorphically) are the forces that permit the transmutation of time through the vehicle of blood and flesh for changing space, history, and memory. Maya Deren writes, "In Vodoun, neither man nor matter is divine. A lwa is an intelligence, a relationship of man to matter."[3] History is the present-future-past, and its enactment in the material realm reinscribes space with new possibilities and meanings. Art grounded in Vodoun aesthetics participates and works in the construction of history by employing the practices of embodiment and rupture, where embodiment results from repeated gestures, acts, and interactions that reinscribe intangible beings into physical bodies and multiple layers of meaning into confined space, and rupture is the primary methodology of ontological reorientation in both time and space. Rupture and embodiment can be conceptualized in what Rachel Beauvoir-Dominique has identified as the "deconstruction of emotion, rhythm, space and time."[4] By anchoring memory and imagination in the material (the body, found objects, etc.), the artist renders history and its detritus — the waste ("refusé," as LeGrace Benson calls it) generated by what is no longer meaningful or necessary.[5] This anchoring in the materiality of art is a process of inscribing memory through form. It is also a process that ruptures the temporality of ritual: the sacred time that expands and contracts through song, dance, prayer, and evocations is marked by material forms that live beyond what the body and the breath contain.

The focus of this meditation centers the discussion that follows within a framework in which the alteration of time and space are necessary givens. It is not possible to discuss *DASH* and the Ghetto Biennale as black queer texts/spaces/performances/projects without understanding that time and space are already different within the construction of these events. This is especially significant because of what takes place in the minds and bodies of the participating artists as articulated by them directly or exemplified by the art they create. All of the works

I discuss here are made by artists, by what James Baldwin has defined as those whose "role . . . is to illuminate that darkness, blaze roads through that vast forest; so that we will not, in all our doing, lose sight of its purpose, which is, after all, to make the world a more human dwelling place."[6] These artists use a range of materials to transform space and, in particular, to transform the possibilities for black queer bodies within space. They do so, as many of them will tell you, because they must. They do so because art is an act of creation and a vehicle for resurrecting memory, future potentialities, refusé, and the human self.

Under the overarching framework of Vodoun aesthetics, I am also discussing the intersections between refusé and *afro-futurism*—a term originally coined by Mark Dery and expanded on by many, but greatly by Alondra Nelson.[7] Both frameworks come together in this meditation through the practice of collapsing metaphorical and material time in bodies and specified spaces. This collapse of time, if considered under the rubric of Vodoun aesthetics (which, I should clarify, is my choice to engage, rather than the underlying assumption of any of the works presented in either *DASH* or the Ghetto Biennale), generates the possibility of a common language between artistic practices across the (queer) (black) diaspora. Though common language may not be of interest or serve the purposes of any artist, I believe there is merit to generating recognition in the face of invisibility.

I begin with how queer black artists attempt to grapple with the invisibility generated by the lack of clearly marked spaces that reflect their embodied erotic or social experiences; spaces that visibly and tangibly welcome, respect, or celebrate divergent and nonnormative erotic orientations; or bodies that move outside class- and racially bound heteronormative expectations. This invisibility and silencing that marks the majority of experiences for black queer artists is also the impetus for the creation and re-creation of the self and of worlds that will sustain the self. This invisibility, as much as it denies what exists, also creates the space for the unexplained: perpetual possibilities in which the gaze, the desire, the subject can be revealed as queer, or even as black.[8] Black queer artists reconfigure the relationship between history and the self, between the self and the future. The future also serves as a tool for defining the present; envisioning queer futures allows for "alternative worlds" or, as Judith Halberstam has theorized, an ever-expansive rendering of "the time at hand."[9] Considering invisibility and temporality as simultaneous conceptual structures, it is possible to say that black queer aesthetics is informed by the creation of time out of nothing as much as the creation of memory out of the unexplained.[10] Without robbing Vodoun rituals or artistic processes of their power, this meditation aims to facilitate an expansive engagement with questions of aesthetics in discussing witnessed performances of blackness, queerness, and art.

DASH

Torkwase Dyson, the curator of *DASH: Metaphor and Connection* dedicates her own work to "preemptive art" — art that answers questions we have yet to imagine. She intentionally pushes her own creative process to procure sounds, smells, tastes, textures that, as of yet, have not even existed, and, in so doing, inherently engages with the question of what existence *is*. Her interest in curating *DASH* arises from a desire to explore what can exist through the vehicle of collaboration between artists and writers. What, she asks, can come into existence that has never before existed? What are the material manifestations of conversations, new systems of information, and interdisciplinary cultural production? Dyson's chosen sites include conferences and other impermanent and transient spaces that provide an intellectual and shifting frame for producing new work. This shifting ground reveals the fissures inherent to artistic processes that are often concealed by the bound spaces of galleries. In *DASH* there is not one landing place but interstitial scapes that artists must grapple with through their material, intellectual, and affective selves. These transient spaces are counterpoints to the usual "locations" of artistic collaboration: galleries, performance spaces, biennials, exhibits, shows. In *DASH* there is no solid ground other than the one created by the artists themselves for the moment of time in which they are working.

The primary organizing principle for *DASH* was an orchestrated collaboration between pairs of artists: one writer and one visual artist or filmmaker. For the 2009 rendition of *DASH* — which took place during the conference "Fire & Ink" in Austin, Texas — Dyson chose three pairings: Ronaldo V. Wilson (writer) and Carl Pope (visual artist), Nalo Hopkinson (writer) and M. Asli Dukan (filmmaker), and Tisa Bryant (writer) and Wura-Natasha Ogunji (visual artist).[11] Each pair was asked to develop a new piece of work that engaged the aesthetics and primary artistic inquiries of each artist in the pair. In one evening, we were privy to a flying Ife head, black vampires, the tearing back of black flesh to expose the pink tendons of an arm, and a body made malleable and vulnerable through the purposeful generation of sweat, dirt, and tears.[12] What was surprising to me as an audience member was that artists whose approaches, forms, and questions are so different generated conceptual overlaps. These included temporal dislocations, reembodied blackness (black bodies flying, reappearing/disappearing, melting into words, sweating, crying, becoming), yearnings for memory and language with which to illuminate notions of human experience as of yet unexposed, and a bending or breaking of the rules of this world to expose what could be possible. The implications of this overlap, of course, are contradictory—as well they should be. All of the bodies presented in the works of art transcended their material limitations as a way to reconfigure the material limits of space and render it impotent, and to resurrect the self through notions of spirits, other beings, and deterioration.

Though Vodoun was not explicitly present in the works of the *DASH* artists, analyzing the bodies of works through a framework of Vodoun aesthetics allows for the rendering of common language and conceptual landing points. For example, in Ogunji's work, when the Ife head—a birdlike creature embodied by Ogunji—flew through the air, a ripple of laughter passed through the audience. Ife's flight mimicked the descent of the Yoruba gods into the material world, and in a moment of recognition, the audience also took flight, imagining ourselves descending into being, becoming what was not existent just before, our laughter a soundtrack marking the creation of time in artistic space: like drums marking time in ritual. As Tisa Bryant responded, "She enters the world on cue, in her favorite clothes, undeniably in her body, watched by everyone, by no one but God, only seen through her own eye. She projects herself onto the world, in her mind, that cinema that must include her."[13]

In their dyad, Dukan's black vampires were also put in conversation with Hopkinson's duppies, wolfies, and other "skin folk"—"people who aren't what they seem. Skin gives these folk their human shape. Peel it off, and their true selves emerge.... And whatever burdens their skins had borne, once they remove them, they can fly."[14] The audience members murmured, moaned, and clicked their tongues, again in recognition of all those who "done seen dat," or "be dat" themselves. Dukan's engagement with black vampires was not just an allusion to and eliciting of racialized and racist renderings of black female sexuality in cinema, of the "bloodsuckers" who steal people in the night. Her reading, next to Hopkinson's skin folk, was also a marking of the alternative ways in which sexually deviant racialized bodies alter the terrains of heteronormative narrative structures. Together with Hopkinson, Dukan was making the tensions between sex and violence visible, specifically as they manifest on sexually deviant (black) bodies. To imagine ourselves as skin folk, to consider the dangers of our individual and collective desires, is to recognize the potential of our desires to unmask the violence historically and materially enacted on our bodies. To imagine the possibility of our flight is to create the possibility of alternative material realities in the now and the future.

In the dyad between Pope and Wilson, there was the ritualistic centering of a black gay man as he confronted his own physical limits in front of another black gay man's unyielding gaze. How often is there public witness to this vulnerability between black (gay) men? Wilson stretched and bent, turned and folded in front of Pope's camera. They were in the grungy darkness of a garage. We, the audience, watched Wilson's body break down into sweat, into filth, until he could do nothing more than melt onto the garage floor, crying. He exhausted himself in the ritual of becoming, offered his body as a path — a moving, shifting vèvè (ritual markings made on the ground that serve as paths for the descent of the lwas into ritual space) so that we could learn the weight of our (collective) breath. This ageless ritual, reminiscent of Damballah's dance around the *poto mitan*, was, in this case, enacted in front of Pope's camera. This dance, transformed and transposed, remade the world.

My choice, then, to consider the works generated and presented for *DASH* alongside the works generated for and as a result of the Ghetto Biennale, comes out of a desire to expand the fields in which we discuss black queer aesthetics to explicitly delineate their transnational context. To do so, I use the metaphor of the *poto mitan* — the ceremonial center pole — to locate how my body connects two spaces that, put into conversation with each other, reveal new insights into black queer aesthetics. The fact of my witness to these two artistic engagements means that I can make visible and mark — in the languages of history, memory, and inquiry — the desires, the gazes, the subjects, and the possibilities of black queer existence. My own crossing of space through time puts the shifting grounds of "Fire & Ink" in relationship to the shifting grounds of the Ghetto Biennale.

Ghetto Biennale

André Eugène, Jean Hérard Celeur, Myronn Beasley, and Leah Gordon, artistic and scholarly collaborators, framed the Ghetto Biennale around the question: "What happens when first world art rubs up against third world art? Does it bleed?" They intentionally created a "contact zone": a "social space where disparate cultures meet, clash and grapple with each other, often in highly asymmetrical conditions of domination and subordination," with the self-conscious mission of uprooting and examining traditional relationships of power through artistic practice and production.[15] The Ghetto Bienniale, the organizers argued, was about reclaiming the biennial model for artists traditionally marginalized by globalized market forces. Bringing together twenty-one international artists with thirty-nine Grand Rue artists (including four master artists) in December 2009 in Port-au-Prince, Haiti, the Ghetto Biennale led to the creation and exposition of numerous major works based in and engaged with the material and social context of the Grand Rue—one of Port-au-Prince's poorest areas, characterized by the massive influx of people occupying public buildings, what Barbara Prézeau-Stephenson has termed a "'theater of the atrocious' . . . a matrix, a home, a workshop and a bearing."[16] The emergent relationships and artistic productions of the Ghetto Biennale generated new "translocal circuits of exchange that subvert[ed] the nation-state through connective flows that translate across cultural differences."[17] These artistic, cultural, and economic exchanges included materials, gestures, sounds, languages, and desires.

On December 16, 2009, I made my way from the Hotel Oloffson down to the Grand Rue; I was accompanied by several of the international artists who were staying at the Oloffson for the ten days of the Biennale. The first thing I saw as I stepped out of the car was an enormous statue, which Richard Arthur Fleming best describes as "a twenty-foot figure of rusted, welded iron, part abandoned bedspring, part truck chassis, sprouting an immense vibrating phallus made from a length of log fixed into the coil of a big rig's shock absorber."[18] I immediately recognized this sculpture as Papa Legba by the telltale hat on his head, the large "cane" that he held, and his placement at the entrance to the Grand Rue exhibition area.[19] Right in front of him was a structure resembling a Haitian country house, only instead of the usual palm wood sideboards and tin roof, it was made completely out of discarded water bags that held potable water, soda bottles, and other trash that is habitually strewn across the city. The front of the church was decorated with a mask made out of an old bleach container, painted over and decorated.

The Ghetto Biennale was launched with rara music and dancing, the animation of bodies in the public space of the open-air galleries: crumbling walls of old, abandoned buildings that had been transformed into exhibit space. Soon after I crossed the threshold, I was lost in the intense maze of metal, rubber, and refuse that was piled across the space, my eyes confused by what Kobena Mercer has described as "African Diasporic Baroque—the classical falling away of simplicity, the artificiality of stylistic excess, and the covering of loss of control through the rendering of spectacular surfaces."[20] Among the assemblage of cybernetic limbs, iron phalluses, tin jaws, and oil drum hauntings were the works of other artists: a tattoo parlor, photographs in the style of Malik Sidibe, paintings, Vodoun flags, murals, and sculptures of other materials.

Of the Ghetto Biennale artists who worked within the bustle generated by Eugène, Celeur, Loko, and Dodi, there are two works I focus on: the bodysuit by Jacquenette Arnette, an African American visual artist, and the flags made by

Ebony Patterson, a Jamaican visual artist. I am choosing to focus on the work of these two artists because of how the content engages not only the material context of the Grand Rue but also the larger question of black queer aesthetics to which this essay speaks.

Arnette's piece most closely approximated the tearing of flesh. That bleeding that the Ghetto Biennale organizers referenced became visible not just in metaphorical terms but also within the materiality of the piece itself. For the Ghetto Biennale, Arnette constructed a full-length bodysuit (approximately six feet), its shell made out of plastic shopping bags from stores in Miami (where she lived). She had worn the bodysuit on the airplane from Miami to Port-au-Prince, and when she arrived, she cut it off, immediately exposing the body's interior and vulnerability. She proceeded to stuff the bodysuit's shell with plastic garbage she found on the street on or near the Grand Rue. She then knit a host of organs for the bodysuit out of yarn she had brought with her. Days before the Ghetto Biennale opening, she was in the lobby of the Hotel Oloffson, knitting a uterus. When I asked her why a uterus, she said, "Because I want to create a balance to all the male energy at the Grand Rue."[21] When she was done with the uterus (complete with vagina and clitoris), she chose to hang the bodysuit in the air, off the side of a building behind the big Legba sculpture.

The bodysuit was as eerie as a vampire: it was a large, hanging female body devoid of head, hands, and limbs, suspended by ropes and on which the organs sat, exposed, red, and raw. Within two hours of hanging the suit, the knitted clitoris inverted itself, undoing a clear reading of sex onto the attenuated body on top of which it rested and firmly placing the piece within a Vodoun lexicon. Many Vodoun lwas are said to be of both sexes, but specifically Legba is said to carry the sexual organs of males and females. Therefore it was quite apropos that the bodysuit, hanging behind Legba, would transform itself in this way and thus render a marked, singular sex untenable. The bodysuit marked the location in which expected notions of sexual normativity were ruptured by the instability of materiality that transformed the moving, hanging body into a new kind of being.

In contrast to the bustle behind Papa Legba, turning the corner through a narrow alleyway, I encountered a small square room that had been converted into an altar by Ebony Patterson. On the walls were five delicate silk scarves on which had been printed images of well-known Jamaican gangstas. Each gangsta was dressed and transformed into a female lwa (and child lwa). There was Madame Brigitte, the two Erzulies (Freda and Dantò), Ayida Wedo, and the Marassa. Each gangsta-turned-lwa was decorated with sequins, boas, and bling: flashy silver and gold jewelry that stood out against the flowery background on which their images had been printed. Along the ground, piles of flowers, toys, candies, and candles were set out in their honor. These pieces riff on Kehinde Wiley's heroic portraits of contemporary black men set in the postures of European saints but redirect our gaze to a specifically Caribbean pantheon of gods and artistic ancestors. Patterson's pieces are based in and incorporate the tradition of Vodoun flags, sequined portrayals of the lwas.

When asked why she chose to make these pieces, Patterson responded that she was curious, as a Jamaican, about the fluidity of gender in Haitian Vodoun and wanted to understand how it might be possible to make men known for their extreme masculinity into more feminine beings. She also expressed her desire to make goddesses out of men who are more often portrayed as criminals, as a way to rehumanize them.[22] Patterson's assertion that the deviant black body must become divine to once again become human exposes the rigid cartographies that black queer beings encounter. Her pieces highlight the notion that we are not inherently human or divine but must become so through a self-creation fashioned through artistic processes. These artistic processes expose the relationships between bodies and matter, between time and materiality, and render the metaphorical bodies of the gods/other beings into material avenues for resurrecting the black queer human. For Patterson, the metaphorical bodies of gods transform the material bodies of criminalized men into human beings who are fully constituted by their specifically feminized masculinity and, thus, become whole.

The Future of the Present Past

In a context where the future is constantly in battle with the present, primarily because of precarious life circumstances, making life out of death is what one does. Yet the assemblage of materials utilized by the Grand Rue artists is a radical critique of what the future portends. The future, much as the present, and much as the past, is materially and metaphorically located in the remains of the dead. The forces of life above ground require a firm rooting in the grounds where the dead reside. Art in this context is a grappling with the refusé in all of its potential for giving life: affective, spiritual, and material.

In Vodoun, life and death are embodied in the Gédé—the *living* spirits of the dead, the mediators between death and the erotic generation of life. LeGrace Benson writes, "The Gédé are not an extinct family who left some garments for latterly others to wear at Halloween. They are the lively, antic spirits of death and sex, conductors of the passages into and out of this visible life. Gédé lives."[23] Like Wilson's dance into deterioration, like the Ife head's flight or like the vampires and skin folk from *DASH*, the Gédé act as "antic spirits" that dance between the realms of the dead, in the erotics of sex that reproduces life not by creating other life but by resurrecting the self into a visible erotic being capable of desire, pain, and flight. In Vodoun it is the embodiment of the gods by the living that queers gender and sexuality. In black queer aesthetics, the queer erotics of artistic practices make the gods visible so that the living may be reclaimed from the dead. Memories and bodies are ruptured by the Gédé, by artists—who transform infertile grounds into gardens and bring the invisible into sharp focus.

The aesthetics employed in the works of the Grand Rue artists are inscribed within a larger circulation of Vodoun and an aesthetic process that Donald Consentino terms *mélange*—where "taxonomies slip, roles reverse, ends become means" in a process of constant accumulation and transformation.[24] Beauvoir-Dominique describes the "magician artist [as] a centralizing figure, [who] directly regroups the latent violence of the community, diffusing charges amplified by the very fact of their immediate centralization."[25] To understand an artistic process grounded in Vodoun, one must understand that death is necessary for life, that it is the body of the living initiate who brings the dead into a careful dance that allows for the continuation and regeneration of life. Therefore, to comprehend an artist's assertion that his or her art has "made this man live again" is to acknowledge that the artist acts as a vessel between the worlds of ancestors and the forces of life and death, between the invisible world of the lwas and the material reality around them. And it is to understand that resurrection is an acknowledgment of the cyclical nature of time and that material reality is transformed by ruptures in the bounded yet porous systems of time and space.

Benson writes, "Nothing is ever totally discarded in Haiti. . . . Whatever defies disintegration becomes another state of being."[26] What is also embedded in these sculptures, besides the human skulls, is the detritus of industrial production: scrap metal from cars, discarded glass jars and cans found floating in the trash amassing itself around the ghetto, old hats and shoes jettisoned from someone's closet in the global North onto the (seemingly absorptive) shores of the global South. Gordon writes of the Grand Rue artists, "Their muscular sculptural collages of engine manifolds, computer entrails, TV sets, medical debris, skulls and discarded lumber transforms the detritus of a failing economy into deranged, post-apocalyptic totems."[27] But here, in the Ghetto Biennale and *DASH*, there is no apocalypse, no final end point in time.

The art from the Ghetto Biennale addresses time through the accumulation of objects; *DASH* artists collapse time inside their bodies. Through accumulation or collapse, the ever-present now is the future is the past is the present, is all at once. At the heart of all creation is the creation/re-creation of the self through creation itself. The Ghetto Biennale makes a point of giving meaning to the space of the Grand Rue through a logic of refusé, of remaking what has been deemed dispensable (waste, black lives and bodies) into objects imbued with meaning, power, history, and life force. In a similar way, the *DASH* artists give meaning to bodies as vehicles for the artistic process, as grounding mechanisms for articulating unforeseen possibilities. The Gédé dance between life and death, between what was not and what will be. The black queer aesthetics present in both spaces are multidirectional, moving inside the fissures of space and time, remaking cartographies in the images of what has always been, rendering visible what is invisible. In zones of discomfort, dystopia, detritus, black queer bodies and their imaginary potentials are recuperated and restored, made visible through the cracks. Within this, an articulated black queer aesthetics ruptures expectations of all that has been, is, and will be. The world takes a new form, again.

Notes

1. Zanele Muholi, *Mapping Our Histories: A Visual History of Black Lesbians in Post-Apartheid South Africa*, zanelemuholi.com/ZM%20moh_final_230609.pdf (accessed August 19, 2010).
2. On what artists do with history, see Matt Richardson, "Critical Reconstructions of History: Black Lesbian Literature and Film" (PhD diss., University of California, Berkeley, 2005); Jennifer DeVere Brody, "Theory in Motion: A Review of the Black Queer Studies in the Millennium Conference," *Callaloo* 23, no. 4 (2000): 1–12; and Brody, "The Returns of Cleopatra Jones," in *Queer Studies: An Interdisciplinary Reader*, ed. Robert J. Corber and Stephen Valocchi (Oxford: Blackwell, 2003), 88–101. On discursive analysis, see Joseph Roach, *Cities of the Dead: Circum-Atlantic Performance* (New York: Columbia University Press, 1996); and Diana Taylor, *The Archive and the Repertoire: Performing Cultural Memory in the Americas* (Durham, NC: Duke University Press, 2003). On reformulating identity politics, see E. Patrick Johnson and Mae G. Henderson, *Black Queer Studies: A Critical Anthology* (Durham, NC: Duke University Press, 2005).
3. Maya Deren, *Divine Horsemen: The Living Gods of Haiti* (New York: Documentext, 1953), 91.
4. Rachel Beauvoir-Dominique, "Underground Realms of Being: Vodoun Magic," in *Sacred Arts of Haitian Vodou*, ed. Donald Consentino (Los Angeles: UCLA Fowler Museum of Cultural History, 1995), 167.
5. LeGrace Benson, "Gédé on Grand Rue: Some Lines of Enquiry to Follow," *Journal of Haitian Studies* 10, no. 2 (2004): 2.

6. James Baldwin, *Collected Essays* (New York: Library of America, 1998), 669.
7. Alondra Nelson, "Introduction to Future Texts," *Social Text* 20, no. 2 (2002): 1–15.
8. Tisa Bryant, *Unexplained Presence* (Providence, RI: LeonWorks, 2007). Bryant theorizes the presence of black (and often queer) bodies as indexes of ruptures in colonial and postcolonial logics. Here I use her notion of the unexplained as the rupturing potentialities of black queerness within spaces of invisibility.
9. Scott Bravmann, *Queer Histories of the Past: History, Culture, and Difference* (Cambridge: Cambridge University Press, 1997), 129; Judith Halberstam, *In a Queer Time and Place: Transgender Bodies, Subcultural Lives* (New York: New York University Press, 2005), 2.
10. "As an international aesthetic movement concerned with the relations of science, technology, and race, Afrofuturism appropriates the narrative techniques of science fiction to put a black face on the future." See afrofuturism.net/ (accessed August 17, 2010).
11. "Fire & Ink 3: Cotillion" was a national conference for gay, lesbian, bisexual, and transgender writers of African descent and heritage. It took place in Austin, Texas, in October 2009.
12. A flying Ife head is a spirit who inhabits the body of the artist Wura-Natasha Ogunji and, in doing so, accomplishes impossible feats. To see images of flying Ife heads, visit wuravideos.blogspot.com/. On black vampires, see M. Asli Dukan, *Black Vamps*, www.youtube.com/watch?v=T9IUG_8rONU.
13. Excerpt from Tisa Bryant's work *The Curator*, presented at *DASH*—"Fire & Ink," Austin, Texas, October 9, 2009.
14. Nalo Hopkinson, nalohopkinson.com/writing/fiction/books/skin_folk (accessed August 16, 2010).
15. Mary Louise Pratt, *Imperial Eyes: Travel Writing and Transculturation* (London: Routledge, 1992), 4.
16. Barbara Prézeau-Stephenson, "Contemporary Art as Cultural Product in the Context of Haiti," *Small Axe* 27 (October 2008): 101.
17. Kobena Mercer, "Intermezzo Worlds," in *Art Journal* 57, no. 4 (1998): 44.
18. Richard Arthur Fleming, "Grotesquerie of Gargantuan Gargoyles, Part One," antarcticiana.blogspot.com/search/label/Grand%20Rue (accessed May 23, 2010).
19. Whether as cord or phallus, Legba—life—is the link between the visible, mortal world and the invisible, immortal realms. He is the means and the avenue of communication between them, the vertical axis of the universe that stretches between the sun door and the tree root (Deren, *Divine Horsemen*, 97): "Legba, then, is guardian of the sacred gateway, of the *Grand Chemin*, the great road leading from the mortal to the divine world." I include both of these descriptions as footnotes because I think it is significant that Legba is the guardian of the Grand Rue. In a sense, the Grand Rue artists are placing themselves on the *Grand Chemin* between life and death through literal means and spiritual metaphors, and Legba, who towers above all the buildings and artworks in the space, guides their path.

20. Kobena Mercer, "Allegories and Emblems: Hew Locke's Post-Colonial Baroque" (speech at Yale University History of Art Department, New Haven, CT, January 19, 2010).
21. Jacquenette Arnette, interview by author, December 16, 2009.
22. Artist panel, Ghetto Biennale, Port-au-Prince, Haiti, December 18, 2009.
23. Benson, "Gédé," 1.
24. David Consentino, "Introduction: Imagine Heaven," in *Sacred Arts of Haitian Vodou*, ed. Donald Consentino (Los Angeles: UCLA Fowler Museum of Cultural History, 1995), 39.
25. Beauvoir-Dominique, "Underground Realms of Being," 175.
26. Benson, "Gédé," 1.
27. Leah Gordon, "What happens when first world art rubs up against third world art? Does it bleed?" Gens de la Caraïbe Call for Proposals, April 22, 2009, www.gensdelacaraibe.org/index.php?option=com_content&view=article&id=3752:what-happens-when-first-world-art-rubs-up-against-third-world-art-does-it-bleed&catid=112&Itemid=200102.

"MY FATHER DIDN'T HAVE A DICK"

Social Death and Jackie Kay's *Trumpet*

Matt Richardson

My father didn't have a dick. . . . My father had a pussy.
—Jackie Kay, *Trumpet*

The epigraph is from Jackie Kay's 1998 black Scottish trans novel *Trumpet*. In this moment in the novel, Colman Moody, the son of the novel's protagonist, Joss Moody, has just found out that the man he knew as his father was anatomically female. This disclosure occurs after his father has died, thereby complicating the son's feelings of loss and also putting his own sense of manhood into crisis. Colman's revelation that "my father didn't have a dick. . . . My father had a pussy" is more than a recitation of body parts: it is a terrified recognition of the uncertainty of gender categories and the fragility of black manhood in particular.[1]

Perhaps the best way to unpack the implications of Colman's crisis of manhood is to begin with an earlier instantiation of gender crisis that took place from the moment that black bodies were ripped away from the African continent. In the now foundational essay "Mama's Baby, Papa's Maybe: An American Grammar Book," Hortense Spillers asserts that black captives were stripped of the genders that they were used to, then regendered at the other end of the Middle Passage—disallowed from continuing with the gender systems from the places they were from and prohibited from participating in the gender systems simultaneously demanded from them.[2] I contend that the undoing and reworking of black gender categories is a key facet of social death.[3] Orlando Patterson defines social death as the condition in which slaves are forced into the position of natal alienation, dishonor, and disrespect from which they cannot recover. Extending from

Patterson's definition, I consider how social death reaches beyond the formal end of slavery and colonialism. As Sharon Holland contends, "Some subjects never achieve, in the eyes of others, the status of the 'living.'"[4] For these purposes, "living" is having available to oneself a full range of subjectivity and citizenship. The gendered aspect of social death gives us a perspective from which to explore its queer implications. Recognizing the continued impact of slavery, Spillers challenges us to make a decision not to futilely follow "the master's" definitions of gender down the (hetero)patriarchal rabbit hole of normativity but to gain "*insurgent* ground" by taking a stand outside the "traditional symbolics" of gender.[5] Of specific interest here is what it would mean for black men to embrace the feminine within themselves.[6]

In this essay, I follow Colman's burgeoning awareness of his own queerness: the fact that gender fragility and uncertainty are a part of what makes black bodies already dead to the Scottish nation. It is this truth that Colman finds unbearable and the condition with which he ultimately has to come to terms. As a queer, Joss is the one to make this aspect of social death salient. His literal death and the subsequent revelation of his queer gender identity bring everyone's gender anxieties into relief alongside their longing for normative gender categories. Colman is unaware of his figurative death until his father physically dies. I am especially interested in how Colman comes to see himself as socially dead as well—a black man who is ultimately in a feminized position in relationship to legitimate patriarchal white masculinity. Here I agree with Darieck Scott's argument in *Extravagant Abjection* that blackness is a hybrid position, at once "hypermasculine and feminine."[7] I would like to depart from his assertions that black male abjection does not have to belong solely to the feminine register in order to examine where male abjection and femininity meet. What if we imagined that the sociologist Robert Park was at least partly right, in that in some fundamental ways the black is structurally the "lady of the races"?[8] The structural meeting of black manhood and femininity does not have to be an occasion for distress. It could be an opportunity to reimagine and improvise other registers for black manhood—perhaps even through the maternal. Misogyny assumes that the feminine is the end of possibility. How can we transform positionality into potential? Perhaps black queerness provides the site from which this burden of decision can be most clearly rendered, given its positionality outside the nation and even outside blackness.

Kay's novel follows this set of circumstances and their consequences after Joss has been exposed and trashed in the press. The story was inspired by the life and death of an actual female-to-male transgendered person by the name of Billy

Tipton, who was a white jazz musician in the United States. When Tipton died in 1989, his body was designated female and his story was told in a book titled *Suits Me* and sensationalized in the press.[9] In interviews Kay reported that the publicity over Tipton's death and subsequent "discovery" of his female birth inspired her to write *Trumpet*.[10] Kay brilliantly adopts some of the context of the Tipton scandal to elucidate the collective implications of gender and racial amnesia rarely discussed in a Scottish context until recently.[11]

While still alive, the main character, Joss Moody, was a jazz trumpeter. "Britain's legendary trumpet player" (6), he falls out of favor with the British public and returns to being an outsider along with other black Scottish people as a result of his gender variance being exposed at the moment of his literal death. The novel reminds us how black Scottish people are cast from the boundaries of nation, invisible in the past and ambivalently part of the present. As Alan Rice has argued, Joss has a problem of "finding his identity in a Scotland that has no place for an African presence."[12] Upon his physical death, all of the familiar categories, such as family, man, woman, marriage, heterosexual, lesbian, and ordinary, are unable to exist in complacent banality for his white wife, Millie, and his son, Colman. The intruding power of the state and media interrupt their private mourning with an entirely new vocabulary of (mis)naming that challenges each of their relationships to normative genders and the heterosexual family. Not only do Millie and Colman lose control over how Joss's body is identified, but the turmoil they undergo exposes the normative as an untenable option, especially for racialized subjects. The revelation that his father was not born with a penis forces Colman into his own painful and terrified recognition of the fragility and social femininity of black manhood.

Kay is an internationally acclaimed poet, playwright, and fiction writer. Before *Trumpet*, she was well-known for her books of poetry, especially *The Adoption Papers* (1980).[13] Kay was born in Edinburgh and grew up in Glasgow, Scotland, the adopted daughter of a "Scottish mother and a Nigerian father."[14] Her poetry, prose, and plays have touched on the experience of children of African descent who are adopted into white families and the "adoption" of black people into predominantly white Britain. Many of Kay's characters in her fiction and poetry are autobiographical in the sense that, as with her own childhood in Scotland, her characters live where they have to find connections with blackness outside their immediate surroundings. They live in towns where there may be only a few other black people; where black people are not visibly a part of the history or recognized as part of the culture; where blackness is understood as being from somewhere else. Kay's books of poetry have been concerned with how black people in the United Kingdom come into political and personal consciousness of their multifaceted identities in nations that reject their claims to the nation by regarding them as permanent outsiders and "newcomers."[15] Christopher Whyte observes that black lesbian Scottish writers such as Kay and Maud Sulter experience the "inescapable fact of being 'other' as Black in Scotland."[16] Despite their rejection from the nation, Kay's black characters have a strong, if complicated, sense of Scottish or English identity. Primarily, Kay's work suggests that people of African descent in the United Kingdom find a precarious (im)balance between their relationship to blackness and black identity and their Scottish or English or Welsh identities. Ultimately, Kay's work suggests that to be black and Scottish is to be absent from national historical imaginary.

Much of Kay's body of work has been dedicated to examining the position of blacks as "dead" to the national imagination of Scotland.[17] The figurative death of black Scottish subjects is very much tied to the literal death of millions of Africans during the transatlantic slave trade. Although the concept of social death is about the condition of the slave, death helps inform the contours of the structural position of blackness well after the formal end of slavery.[18] One place where this is evidenced is in the continued interruption of black ancestral genealogy, which forces blacks to create their own histories through memory and creativity. Holland comments on this by pointing out that in an antiblack imaginary, there is "an unaccomplished imaginative shift from enslaved to freed subjectivity."[19] In *Trumpet*, while Joss was still physically alive, he did what he could to militate against acknowledgment of his own positioning within Scotland—the figurative death that befalls other black Scottish people. Without his celebrity, Joss too would have been denied national belonging and relegated to a place of limbo. From this viewpoint, Joss did not die suddenly; from the perspective of the nation, he was never a "living" subject to begin with.

The novel gives us an example of how the slave and the freed subject are dangerously close to each other in the figure of John Moore, Joss's father. Moore stands in for the disremembered black Scots whose history is rendered "dead" in the national imaginary. In a letter to Colman, Joss explains how Moore came to Scotland from an unremembered African country as a six-year-old child through a less-recognized middle passage—between Africa and the United Kingdom—at the beginning of the twentieth century. What Moore finds is that his life and the lives of slaves less than a century earlier are eerily similar. Surrounded by "shadow people," his life was "something that happened to him. Other people pulled the strings and he moved his limbs" (271). His life before arriving in Scotland is lost (including the name he was born with), "drowned at sea in the dead of dark, dark night" and enshrouded with a mournful wailing beyond conscious reach (273). Moore's brief story, including his tale of learning to read, is reminiscent of slave narratives. Although brought to Scotland for an education, Moore spends his days polishing the white master of the house's boots, "till he could see his own dark face" (275). Using the ingenuity that many blacks had to muster in similar circumstances, he polishes the boots in the library and consequently manages to teach himself to read.

Although he spends many years in Scotland, Moore is not considered among the "living," meaning liberal citizen-subjects, but in fact remains illegible to the people around him. Moore's story ends abruptly with a painting. The last remaining vestiges of Moore exist in Joss's memory of a painted portrait of him by a local Scottish artist titled *Mumbo Jumbo* (276). The title makes Joss "more angry than anything [he] can remember" (276). It is an indicator of the fact that despite all the years in Scotland, marrying a white Scottish woman, being steadily employed as a house painter, and having a child born there, Moore is still rendered an unknowable absence. Joss's retelling of his father's story comes at the end of his life, when he is about to physically die and wants to pass on more information to Colman before it is too late. Having Moore's story arrive at the end of Joss's life suggests that part of his preparation for death is his recognition that he (and his father) were "dead" all along. Joss had put away the pain and anger of the *Mumbo Jumbo* painting because it would be a reminder that his celebrity is temporary, and obscures a structural relationship of absence that he does not want to face. Death makes him able to face this condition of social death and willing to share it with his son, Colman, whom he has sought to shield all of his life.

The public revelation of Joss's queerly gendered body immediately turns him from a beloved icon into a figure of revulsion and derision. He easily slips from being claimed by Great Britain as its own "legend" to "the Transvestite Trumpet Player" without a home in public discourse (125). Joss's fall from grace demonstrates the provisional nature of his acceptance into the world of the "living" and that social death had never gone away. For the colonized, life is meted out by the colonizer according to his or her discretion.[20] In *Trumpet*, a reporter, Sophie Stones, represents the voice of the dominant society that relegated Joss back into the world of the "dead." She is an opportunist who attempts to seduce Colman to get at Joss's story, exploiting Colman's grief and anger at his father for keeping his past a secret. Her role in the novel as the villain is made poignant by the fact that she delivers a sobering look at Joss's position as a tool to be manipulated according to the nation's needs. She says,

> The word transvestite has got more in it than the word cross-dresser. What is a cross-dresser anyway when he or *she* is at home? . . . Transvestite has a nice pervy ring to it. When we have finished the book, Joss Moody's records will be selling better than they ever did. We're doing *her* a favour. We're making *her* immortal. (126; italics mine)

If "Britain's legendary trumpeter" can be both black and Scottish, male and female, heterosexual and transsexual, then societal categories would begin to unravel. In *Freaks Talk Back*, Joshua Gamson argues that when disruptions confuse the strict binary order of sexual and gendered identity arrangements, it is the role of the mass media to "stitch things back together, to hide the seams and make sure the either-or categories are still intact."[21] Stones's insistence on using female pronouns and terms for Joss that she considers more "pervy" or perverse is part of the way she degrades his life and memory. Cultural memory is easily manipulated to maintain categories of normalization. Stones is, in Foucauldian terms, part of the regulatory matrix of society that keeps categories from slipping into ambiguity. When the nation cannot fold individuals into its plot, it must displace them to recover its rigidity. The nation needs exemplary blacks to maintain its facade of multiculturalism. As the token black Scottish person, Joss — putatively "living" — is the example of the nation's tolerance of difference. When Joss ("the good black") turns "bad" — that is, rendered just another (socially) dead Negro subsequent to his actual death — the nation recovers itself, through the media, with claims of being duped. As a "pervy transvestite," Joss is unthreatening and made palatable to a public culture anxious about its own hybridity and ambiguity.[22] In addition, Scottish manhood is on the line and a premium is placed on not acknowledging gender and sexual uncertainty and unfixity. For example, Joss's friend and bandmate, Big Red McCall, admits to Stones that he "beat up anybody who said [that Joss had a baby face]" (148). To let the comment stand would open up Big Red's own ambiguous desires to public scrutiny.

For a nation that has difficulty admitting that there is a history of blacks in Scotland, Joss, postmortem, is the ultimate "unadmittable" figure because he is both black *and* gender nonconforming.[23] Public acknowledgment of Joss would release the open secret that gender and sex are not immutable; that patriarchal manhood in particular is vulnerable to "trespass" by female-bodied persons; and that gender transgression happens often *undetected* both by the state and by its subjects. Stones places her career on the line by pursuing the book because she counts on the public's revulsion toward and (perverse) attraction to those it considers "abnormal." She laments, "The public may hate perverts, but they love reading about them" (264). By sensationalizing difference, the dominant culture can deny that "every person goes about their life with a bit of perversion that is unadmittable, secretive, loathed" (264).

How Joss is described after his physical death suggests the extent to which he is no longer considered a special case and becomes again the outsider to Scottish culture that he occupied before his rise to fame: a black queer monstrosity that can be met only with derision and turned into spectacle. Thus Colman is given a gift in his father's death that Joss could not give him in life—the choice either to continue on, pretending not to be conscious of the limitations of normative masculinity and manhood, or to "make it up" (58), to re-create without fear of his own queerness. Once Joss actually dies, the pretense of the stability of the "normal" crumbles, revealing a crisis of black masculine identity for Colman. Colman feels inadequate in every way to his father: his talent, his clothes, his style. Moreover, Joss has managed to have the patriarchal dream of a wife, a son, and a successful career even without the infamous black male penis. However, Colman's revelation that "my father didn't have a dick. . . . My father had a pussy" (61) forces Colman to face the fact that black masculinity is socially feminized. The conversion of Joss from "man" to "woman" in the press reveals Colman's own fears that he has suddenly "lost" his patriarchal black father figure, leaving him vulnerable to never being able to be recognized as a "man" himself.

To shield himself from the creeping awareness of his own status as "dead," Colman takes refuge in his penis. No matter how much Colman appreciates the life that his father has given him, he still says, "No man wants a lesbian for a father. Maybe for his mother. But for his father!" (66). His father's absent penis leaves him with a need to reassure his own manhood and convince himself that his "cock is bigger and harder now that his father was dead" (140). With the desire to have a "hard" and "big" cock comes the desire to use his penis as a tool of domination and revenge. He fantasizes about having anal sex with Stones:

> He imagines lifting Sophie Stones onto the desk in the office he has not seen. He pulls down the zip of his jeans. He gets it out. He runs his finger up the crack of her arse. This is what she'll like . . . Fucks full of cruelty and sleaze. (140)

As a white woman, Stones is what Frantz Fanon called the black man's "revenge."[24] The white woman's body has often been a source of imagined redress in black male imaginary. She is the instrument of a lost humanity and manhood to which black women are not a vehicle because of their alleged "worthlessness."[25]

By "fucking" Stones, Colman wants to unleash his own rage at being "fucked" by her and everyone else (including his parents). Colman seeks revenge and the reassurance of his manhood through sex with Stones, as he seeks to evade figurative death—which is ironic given that white womanhood has historically been the excuse for the real death of black men. Colman's fantasy of penetrating and therefore dominating white femininity speaks to his attempt to save himself from what he considers the death of black feminine association by overidentifying with his sexual prowess.

Stones insists on constructing Joss as "freakish." When Colman will no longer cooperate with her schemes and withdraws his agreement to give her an exclusive, Stones writes in Colman's voice: "On the person who I thought was my father, breasts and the pubic hair looked disgusting. Freakish . . . His pubic hair and breasts looked grotesque, monstrous" (265). Stones's appropriation of Colman's anger and shock turns into an opportunity to produce Joss as "monstrous" and "disgusting." Stones's words are reminiscent of Colman's first memory—that of another black man being called an "ape" (54) on the public bus in Glasgow. Colman remembers not being able to stop looking at the black man who "was just sitting with his eyes low, looking at the bus floor" (54). Colman comes into consciousness of his race at the moment the adult black male is animalized by the whites on the bus, which provokes him to look at the color of his own skin. The black man on the bus is displayed by the racist passengers who have the power to force him to bow his head in shame. The scene is a reminder of black male (structural) castration. Joss too becomes an example of black monstrosity and a "nasty man" (54) to other people. When asked about his earliest memory of his father, Colman remembers the man on the bus in connection with his anger about discovering his father's female anatomy. He is afraid of what has already happened—that black genders are nonnormative and unstable. Colman is mourning not only his father but also black gender coherence. Colman's rage and pain over the loss of the black male phallus is not unique to his character but speaks directly to the ongoing condition of black men's melancholic desire for their fathers, not just their father's presence but for his (potential) gendered position in society.[26]

After remembering the man on the bus, Colman is haunted by the realization that to the white people who surround him, he is like all the other black men—a criminal. He recalls the *imago* of the black male "mugger," observing that "men who look exactly like Colman are always on the news," identified as "more likely to be muggers" to the racist eye of the police (224).[27] He recognizes himself as the epitome of criminality in the white mind and, as such, always at risk for some form of racial brutality often symbolized in the specter of the incarcerated black man.²⁸ In remembering his father, he remembers that he himself is "dead"—a mugger/nigger—and that his father's celebrity does not shield him from this reality. Black men have no history and no place in Scotland except in the nightmarish visages of the mugger/nigger, or the debased "ape." They are two sides of the same symbolic figure, representing the hypermasculine and feminine parts of black manhood.

In the novel, Joss and Colman prioritize the relationship with the father to the exclusion of the mother. In *Trumpet*, the father displaces the mother entirely and becomes the first primary love object, with whom the child experiences the feeling of wholeness and perfection. Since his position in a patriarchal culture is always vulnerable to disappearing, the "father" for black men is an elusive and illusory figure, even if he is physically present.²⁹ As David Marriott has stated, black fathers are "murdered, usurped and withheld, by a culture, and a nation" intent on representing black fathers as "inadequate," "weak," "brutal," and (irresponsibly) absent.³⁰ Black (male) death exists as a "reminder of how fragile his possession of himself, his 'manhood' can be."³¹ If the son rejects identification with the white "father," then he is left to a disappointing eternal search for the phallic black father who will lead him into the realm of self-determination and presence.

At the depths of black male melancholic mourning and longing for "daddy" and anxiety about legitimate paternity is a phobia of black female uncontrolled sexuality. (Black) femininity haunts (black) male psychic dramas. This nightmare of uncertain paternity and usurped masculinity has double meaning for Colman, who thought that he was gifted with the perfect black father only to be faced with the ultimate Oedipal nightmare of the father with female biology. For this reason, the primary bond in this text is with the father. In the Lacanian terms of development, this black father-son bond is the primary interaction at the crucial stage before language and before the recognition of difference. Though the pre-Oedipal is usually associated with the pure bliss of being one with the mother, the black male is connected to the father, and all subsequent relations are of the loss of that oneness, even as the yearning to experience pure father-love is never without the feminine. This primary father-son bond is demonstrated in the novel in the scenes where Colman remembers his childhood:

> *I goes in my father's bedroom. I am six years old. I opens their wardrobe. My daddy keeps his trumpet in here. I opens the big silver box, and there it is, all shiny inside. I touched it. I did touch it. Then I strokes it like I've seen my father do and it purrs. I runs my finger over the keys then along the fur, the purple fur in the box. My fingers are burning hot . . . Then my*

mum finded me . . . She says, Colman, what are you doing? Get out of your father's trumpet. (49)

The trumpet is an obvious phallic symbol; however, like a dildo, it is detached from Joss's body, able to be taken with him or left behind. Colman experiences reassurance in Joss's absence and pleasure in being close to his father's phallus. He "strokes" it, imagines that it purrs under his fingers. But Joss's instrument of black manhood is also hybrid. Like Gordon's description of the male penis as an "ambiguous organ," Joss's trumpet has a hole (at both ends).[32] Colman claims to Stones that he is "one hundred percent heterosexual" (57); however, masculinity can never be completely sealed off from the feminine, and its claims of purity are a "chosen falsehood, a form of denial."[33] In this way, Joss is like any other black man, ambiguously gendered and caught in tangles of denial of his own femininity in order to claim manhood.

The mother is an interruption of the bonding between black fathers and sons. Millie disturbs Colman's fondling of his father's phallus, which is tucked away inside a "fur" case lining, creating the image of pubic hair surrounding a vagina. Both the case, or "box," and the trumpet are soothing to young Colman, who enjoys touching them without anxiety or ambivalence. His fascination with his parents' genitalia begins early in life. Colman has urges as a child to see his father's penis. His friend Sammy compares his father's penis to his own only to be disappointed in his own lack. Colman is too afraid that he won't "measure up" to his father's manhood and therefore fights his temptation to peek into the bedroom (55). He satisfies his need for reassurance and curiosity with the trumpet as a stand-in. However, when adult Colman finds out about Joss's female past he is repulsed that he could have been confronted with Joss's "big frigging mound of venus" (55). The feminine is only tolerable in displaced subordinate association with masculinity. The fur lining is there to protect the trumpet, not to usurp its place as the primary object. Joss's "mound of Venus," however, strikes fear into the hearts of both Colman and the funeral director, stalking their manhood, threatening to render it obsolete. If black masculinity is not in the penis, then what is left for Colman?

Colman models his own black masculinity on Joss's. Colman lives his life in his father's shadow as his "father's disciple" (62), desiring his approval of him "as a man, as a black man" (49), and finally admitting, "I fucking worshipped him" (49). He studies his father's look, his way of walking and talking in the world, with awe and admiration. Colman also attempts to make up for what he lacks in masculine status by yearning for the story of his forefathers.

John Moore is resurrected at the end to finally give Colman the "father story" of origins that he craves.³⁴ At first Joss scolds him, saying that he lacks the imagination to "pick" from the richness of the African diaspora to make up his family's story (58–59). Joss finally clarifies the Moore/Moody patrilineage, relieving some the "cultural unconscious fantasies of black men" to "lay claim to particular accounts" of the diaspora.³⁵ Moore traveled across the Atlantic from Africa to Europe, bringing with him very little cultural knowledge, leaving his then daughter, Josephine (the name assigned to Joss at birth), in the predicament of loss, displacement, and alienation and a vague memory of music. Josephine uses the memory of music and the practice of jazz to construct a black male identity.

In the novel, jazz is a practice of creating and re-creating black manhood. Until his encounter with his father's corpse at the funeral parlor, Colman had been certain that his father had successfully negotiated black erasure to attain black manhood through jazz, and that Colman himself was the failure. In fact, jazz grows into its identity with Joss. Millie observes that it was the "early days for jazz and early days for [Joss], for his new life" (16). Joss creates himself and . . . Millie watches Joss "walk up the street, hands in his pockets. He has a slow deliberate walk, like he's practiced it" (15). Joss derives his manhood from copying other black male jazz artists. But Colman notes that the black men who are Joss's professional and political role models are (to Colman's frustration) from the United States.³⁶ He says, "All jazzmen are fantasies of themselves, reinventing the Counts and Dukes and Armstrongs, imitating them" (190). Black men become ideals of civic or cultural manhood through copying other (black) "icons and models" to mitigate their "demoniac or bestial typecasting."³⁷ The resistance to white imagination is also a disclosure that (black) manhood is not "natural" or an "original" but socially constructed and performative, [a copy of a copy] and therefore not restricted to the born-male individual.³⁸ In Joss's world black men reinvent themselves outside the *imago* of the "criminal" and the "mugger," but often maintaining an attachment to hypersexualized versions of masculinity. The jazz ensemble is also a site of black male re-creation through its homoerotic potential.

The performative nature of heterosexual black masculinity is occluded in the pressure to naturalize it in the face of black erasure and death. Black manhood is authenticated by the successful reproduction of aesthetic principles. Everyone who meets Joss is impressed with his smooth appearance. His black masculinity is studied, copied, and performed to perfection. Here seemingly immutable and stable gender identities become "special symbols" of racial subjectivity.³⁹ To question naturalized gender norms is to "place oneself outside of the racial kin group."⁴⁰ Joss experiences his African diaspora consciousness partly through mimicking the gender performativity of other black men, just as transatlantic racial connections often take place through the circulation, consumption, internalization, and recirculation of "particular definitions of gender and sexuality."[41]

As much as music is a location for authenticating black (masculine) gender, it is also a site of gender ambivalence and dislocation. Instead of using the transmasculine body as a metaphor of some other narrative, it is more productive to look at jazz as a metaphor (and a mechanism) for black gendered and sexual improvisation. Joss turns to jazz to create his black masculinity; he practices his trumpet as he practices his walk (and vice versa). The mastery over a jazz instrument gives him access to the closed world of the male jazz ensemble. As Joss's bandmate Big Red recalls, Joss is well loved by the other members of the "Moody's Men" jazz ensemble.[42] Big Red defends Joss against people who question his gender.

> One time he caught a guy saying, "there's something strange about that Moody" . . . He cornered the guy, poked him hard with his fat fingers. "Who, jab, are, jab, you, jab, calling, jab, strange?" (144)

Big Red is one of Joss's "disciples"; faced with various questions about Joss's "squeaky voice" and "baby face," Big Red "rushed to [Joss's] defence" (147). In the "ensemble's internal space," intimate devotion to ensemble members is permitted.[43] In Big Red's dream, Joss comes to him and challenges his idea that he did not know of Joss's birth sex until the funeral. Joss says to him, "Don't be soft, McCall. You knew all along!" (150). After he finds out about Joss's physical death, Big Red cries (sobs, actually) for the first time in years. Joss's death brings out the softness and vulnerability in his overwhelming tough masculine facade. The intimacy of the ensemble initiates uncontrollable feelings and deep urges to protect each other, exposing the "effeminate" and "overemotional" side of the jazz collective.[44]

During the first stages of their relationship, Millie accompanies Joss to his performance at a club where she witnesses some of the queerness of the experience of the jazz ensemble.[45] She says, "When the sax starts Joss closes his eyes and keeps them closed for the longest time" (17). Millie experiences the rapture that the erotics of the jazz ensemble produces for itself and the audience. Gradually, the rest of the audience is pulled into the music as well. The audience is "rapt," "euphoric," and "dedicated" to the music (17). In the performance, "heterosexual and homosexual cut and augment one another," creating an environment where "ecstasy is the end of a perverse, interracial consumption."[46] Big Red lets the tears flow for Joss, he gives in to his love for him, letting "the snot run down his face till he has to wipe it with the back of his big hand" (151). Big Red's final display of possible homoerotic emotion foreshadows the affective gate that opens for Colman once he becomes open to his own queerness and begins to embrace the feminine within himself.

Joss's final letter is a love song to John Moore, which produces a synchronous riff between father and son that allows Colman to approach his mother, literally and figuratively. In his letter Joss describes how he made the decision to leave his mother's love behind and to embrace the position of man. The loss of black father-love fills Joss's letter to Colman. In the letter Joss gives Colman the opportunity to write his own "father story": "I am leaving myself to you . . . I will be your son in a strange way. You will be my father telling or not telling my story" (277). This reversal of father and son presents a possible way to feed the black father-hunger starving black men's ability to reinvent themselves. Joss writes,

> When I was eleven, he died, my father. I remember my mother's pinched face, Her terrible hush. I remember the awful quiet in our house without him. The dreadful dream-like quality the whole thing had. . . . I remember the sadness in my mother's baking; once I caught her weeping into the dough. We were both changed for ever [sic] by the death of John Moore. There was no one to look at me like he did, with shining, adoring eyes. . . . My mother's love was sensible, but different. Not like him. I missed holding his black hand in the street. Looking at it, comparing it to my own. I was on my own then. Looking at my own hand, trying to remember my father's lines. They were darker than mine, his lifeline, his heart. (276)

As a little girl, Josephine's home falls into a silent void without her father's presence. He is her only link to blackness; without him, she sinks into a lonely absence in all-white Greencock, Scotland. As an adult, Joss remembers Edith Moore as a sad and vacant figure of sorrow without her husband. Edith's love is inadequate, "sensible, but different" from the "adoring" and validating look that Josephine craves from her father. Young Josephine's comparison of her father's dark hands to her own symbolizes her evaluation of her male future. She follows her father's lifeline in pursuit of the position of black husband and father. For Joss to achieve black manhood, the mother is left behind.

Josephine is a phobic presence for Joss. He tells Millie to "leave her [Josephine] alone" (93), but at the same time it is Josephine/Joss who sends his mother letters and checks. He is still Josephine in Greencock. Joss's request that Josephine be left alone is the only moment in the novel that he speaks of his former female self until the letter to Colman. Josephine is the absent presence of black female experience in the diaspora, the denied past that sustains the present and the future silence. Without her, there can be no Joss. He (erroneously) determines that he has to be his own mother, that to be a (black) "man" he has to deny his own reproduction: his biological mother and his figurative "mother" in Josephine constitute the feminine that must be displaced. Ironically, Colman's search for his father leads him back to Edith and to Josephine. In the novel's final dream sequence, Colman sees Edith "in front of him at the seaside, holding the hand of a small girl, his father" (260). Colman follows little Josephine into a house that suddenly starts to fill with water that is "leaking from everywhere" (260). The seaside has been associated with the family's life in Scotland throughout the novel. Kay invents a coastal town named Torr that represents their seclusion from reality. The house in Torr is where things are most ideal. The barriers to awareness of his and his father's "dead" position within Scotland have begun to break into Colman's mind. The leaky house represents the edifice (and artifice) of heterosexual, patriarchal, middle-class black manhood that Colman is beginning to understand as an impermanent and vulnerable construction.

In the dream, Colman is determined to save Josephine, putting her on his back to keep her from drowning. He thinks, "He has a little girl's life on his back. He has to save her. Has to" (260). The need he has at the beginning of the book to prove his manhood through his penis is replaced by a drive to recuperate the female part of his paternal heritage. It is Colman who saves Josephine from the annihilation of being not only "dead" but also forgotten. Colman's internalization of Josephine is an indication that he is coming to terms with the parts of himself that are queer. The dream compels Colman finds his mother in her childhood home in Torr. Colman's dream is a symbolic turn to the (black) maternal. Perhaps this place of gentle caretaking is a hint toward the potential future of black manhood that would otherwise be despised under the phallic-centered goals Colman begins with in the novel.

The novel's last line leaves us Colman and Millie together with a soaring bird, singing its flight: "its wings dipping, faltering and rising again . . . and scatting to the wind" (278). Scatting is the process by which a jazz singer extemporaneously vocalizes along with the instrumentals. The reference to scatting takes us to the contributions of vocalists to jazz, which is dominated by women singers (as opposed to the male-heavy instrumentalists). Scatting shows up earlier in the novel when Joss scats to Colman at the breakfast table. This practice is a constant reminder to Colman that he belongs to an "untraditional house" (46). The bird's scatting symbolizes the potential through the improvisation of black manhood. Improvisation is a strategy where each player creates his or her own take—moving the song forward, signifying on past melodies, changing and commenting on them. It is a process wherein familiar tunes are reworked through improvisation to fit the artist's harmonic sensibilities to the extent that the tune becomes "radically defamiliarized" to the listener.[47] Legibility has been abandoned or lost, the object has gone past the stage of recognizability, and only traces of the familiar remain. Although John Moore, Joss, and Colman are rendered "dead" by the nation partly by destabilizing black manhood, the search for legibility and coherent (patriarchal) gender fails to resurrect them as "living" subjects. The bird's appearance with a reunited Millie and Colman at the end of the novel suggests that Colman is integrating queerness into his sense of self. Kay's text suggests we can become accustomed to new harmonies. They do not have to make us comfortable or relaxed; the song does not have to march toward an inevitable resolution or conform to explicit or implicit goals. At a time when melancholic attachment to black manhood and masculinity erases all other possibilities, we need to look to different models of self-invention. African musical heritage is one that privileges polycentricism; allowing the music to weave different melodies into one song is an opportunity to learn from jazz.

The fact that Joss was designated female at birth and became a man in adulthood does not exempt him from the (misdirected) desire of black manhood to occupy a position ("living") liberal citizenship that dominant cultures promise comes with patriarchy.[48] As a result of the demand that manhood makes on family structures and gendered relations, Joss becomes, for a time, the diaspora patriarch so woefully desired and mourned by the larger black collective. Joss's queerness exposes how impossible that desire ultimately is. For Colman, this means that the ideal of the heteropatriarch, which is based on assumptions of an impenetrable black manhood that he thought his father embodied, is a facade. Instead he becomes aware of black manhood's structural vulnerability as feminine and of black dispossession from the normative heterosexual nuclear family.

Colman's attachment to limited, patriarchal facets of manhood is indicative of a generalized black male melancholic mourning for legitimized manhood and masculinity.

Jazz's dual nature of featuring the individual and privileging the collective is a useful vehicle for black queer improvisation on the relationship between the collective identities of race and nation and the expressions of gender. At the end, Colman is introduced to the possibility of embracing the maternal within himself. Colman's glimpse into the black male potential for the maternal symbolizes the broader queer horizons possible for black manhood and masculinity. Joss advises us to "make it up" (58), leaving us with the burden of decision: To keep chasing the genders of white society that we are excluded from or to embrace other possibilities.

Notes

1. Jackie Kay, *Trumpet* (London: Picador, 1998), 61. Hereafter cited in the text.
2. Hortense Spillers, "Mama's Baby, Papa's Maybe: An American Grammar Book," in *Black, White, and in Color: Essays on American Literature and Culture*, ed. Hortense Spillers (Chicago: University of Chicago Press, 2003), 203–29. Although her essay title calls attention to the crisis of the American black, I contend that her descriptions of the damage and potential caused by African capture and delivery to the West has diasporic implications.
3. Orlando Patterson, *Slavery and Social Death: A Comparative Study* (Cambridge, MA: Harvard University Press, 1982). Patterson's landmark study is an all-encompassing investigation that defines slavery across cultural contexts as a condition of social death.
4. Sharon Holland, *Raising the Dead: Readings of Death and (Black) Subjectivity* (Durham, NC: Duke University Press, 2000), 15.
5. Spillers, "Mama's Baby," 229, 228.
6. Lewis R. Gordon, *Bad Faith and Antiblack Racism* (New York: Humanity Books, 1999), 227.
7. Darieck Scott, *Extravagant Abjection: Blackness, Power, and Sexuality in the African American Literary Imagination* (New York: New York University Press, 2010), 19.
8. Robert Park, *Race and Culture: Essays in the Sociology of Contemporary Man* (Glencoe, IL: Free Press, 1950), 280.
9. Diane Wood Middlebrook, *Suits Me: The Double Life of Billy Tipton* (Boston: Houghton Mifflin, 1998).
10. "Writers; Jackie Kay," 2011, literature.britishcouncil.org/jackie-kay.
11. Only since 2002 has there been a recognized black history month campaign in Scotland. "Black Affronted; Ed McCracken Reveals That Many Blacks in Scotland Still Feel the Chill of Pernicious Racism, yet Hope That an Exhibition on Black Culture Could Help Instil a Greater Understanding of a Troubled Past," *Sunday Herald*, October 12, 2003, findarticles.com/p/articles/mi_qn4156/is_20031012/ai_n12585853/ (accessed July 8, 2010).
12. Alan Rice, "'Heroes across the Sea': Black and White British Fascination with African Americans in the Contemporary Black British Fiction of Caryl Phillips and Jackie Kay," in *Blackening Europe: The African American Presence*, ed. Heike Raphael-Hernandez (New York: Routledge, 2004), 227.

13. Kay's poetry includes *That Distance Apart* (London: Turret, 1991); *The Adoption Papers* (Highgreen, Wales: Bloodaxe Books, 1991); *Other Lovers* (Highgreen, Wales: Bloodaxe Books, 1993); *Three Has Gone* (London: Blackie, 1994); and *Off Colour* (Highgreen, Wales: Bloodaxe Books, 1998). Her fiction includes *Bessie Smith* (London: Absolute, 1997); *Trumpet* (London: Picador, 1998); and *Why Don't You Stop Talking?* (London: Picador, 2002). Kay is also an accomplished playwright. She has published two of the few black lesbian plays in print, most notably *Chiaroscuro* (London: Methuen, 1986) and *Twice Over*, in *Gay Sweatshop: Four Plays and a Company* (London: Methuen, 1989).
14. From "Author Profile," Booktrust, British Council, the Authors, the Photographers, September 12, 2004, www.comtemporarywriters.com.
15. A term most often used to refer to recent immigrants to the United Kingdom.
16. Christopher Whyte, *Gendering the Nation: Studies in Modern Scottish Literature* (Edinburgh: Edinburgh University Press, 1995), 10.
17. As we have learned from Benedict Anderson, the construction of the nation is a process of imagining its borders.
18. Patterson, *Slavery and Social Death*; Holland, *Raising the Dead*.
19. Holland, *Raising the Dead*, 15.
20. See Achille Mbembe, "Necropolitics," *Public Culture* 15, no. 1 (2003): 11–40.
21. Joshua Gamson, *Freaks Talk Back: Tabloid Talk Shows and Sexual Nonconformity* (Chicago: University of Chicago Press, 1998), 141.
22. The influx of people of color in greater numbers caused a crisis in British self-conceptualization. White Britain had made the collective decision to look inward and was suddenly forced to recognize the demands of the colonized inside the metropole. To preserve the racial order from the perceived threat of "newcomers," there was a public "reconfiguration of British national identity" as a "reinvented white national identity" (Barnor Hesse, *Un/Settled Multiculturalisms: Diasporas, Entanglements, Transruptions* [London: Zed Books, 2000], 5).
23. "Black Affronted."
24. Frantz Faron, *Black Skin, White Masks* (New York: Grove, 1967), 70.
25. As Lewis Gordon states, "To be desired by a Black woman is denigrated as presumed desire. . . . Blacks desire to be desired by whites" (*Bad Faith and Antiblack Racism* [Atlantic Highlands, NJ: Humanities, 1995], 101).
26. Melancholia is the inability to cease the mourning process and replace the lost object. Sigmund Freud, "Mourning and Melancholia," in *The Standard Edition of the Complete Psychological Works of Sigmund Freud*, Vol. 14 (London: Hogarth, 1974), 239–60.
27. *Imago* is a psychoanalytic term that refers to the images perpetuated through someone else's desires. See Paul Gilroy, *Ain't No Black in the Union Jack: The Cultural Politics of Race and Nation* (Chicago: University of Chicago Press, 1991), 74. Gil-

roy discusses the predominant framing of blacks as inherently criminal through the image of the black male mugger in Britain. See also Faron, *Black Skin, White Masks*, 169.

28. Of course, though it is rarely acknowledged, black women also are criminalized in the eyes of a racist society and face the possibility of racialized and sexualized brutality every day from within and without their homes and families.
29. According to Lacan, this pre-Oedipal feeling of wholeness is always an illusion. See Jacques Lacan, *Ecrits: The First Complete Edition in English*, trans. Bruce Fink (New York: Norton, 2010).
30. David Marriott, *On Black Men* (New York: Columbia University Press, 2000), 96.
31. Marriott, *On Black Men*, 15.
32. Gordon, *Bad Faith*, 127.
33. Gordon, *Bad Faith*, 127.
34. Marriott, *On Black Men*, 95.
35. Marriott, *On Black Men*, xiv.
36. Black British appreciation for African American images and other cultural products are a part of black British culture. See Jacqueline Nassy Brown, "Black Liverpool, Black America, and the Gendering of Diasporic Space," *Cultural Anthropology* 13, no. 3 (1998): 291–325; and Heike Raphael-Hernández, ed., *Blackening Europe: The African American Presence* (New York: Routledge, 2004).
37. Marriott, *On Black Men*, 44, 55.
38. From *Gender Trouble*, 31. Or we could say that black cultural expression is not restricted to the born-black individual, as white men and a variety of other races of people have copied black masculinity with varying degrees of success from the days of blackface until the present.
39. Paul Gilroy, *Black Atlantic: Modernity and Double-Consciousness* (Cambridge, MA: Harvard University Press, 1993), 85.
40. Gilroy, *Black Atlantic*, 85.
41. Gilroy, *Black Atlantic*, 85.
42. This kind of love, Fred Moten argues, is a "love that is never not sexual." Fred Moten, *In the Breach: The Aesthetics of the Black Radical Tradition* (Minneapolis: University of Minnesota Press, 2003), 161.
43. Moten, *In the Breach*, 161.
44. Moten, *In the Breach*, 161.
45. Moten calls these dynamics the "(primarily male homo)erotics of ensemble." Moten, *In the Breach*, 161.
46. Moten, *In the Breach*, 151.
47. Scott Knowles DeVeaux, *The Birth of Bebop: A Social and Musical History* (Berkeley: University of California Press, 1997), 224.

48. The *Moynihan Report* makes the assessment that because black people do not have proper patriarchal families, that they are pathological. If they can assume them, they can get back in step with the rest of society. Although it is in a US context, the pressure for patriarchy and the promise of instant citizenship still applies here. Daniel Patrick Moynihan, "The Negro Family: The Case for National Action," in *The Moynihan Report and the Politics of Controversy*, ed. Lee Rainwater and William Yancey (Cambridge, MA: MIT Press, 1967), 39–124.

Image Gallery

Figure 1. *The Epic Crossings of an Ife Head*, video still and performance by Wura-Natasha Ogunji. Courtesy of the artist

Figure 2. Untitled, sculpture by André Eugène; photo by Jacquenette Arnette.
Courtesy of Jacquenette Arnette

Figure 3. Untitled, sculpture and photo by Jacquenette Arnette. Courtesy of the artist

Figure 4. Grand Rue's Church, house structure made by multiple artists; photo by Ana-Maurine Lara. Courtesy of Ana-Maurine Lara

Figure 5. Untitled, detail: Ayida Wedo, by Ebony G. Patterson;
photo by Ana-Maurine Lara. Courtesy of Ana-Maurine Lara

Book Review

QUEER HISTORIES AND THE GLOBAL CITY

Robert G. Diaz

Metropolitan Lovers: The Homosexuality of Cities
Julie Abraham
Minneapolis: University of Minnesota Press, 2009. 244 pp.

Undercurrents: Queer Culture and Postcolonial Hong Kong
Helen Hok-Sze Leung
Vancouver: University of British Columbia Press, 2009. 149 pp.

Queer Visibilities: Space, Identity, and Interaction in Cape Town
Andrew Tucker
Oxford: Wiley-Blackwell, 2009. 256 pp.

San Francisco, Los Angeles, New York, Berlin, London, Cape Town, Prague, Taipei, Hong Kong, Bangkok: the list of cities that have, in the last decade, been touted as catering to a gay consumer continues to grow. In its 2009 Autumn–Winter issue, the Singapore-based magazine *PLUTO: People Like Us Travel Orbit* added Copenhagen to this list.[1] *PLUTO* promoted the city's tolerant nature and "queer friendly" tourist amenities. These characteristics provided the perfect environment for the 2009 World Out Games (the largest gay-themed international sports and cultural event held in the area), which consequently cost 4.5 million dollars to host. The magazine also focused on John Goss, the inventor of Utopia-Asia (www.utopia-asia.com), a website that provides detailed descriptions of gay business and social services (saunas, bars, clubs, and restaurants) found in a gamut of Asian cities. Goss, a white gay man, invented the site after falling in love with Bangkok as a tourist.

PLUTO embodies the coupling of neoliberal politics with queer cultural discourses. It highlights the emerging importance of the globalized gay subject in the formation of queer life in the city. Goss eerily echoes this fact in his interview. When asked about the challenges that gay businesses face, he responds by saying: "Maintaining quality! Too many businesses fall flat fighting for scraps at the bottom of the budget barrel. Aim for high quality and you can maintain higher prices for quality service. Gays are famously picky but they are going to spend money for fun no matter what. I think that's the reason they prove more resilient than their straight counterparts. An economic downturn is the time to promote your business: not only will it help you survive, but you'll be reaping the benefits when cash starts flowing again."[2] Goss registers the homonormalizing impulses of capitalism in the contemporary moment. His remark encourages the acceptance of particular forms of queerness as long as juridical and economic liberation would further the production of material wealth. Absent from his statement are the many issues queer- and non-queer-identified subjects experience as they are directly affected by economic inequity, uneven development, and poverty. Goss sees a future where only the stylishly spendy queer mobile cosmopolitan will survive, for he is the only one who matters. Interestingly, this cosmopolitan is oftentimes male.

Amid this backdrop, how might we locate other conditions of possibility for the queer subject who does not fall into the "gay consumer" category? Could the histories of these cities themselves beg further complication?[3] Is it possible to imagine the "gay subject" in the postcolonial Third World as not merely mimicking the West? How might we resist seeing the homogenization of queer subjectivity through a more thoughtful unpacking of the hybrid practices and disparate communities present in the postcolonial metropolis? How might the local and the global intersect? Could we reimagine the city as still producing the possibility of queer intimacies, knowledges, and interactions that challenge dominant forms of heteronormative and even homonormative culture, even if the latter continues to shape the urban landscape? How might recent scholarship in the field examine linkages between queer politics and the continually evolving transnational metropolis?

To varying degrees, Andrew Tucker's *Queer Visibilities: Space, Identity, and Interaction in Cape Town*, Helen Hok-Sze Leung's *Undercurrents: Queer Culture and Postcolonial Hong Kong*, and Julie Abraham's *Metropolitan Lovers: The Homosexuality of Cities* all center on the city as the key site for unpacking disparate queer cultures. Discussing Tucker and Leung's works more thoroughly and

Abraham's more briefly, I argue that the first two authors are more successful at deterritorializing and reshifting queer studies as a theoretical and political project outside the West. In a moment of intensified counterterrorism, necropolitical nationalism, and resurgent yet covert forms of empire, both Leung's and Tucker's projects have much to say about queer subjects who are simultaneously affected by and resist Western imperialism's effects. Thus they also enter into an ongoing political discussion in contemporary queer studies, the thrust of which is to challenge the normalization of queer politics as a product of expanding capital both locally and abroad.[4] Although these projects cover distinctly different metropolitan spaces and populations (Cape Town, Hong Kong, and such US cities such as New York and Chicago), I would also argue that they nonetheless show us what is still possible within the field, as we continue to think about the relationship between queer identity and cosmopolitan life. As a general (and of course, limited) schematic, all three books focus on the following analytic nodes: (1) the city as having a local history that is inherently linked up to national history, (2) the urban landscape as fostering an array of queer resistances and queer intimacies and, (3) queer performances of the everyday that, in their very acts, destabilize and expand the limited understandings of their respective cosmopolitan and national imaginaries. In differing detail, the works elaborate all these schematics as they seek to locate what, in these particular cities, queer communities look like.

Tucker's *Queer Visibilities* examines the many facets of queer cultural life in South Africa's "most liberal" city. Although serving as the metonym for the country's turn away from a history of systematized racism into a more tolerant future, Cape Town could also be characterized as a space filled with contradictions stemming from this vexed history. For instance, although gay-owned businesses are generally open to everyone in the queer comjunity, these businesses still discriminate against "black" and "colored" South Africans. Inhabitants embody these contradictions as they navigate and interact with each other. The exclusionary history of the past affects socializations of the present, in that national, racial, linguistic, and class boundaries shape Cape Towners' everyday lives. As Tucker notes, "In a country like South Africa, queer experiences are further complicated by the extraordinary way in which communities have historically been spatially regulated by the state. The use of 'race' as the basis of a system of discrimination has left the country with deep social, economic, and political scars. Queer communities today have therefore also remained strongly influenced by the way colonial and later apartheid mechanisms compartmentalized, regulated, and manipulated groups" (2). Being a geographer, Tucker is ultimately interested in the relationship between Cape Town's racial history and its urban spatialization. The project moves through various enclaves, beginning with the most "visibly" queer space in the city (De Waterkant) to the larger outlying townships (moving from a predominantly "white" community to "colored" and "black" ones). Although the book's chronology makes sense, I did wonder whether starting from the city's center and most visibly gay area (which is also, consequently, the "whitest" area) does not repeat the very privileging of whiteness that *Queer Visibilities* seems to resist. It seems that in Tucker's attempt to contextualize whiteness, he also centers the book's overarching narrative thread on it. What I do find useful about the project's beginning is that the author makes a point of contextualizing the various polarizations in the city. He asks: How might these specific queer spaces bleed into and regulate each other? Tucker notes that "a study of queer visibility in Cape Town must consequently be seen both as a project that draws on geographical concepts of sexuality and race and also an attempt to offer a new perspective on dealing with cross-cultural queer communities in postcolonial environments" (26). Of particular interest are the ways racial enclaves produced different queer cultures. The theoretical move here is reminiscent of ethnographic projects that acknowledge how postcoloniality creates new queer vocabularies and queer modalities.[5] *Queer Visibilities* adds to this growing archive by shifting the subject and site of inquiry outside the West, to find new ways to think about queer subjectivity delinked from Western epistemologies.

Visibility and invisibility become key frameworks for the book. Instead of marking a process whereby queer persons make themselves legible to the state, visibility is understood as a form of sociality between and within competing marginalized groups. "Queer visibility" is an "attempt to explore why difference may or may not exist within and between communities and how visibility and appreciation of difference depends on how groups have developed elsewhere. It therefore also initially shifts that argument away from the 'global' or 'the local' and instead focuses on how difference becomes possible when communities interact internally" (5). Although this framework does not seem all that new, given that queer scholarship in the last few years has begun to unpack how queer communities get stratified according to various boundaries of affiliation and kinship (the most recent works on state-sanctioned queer narratives that espouse gay marriage at the expense of queers of color, noncitizens, and the underclass are the most concrete example), what I do find refreshing about Tucker's use of visibility is that he specifically thinks of it as inter-/intracommunity contact marked by the city's (and nation's) specific historical legacy. The evolution of localized queer subjectivity is always already connected to national practices of racism. This is especially relevant in South Africa, since "visibility" *is* one of the most oft-used identifiers for classifying individuals as "white," "coloured," or "black" by the state in the first place.

The first few chapters discuss Cape Town's queer groups as they have settled in disparately located areas. In the first chapter, Tucker focuses on white gay men in De Waterkant and the outlying suburbs. Although similar in their racial classification, white gay men are separated along class, linguistic, and migratory lines. Tucker suggests that "in Cape Town, class divisions between white queer groups have been perpetuated by a uniquely South African (and unique to Cape Town) historical factors" (56).[6] This perceived ethnic and linguistic divide shapes their interactions. The assumption, he argues, is that Afrikaans speakers (who are of "Boer" ancestry) possess lower class status than their English-speaking (and thus British) counterparts. English speakers are seen as more wealthy and urbanized than Afrikaners. This discrepancy is palpable when Tucker observes Gat parties and the individuals who participate in them. Gat parties are gatherings (*Gat* is Afrikaans for "hole") where Afrikaner men who live in the suburbs meet to create opportunities for mingling and networking. Tucker interviews those who frequent these events and those who shy away from them. He comes to the conclusion that "for some men from the City Bowl or Atlantic Seaboard, Gat parties and the lives of men who inhabit the suburbs (especially the Northern Suburbs) appear at times incongruent with their own lifestyles" (64). The parties signify a move away from the cosmopolitan vibe of De Waterkant, since they do not require one to buy into the city's consumer culture.

Tucker then shifts his attention to the predominantly colored (and larger) areas outlying Cape Town in the next chapter, "Coloured Visibilities." Similar to the historical contextualizing of De Waterkant and the northern areas of Cape Flats, he begins with a discussion of how "coloured" enclaves formed during apartheid. He specifically tracks this formation by focusing on the vibrancy and destruction of District Six (which is now called Zonnebloem). District Six at its peak "was home to a vibrant coloured community. It had come into being during the late nineteenth century as a racially mixed community of freed slaves, merchants, artists, labourers, and new migrants" (69). These populations were then moved as a consequence of the 1966 Group Areas act, since the area was deemed white only. Relocating these communities into the sand flats destroyed their way of life. Colored communities had provided a space for queer persons to act as visible participants. In a sense, "such relocations affected the lives of coloured queer men who, alongside merchants, shop owners, labourers, and mixed-race families, had also found an open and accepting space to express a very visible and unique culture" (74). Moffies and their accompanying drag are the remnants of this vibrant culture. Even though both terms have come to mean any queer man, in common parlance, *Moffie* and *Moffie drag* trace their roots to the practices of queer effeminate men in District Six and similar colored communities. Tucker argues that in District Six, colored queer men "were freer to experiment with different social configurations" (77). This openness is tied to the fact that colored areas were made up of a conglomeration of other marginalized groups, whereby a family could live side by side with sex workers, or merchants beside "gangs." Even "coon carnivals" (a minstrel festival held annually on January 2), which often promoted the way of life in colored areas, featured Moffies and cross-dressing men as active participants.

This "acceptability," however, was also policed according to outward signs of gender difference. Tucker notes that effeminate queer men could have relationships with heterosexually identified men, as long as both parties conformed to performances of masculinity and heteropatriarchy. Discussing gang members and their taking on of cross-dressing sexual partners, Tucker concludes that

> the reinforcement of gender roles plays an important part in the social and sexual relationships that occur within these coloured communities. Similar to cross-dressing men who lived in District Six, these men's attempt to emulate the social mannerisms and dress of women marks them out as a very visible and unique category of individual. . . . The very "obviousness" of many queer men in drag tied to the femininity inherent in such acts, permits these men a degree of social safety when socializing with the "straight" community. (86)

In other words, the seeming openness of colored enclaves comes at the expense of particularly rigid notions of masculinity that these intimacies nonetheless uphold. In terms of Tucker's reading of drag and queer identity, I have some hesitations about his constant valorization of the "obviousness" of the cross-dressing these men enact. Continually referring to the cross-dressers as men, or *only* as gay men dressing in drag, he does not really consider the fact that these might not be "gay men in drag" at all. Moffies in drag, and those who cross-dress in general, could also claim positionalities that exceed normative notions of homosexuality and Western gay identity. Moreover, throughout the chapter, Tucker seems to suggest that dressing as women offers these men some safety from retribution within the community (86), yet he does not seem to question how this safety is brokered on an assumption of both appropriate "female" attributes and strict gender codes. In many ways, this safety already conforms to social structures that allow patriarchal assumptions about women (and other sexually marginalized people) in the first place—through male patronage and notions of a kind of helplessness in need of relief. What does resonate in this chapter, however, is the interesting notion that "in some coloured communities, concepts of sexual identity and gender identity, tied to a specific spatial appropriation of heteronormative space, have led to different ways of becoming visible than in some historically white communities" (99).

In this regard, Tucker also focuses on black African townships and their accompanying queer communities. He studies how black queer men have strategically deployed unique visibilities. He historicizes the creation of black townships to show how residents in these areas "inhabit a totally different world to that of many coloured and white individuals" (106). Although little research has been done on black townships and queerness, Tucker writes that documented narratives of mining towns suggest close same-sex relationships. During the mining period, young black men who had taken part in "mine marriages" were referred to as "wives." These individuals performed the domestic labor associated with women in the larger community (108). Same-sex activity, penetrative and otherwise, would also occur in these couplings. Tucker uses these data to contradict the assumption during the 1990s (made most infamous in Winnie Mandela's speech) that homosexuality is inherently "Un-African" and that it was brought on by colonizing powers from the West. He notes that such an assumption "not only attempts to foreclose the discussion of how same-sex sexual relations have been part of black African communities in southern Africa, it also robs contemporary queer-identified groups of any 'authentic voice' with which to speak" (112). Contemporary examples of a black queer culture could also be seen in Xhosa communities, for instance, through the figures of the Ivy and Pantsula. As Tucker notes, "Ivys were seen 'to take care in appearance' and Pantsulas were men who dressed and behaved in more overtly masculine ways" (116). After apartheid, the figure of the Ivy "developed in unison with 'Pantsula'" to "denote music, dance, fashion styles rather than sexualities" (116). Tucker's research suggests that aside from being aesthetic figures that conformed to gender norms, the Ivy and Pantsula were also sexually active in their communities (116). Compared with other queer communities, black Africans also experience the most homophobia. Tucker argues that "it is among black African township men that this violence is most forceful. Cases of gang rape against black African queer men, along with premeditated beatings and frequent verbal attacks, were often documented during the research period" (129). He attributes this violence to the conflict arising from black visibility and contact with Xhosa community values. Although understandable, I find Tucker's automatic paralleling of violence to cultural values also suspect. He locates violence in "tradition," which in the end might limit other possible explanations for the intensification of homophobia in these spaces. Is it not plausible to imagine that precisely because Xhosa communities (and other black townships) have experienced the worst forms of violence from the state, this violence is then displaced onto queer bodies within the community? It would be as easy to see this aggressivity as stemming from the systematic oppression that the state enacts on black bodies (both before and after apartheid). I would have hoped for more thorough analysis of these possibilities, which Tucker does not provide.

The book's last chapters are grouped according to the theme of invisibilities. The chapter on social invisibility suggests that although apartheid had officially ended, immense material disparities continue, which shape queer interactions. There is a sizable difference in income between groups formerly classified as white, colored, and black. This disparity has affected how queer populations both perceive each other and move between queer spaces within Cape Town. According to Tucker, "The most basic and limiting factors that can stop some coloured and black African queers accessing the gay village is simply the distance" (146). The city's spatialization *is* a remnant of apartheid, and thus it shapes the economics of the seemingly "cosmopolitan" gay village. When nonwhite queers do reach De Waterkant, traces of material unevenness come to the fore, as businesses informally limit their clientele to white gay men, whom they perceive to possess the most capital. The chapter "Political Invisibilities" tracks the life of specific activist groups. It particularly follows the development of Cape Town's Pride parade. Similar to other Pride celebrations in Western cities, Cape Town's parade shifted from being a grassroots event to a profitable endeavor that also fosters South Africa's image as a newly tolerant nation-state. The chapter "The Costs of Invisibility" centers on the lack of contextualization around Cape Town queer populations, even within the contemporary moment. It specifically uses the outbreak and subsequent representation of HIV/AIDS as a marking point for this lack. If, in the United States and in other European countries, the queer body has stood in as the metonym for AIDS, in Cape Town HIV/AIDS has predominantly been associated with images of women and heterosexual relationships. Tucker suggests that by providing in-depth analysis of queer lives and sexual practices in Cape Town, his work subtends the overrepresentation of HIV/AIDS transmission through heterosexual contact in South Africa. He writes what would at best be perceived as a gross generalization (190).

If in Tucker's *Queer Visibilities* the spatialization of Cape Town becomes a key trope for analyzing national history and local queer life, in Helen Hok-Sze

Leung's *Undercurrents* cinema becomes the focal site for unpacking Hong Kong's history and queer culture. While discussing Asian Pacific films that highlight urban scenery, in *Geopolitics of the Visible* Roland Tolentino suggests that, on the one hand, "the city is the space against which to symptomatically read the affects of historical and geographic developments of late capitalism as experienced in the Asia Pacific. On the other hand, the 'city' films map out tensions between the hegemonically planned (city developers and urban planners) and those who struggle with it every day (individuals and groups). Thus, the city is the space where individual subjectivity and group or national identity are to be deciphered and contested" (137). In Hong Kong cinema's case, deciphering these contestations requires an understanding of the city as a (post)colony. Indeed, it would be difficult to imagine an allegory for capitalist development in Hong Kong film without linking this allegory to the anxieties that the 1997 handover to China produced, especially because of the immense capital amassed during British rule. These historical linkages are certainly felt through the pages of *Undercurrents*. As Leung notes in her reading of Wong Kar Wai's *Days of Being Wild*, which for many Hong Kong film critics is *the* most influential Chinese-language film of the 1990s, "the film's obsession with time, dates, and memory—a theme that recurs in all of Wong's subsequent films—mirrors a collective fixation in Hong Kong during the time leading to the handover" (25). She indexes Aihwa Ong's notion of "flexible citizenship," since the narrative of departure from and inevitable return to the city post-1997 has been the predominant model for thinking about how its inhabitants connect to the urban space during this period.[7] However, Leung moves away from the notion that the city's value is tied only to these migratory flows. Decoupling her framework from this stereotype, Leung challenges the temporal logics that equate Hong Kong with outward postcolonial migration. She examines how queer subjects navigate Hong Kong from within, thereby utilizing queerness and queer performance as effective ways to reinvigorate the seemingly fixed urban landscape. She locates peripheral spaces within the metropole—islands, nooks, spaces for cruising, outlying undeveloped or soon-to-be-developed areas—to think about how these reflect local forms of queer cultural life that seek to escape their cultural constraints. She argues that in many postcolonial Third World cities, the rural and the urban commingle, and thus she espouses, following the work of Judith Halberstam, a persistent critique of "metronormativity." She questions queer theory that has traditionally privileged limited understandings of the city as the locus of a liberatory queer life.

In the first and meatiest chapter of the book, "Sex and the Postcolonial

City," Leung goes through a gamut of films—from Stanley Kwan's *Still I Love You* to Yonfan's *Bishonen*—to highlight "how queer relationality strains to (mis)fit the cityscape, and, in so doing, reveals the city's secret nooks and crannies, its margins and borders, its unreality and its possibilities" (39). She begins the section with the city's most visited tourist area, Victoria Peak, noting how the historian Lu Wei-Luan writes of the peak's view, which the latter characterizes as a certain "opaqueness."[8] Leung suggests that even in one of the most often traveled (and marketed) areas in Hong Kong, which should provide a clearer view of the metropolis, Lu re-visions this perspective as ironically unable to fully capture the complexity of the urban space. Leung uses this metaphor quite powerfully, as an effective metaphor for the possibilities inherent in trying to "find" queerness in a city as overdetermined as Hong Kong. She suggests that it is precisely this opaqueness amid the networked or "efficient" landscape that allows for furtive and unexpected queer encounters. Supporting this argument, she then reads Kwan's *Still I Love You* as the director's rumination of a queer subject's ambivalence as he reflects on how postcolonial Hong Kong has shaped both his Chineseness and his queerness. The film, made during the months preceding the handover, is preoccupied with notions of passing as Chinese, and of the act of navigating the urban space through uncertainty and detachment. Leung remarks on a statement by Kwan that "in Hong Kong, we know that we are 'Chinese' but also that we are distinctly different from Chinese in other places" (13). Kwan also recalls his inability to connect with Cantonese and English tunes being taught in school. In both these instances, Leung locates the queer subject's mourning, stemming from the inability to fully embody appropriate modalities of nationality, ethnicity, and sexuality. Instead, what Kwan ends up valuing in the film are his experiences of transience and fleeting connections with the city. According to Leung, this movement allows Kwan to play on the ironies effected by his ambivalence. For example, reading the director's mentioning of various Hong Kong streets that have colonial names (such as Princess Margaret Road and Tonkin Street), Leung writes that

> what comes across as queer in *Still I Love You* is thus not Kwan's certainty of being gay (or Chinese) but his loving evocation of a disappearing timespace that is not bound to such reassurance. . . . In *Still I Love You*, Kwan attempts to map, through his camera, this queerscape as Hong Kong's postcolonial space—the hybrid everyday locales, caught up with speedy changes and traces of half remembered histories, that contribute to their inhabitants' sense of being somehow "distinctly different" from people whose identity they otherwise share. (14)

Borrowing from Gordon Brent Ingram's notion of queerscape, Leung sees this ambivalence as an interesting counterpoint, noting that "just as the globalization of sexuality results not in the homogenization but in intricate processes of transcultural exchanges, translations, and appropriations, urban queer spaces that are produced at the confluence of global and local forces do not necessarily replicate a predictable metropolitan sexuality but most likely result in hybrid spaces that retain varying degrees of local traces" (15).

In another section of the chapter, Leung links this notion of movement to cruising. Cruising becomes an important act that opens up the central business district in Hong Kong, as a film like *Bishonen* demonstrates. In Yonfan's work, Leung seizes on the character Jet's various points of connection with the people he cruises (first a man he encounters and he sleeps with, then a couple who beckon him after the sexual encounter). These quotidian moments in Lan Kwei Fong (a street that has become synonymous with gay bars and bohemian trendy establishments) open up the entire city to a different reading, one that suggests that even within the business district's rigidity, it is still possible to foster queer interactions and unscripted adventures. As Leung notes, "*Bishonen* is most interesting when it uncovers latent queer spaces of the neighborhood and shows in unexpected ways how they become activated by sexually adventurous inhabitants" (23). In many ways, then, the city's queerness is precisely dependent upon the performance of queer sociality by its citizens, in the act of cruising, for instance. Leung also focuses on Hong Kong's geographically marginal sites, such as Mayfly Island. Particularly in the movie *Island Tales*, she connects the film's looping nature and the inability of the island's inhabitants to leave (again, an effective allegory for Hong Kong during this moment) as a way to think about enforced contact between individuals and what these contacts offer them. Leung's usage of contact reminds me of how Samuel Delany thinks about the term when he describes sexual subcultures in Times Square porn theaters. According to Delany, while often nonnetworked, fleeting, and random, moments of contact nonetheless offer crucial conduits for queer knowledge production, interclass interaction, and survival amid governmental policies of erasure.[9] As Leung notes when she observes the film, "Once the option of leaving has been taken away, there is little else for the characters to do than to give in to spontaneous and accidental encounters. The philosophy behind such an impetus offers an alternative perspective on Hong Kong as a community" (28).

In the next two chapters ("Between Girls" and "Trans Formations"), Leung focuses on topics that have often been ignored in the queer studies of postcolonial cities: female intimacies/kinships and transgender identity in the urban space.

She examines "films with subplots that portray girls in intimate relations with each other: they are daughters, neighbors, or best friends of the main characters. While their sexual intimacy often remains underdeveloped or unresolved, their very presence significantly troubles the main plots, especially in relation to adult heterosexuality" (50). What is refreshing about this section is that it recuperates films that do not necessarily have explicitly "queer" characters. In fact, the queerness of these films is directly linked to the intimacies of the women in them — intimacies that escape codification as heteronormative melodrama. These intimacies then question the pejorative quality of stories that depict women coming of age, a common theme in Hong Kong cinema. Even lesbian characters in films like Sylvia Chang's *Tempting Heart* proudly display their inability to have children, thus flaunting what Leung refers to as an inability to follow repro-time. "These stories, while often truncated and unfinished, are traces of what has been obscured, overshadowed, or bleached out of existence in the inexorable narrative of heterosexual womanhood" (64). Leung is also concerned with rethinking notions of transgender identity. She borrows from Peter Jackson's "pre-gay/post-queer" as markers of sexuality in Asia: *pre*, meaning a sexuality that predates the advent of lesbian and gay politics in the West, and *post*, meaning sexuality that confounds Anglo-American constructions.[10] Offering a rereading of the film version of *Swordsman 2*, Leung suggests that through the figure of the aggressive, manipulative, and ever-present Dongfang Bubai (who consequently is given more importance in the film than the novel), the film gives "a spectacular display of transsexual femininity that has successfully eclipsed the centrality of masculine heroism in the genre" (77).

In the most moving chapter in the book, "In Queer Memory," Leung reflects on Hong Kong actor Leslie Cheung's legacy. She follows the actor's iconicity and the criticism around his ambivalence in the public eye. Cheung never "came out" as a gay man, and thus he has been accused of strategic concealments by the press and his fans. Leung asks what the value of such concealment would be in reconfiguring expectations around sexuality and kinship within the local culture. She writes that "by exploring these aspects of his legacy, I want to suggest that Cheung is a queer icon *because* — not in spite — of his ambivalence" (88). In this regard, Leung provides a good counterpoint to narratives of visibility such as Tucker's, in that she calls for a more nuanced understanding of practices of queer identity that cannot be simply categorized as either visible or invisible, out or not out. What of visibility that has its delays, hesitations, and playfulness? What is fascinating about Leung's reading is that the constant desire for Cheung to be out, and the latter's refusal to state definitively that he is gay, produces a version of queerness that refuses pejorative connections to knowledge or authenticity. Queerness in this instance is a process of refashioning and re-creation. Studying the gossip around Cheung (in the form of blogs and magazine articles), Leung is "interested in the way gossip can function through the mass media as a site of *self-making*, both for the celebrity whom the media is bent on 'outing' and for the queer spectators 'in the know' who must read between the lines to wrest queer meanings out of ambivalence" (91). Leung also suggests that Cheung's depictions of his queerness demand reconsidering traditional notions of kinship and family within Hong Kong society. In another moving moment in the chapter, Leung narrates a concert where Cheung thanks both his mother and his partner, Daffy Tong. In *Across 1997*, Cheung stuns the audience by referring to Tong as his mother's "bond son" (*qizai*) (98).[11] According to Leung, Cheung reconfigures familial scripts within Hong Kong culture through this act. In doing so, he has also subtended the most dominant stereotype around queer coupling in the last decade: gay marriage. As Leung notes:

> The struggle for gay marriage imposes parameters for figuring queer lives, and as a result, renders what falls outside of these parameters not only illegitimate but also *never* (to be) legitimate. By contrast, Cheung invoked a much older form of relational practice whereby kinship terms within the family are appropriated to accommodate affective and sexual relations not intelligible within the familial and social order. (100)

Cheung's displacement of the marriage narrative with an older kinship structure legitimates queer intimacy through moments of self-making that also go beyond Western familial models. Even in Cheung's death, his family refers to Tong as a "quasi kin." This, according to Leung, opens up the kinship structure, since "the 'quasi-kin' relations of nonblood 'brothers and sisters' bestow a certain fluidity and openness on the familial structure, whereby queer relations may be accommodated from within rather than reinvented from without such as a parallel structure (such as gay marriage)" (100).

Similar to Tucker's *Queer Visibilities* and Leung's *Undercurrents*, Abraham's *Metropolitan Lovers* offers a reading of how queer life has been affected by the ever-changing urban landscape. Abraham focuses much of her attention on the historical shifts occurring in major cities in the United States, Britain, and France since the nineteenth century. The representations of these shifts—whether celebratory or ambivalent—then depend on accompanying "representative" sexualities. Departing from Tucker and Leung's projects, however, Abraham seems to make a larger claim about the functioning of metropolitan queerness in the perceptions of modernity itself (Western modernity specifically). She "maps the convergences, the exchanges of meaning, the transfers of value, and the intertwined fates of the understanding of homosexuality and the city that have in turn shaped our comprehension of modernity" (xvii). Throughout the book, one gets the sense that although the times have indeed changed, the fate of the homosexual continues to be tied to the city's evolution. This is especially true within the Western literary and sociological tradition that Abraham reads. *Metropolitan Lovers* examines the works of figures such as Honoré de Balzac, Émile Zola, Oscar Wilde, James Baldwin, Alfred Kinsey, and Ebbing, moving from a discussion of lesbian sexuality in Balzac's *Girl with the Golden Eyes*, to the presence of prostitution in Zola's *Nana*, to the discussion of secrecy in Wilde's *Picture of Dorian Gray*. In all of these gestures, Abraham suggests that the quintessential tension between what is "natural" and what is "artificial" affects notions of the urban (152). These notions of authenticity and artificiality have plagued notions of queer intimacy and sociality from the onset. Abraham also writes that "it is possible to argue, in fact, that despite the tectonic shifts in social and intellectual possibilities initiated by gay liberation and feminist politics in the late 1960's, there has been a remarkable consistency in cultural conceptions of homosexuality in the West, from the era of Wilde and James to the present" (44).

While it is certainly possible to argue for the consistency of such figurations of homosexuality in the West, I wonder about the politics of such an assertion when it does not provide a more thorough critique of how this historical consistency matters in the contemporary moment — especially outside these major cosmopolitan centers. Although Abraham provides a lucid tracing of how these authors and their works affect each other's notions of homosexuality — how the notion of secrecy in James differs from that of Wilde, how the notion of "overstimulation" differs in the study of various Chicago School sociologists — I often felt like the project's main purpose is to provide a lengthy comparative description of the queer representations of various artists without noting the significance of such a move theoretically. I am left to ponder, even after finishing the book, what these revelations do. In light of Tucker's and Leung's writing, I wish that Abraham had placed her work in larger conversation with critics within postcolonial, ethnic, and queer studies, beyond gesturing toward Eve Kosofsky Sedgwick's notion of the closet and David Harvey's take on the "postmodern" city.[12] While Abraham does discuss the writings of Martin Manalansan and Delany in her afterword, this citational practice deploys their work to exemplify the presence of minority communities in New York rather than mobilize their theoretical claims (i.e., Manalansan's claim that the Filipino diaspora, especially in urban areas, is also a queer one and Delany's work on the functioning of "contact" in understanding knowledge production in Times Square). Nor is there discussion of HIV/AIDS except for a passing mention of *Angels in America*, and a description of how AIDS representations reiterate narratives of migration out of cities into small towns (280). This seems rather odd to me given that her study is concerned with large-scale tropes and their effects on queer representation. Moreover, given that Abraham favors the literary, I was perplexed by the lack of discussion of HIV/AIDS literature and performance. In the United States, HIV/AIDS and the dying of a large population en masse was the strongest catalyst for understanding queer politics, activism, and policing. HIV/AIDS is one of the flashpoints of the urban queer population in the United States that forced a rereading of the history of the past — around issues of sexuality and populations, and how narratives of disease are used to police others.[13] Instead, Abraham seems to be concerned with the chronology of queer representation as a linear mapping of changes and representative affinities, rather than with, say, thinking about how queerness itself affects the project of historiography or even, as many have argued, the very notion of time.[14] Thus when Abraham ends her introduction by saying her book is "an exploration of how we arrived here" (xix), I am left wondering whom she means by "we" and if indeed *arriving* is the most effective term to use when thinking of queerness in these complex times.

What is a notable, however, is that Abraham presents a strong and valid critique of current queer scholarship that focuses mostly on gay men. She even critiques Delany's own anecdotes in *Times Square Red, Times Square Blue*. She suggests that in one encounter with a woman in the theater, Delany's lack of curiosity highlights a certain illegibility of the female subject before him. This argument, which is consistent through the book, is enlightening. She shifts our attention to lesbian sexuality and the role of women within urban spaces. She writes that "women, and especially lesbians, were at the center of this complex of understandings of cities — whether the terms of discussion were vice and capital or nature and history — because of the ways in which dominant cultural understandings of gender and sexuality allowed for the entangling of these terms" (21). Abraham rightly criticizes the unchallenged centrality of gay subjects in historical discussion of queerness in the city (as manifest in the writings of such historians as Martin Duberman). In one chapter, she works through Balzac's description of the lesbian in *The Girl with the Golden Eyes*, an image of Paris as an urban hell obsessed with artifices and gold. Through the secretive character of Paquita, Balzac locates the city's falsities: "Balzac's novella turns on a particular set of ideas about lesbianism, which he draws on to express most fully — most personally — the threat of his hellish Paris and the ultimate baselessness in this threat" (8). Lesbianism also becomes a key space for discussing intimacies between prostitutes, which she locates in Zola's depiction of *Nana*. According to Abraham, *Nana* is a threat to Parisian social order precisely because her sexuality is uncontrollable. Thus "lesbianism as the vice of whores, sexuality at its most abandoned, does not simply confirm the utter degradation of prostitutes but represents the fundamental threat of vice itself to the social world of the city, which is the possibility that even gold might cease to control pleasure" (12). Outside the literary, Abraham also focuses on the figure of Jane Addams and her building of Chicago's Hull House. As Abraham suggests, Addams "lived the model life of lesbian social political engagement that came to be described with praise by Carpenter and Hirschfield and with suspicion by Ellis and Freud" (117). Her life and activism produced a gamut of interpretations of female sexuality from key sociologists of her day. These interpretations are closely tied to the city, in that both Addams's choosing of where to place Hull House and her activist work are affected by Addams's views of Chicago's metropolitan landscape. In almost all of the chapters, Abraham makes a point to discuss lesbian sexuality as shaping and being shaped by representations of the city. The new cosmopolitanisms promised by North Atlantic centers are certainly alluring to those living under geographic and ideological constraints. As Pheng Cheah declares in his treatise on the relationship between cosmopolitanism and human rights, they purport to connect individual freedom and the "power of transcendence with travel, mobility, and migration."[15] In arguing that this ruse fails, Cheah writes that

> in each of these cases, the freedom that is promised is inaccessible to the world's populations, who inhabit the other side of the international division of labor and are unable to move to OECD countries and top tier global cities. It is also severely undermined by the fact that the efficacy of these new cosmopolitanisms is generated by, and structurally dependent on, the active exploitation and impoverishment of the peripheral majorities.[16]

Given Cheah's warning, how might queer studies offer useful correctives to actively engage cosmopolitan life within major cities in the West while also being attentive to queer communities within the peripheral majorities, the peripheral cities, and the marginal urban locales? How might we examine unequal queer communities and their cultural practices in relationship to varying notions of what it means to be a "queer cosmopolitan?" Could queer subjects in the global South resist the ruses of these new cosmopolitanisms through their everyday actions? How might they contradict, enact, and complicate these desires? These three works highlight the possibilities of re-viewing the metropolitan through a queer lens. While their studies span multiple cities deemed "global" in nature, Tucker, Leung, and Abraham also show us the inherent contradictions and fissures within these "global" spaces. Queer inhabitants—their policing, their active engagement, their vocabularies, and their ways of surviving—reflect the local and historical shifts experienced by the city and the nation-state. As Tucker notes, "To assume that a global queer culture is usurping all those it encounters around the world could be to deny the possibility of hybridization and an appreciation of diversity" (60). By refusing to accede to the axiom that queer subjects are always being homogenized by cosmopolitan cultural norms, Tucker, Leung, and Abraham offer us a rich archive of queer practices that, I would hope, encourage future debate and analysis.

Notes

1. For the full story on the Gay Games on Copenhagen, see "Out Is In at Copenhagen," *PLUTO: People Like Us Travel Orbit* (Singapore: Neu Ark Multimedia) Autumn–Winter 2009, 52–67.
2. Koh, Amos. "Finding Utopia," *PLUTO: People Like Us Travel Orbit* (Singapore: Neu Ark Multimedia) Autumn–Winter 2009, 41.
3. *PLUTO* skipped over Manila as it located queer businesses in other Asian cities. Having been to queer spaces in the city (spread out over Malate, Pasig, and Ortigas), I wondered whether this elision could be connected to what critics such as Neferti Tadiar have argued as the geographic incommensurability of metropolitan Manila and the refusal of its urban excess to be contained. Even though foreign capital has invested in the city and the local government has attempted to channel the flow of bodies in a more effective fashion, the urban population itself complicates these efforts through its viral proliferation. For more on metro Manila, see Neferti Tadiar, *Fantasy-Production: Sexual Economies and Other Philippine Consequences for the New World Order* (Hong Kong: Hong Kong University Press, 2004).
4. Some examples of these studies are Lisa Duggan, *The Twilight of Equality? Neoliberalism, Cultural Politics, and the Attack on Democracy* (Boston: Beacon, 2003); and Jasbir Puar, *Terrorist Assemblages: Homonationalisms in Queer Times* (Durham, NC: Duke University Press, 2007).
5. Some examples of these ethnographies are Martin Manalansan, *Global Divas: Filipino Gay Men in the Diaspora* (Durham, NC: Duke University Press, 2003); Tom Boellstorff, *The Gay Archipelago: Sexuality and Nation in Indonesia* (Princeton: Princeton University Press, 2005); Larry La Fountain-Stokes, *Queer Ricans: Cultures and Sexualities in the Diaspora* (Minneapolis: University of Minnesota Press, 2009); and Peter Jackson and Nerida Cook, *Genders and Sexualities in Modern Thailand* (Chiang Ma: Silkworm Books, 2000).

6. Ironically, even though De Waterkant's gay clientele states an affinity with other urban queers in the United States or Europe, South Africa's past forces a rereading of this seemingly cohesive urban vibe. Tucker notes that contrary to their counterparts in the cities of Western nations like the United States and Britain, white queer communities in South Africa did not gain recognition through piecemeal confrontation with the state, either through mass protest or the legal contestatory process. Rather, their inclusion in mainstream culture through the granting of such rights as gay marriage, pension, and the right to adopt was a direct result of the government's ratification of the new constitution in 1996, and of the ANC's desire to resist all forms of discrimination, including discrimination based on gender and sexuality. Thus, in many ways, it was precisely the shift to a removal of race-based discrimination that then precipitated the inclusion of queer rights in national legislative discourse. As Tucker suggests, in South Africa unlike other countries, "It is debatable how far white queer men themselves were actually responsible for such a shift" (46). In fact, white men did not have to contend with the harsh racial policies of apartheid and thus were not policed (or resistant) in the same way.
7. For a discussion of how "flexible citizenship" relates to economic migration out of and back to Hong Kong, see Aihwa Ong, *Flexible Citizenship: The Cultural Logics of Transnationality* (Durham, NC: Duke University Press, 1999).
8. See Lu Wei-Luan, *Xianggang gushi: Geren Huiyu yu wenxue sikao* (*Hong Kong Stories: Personal Memories and Literary Reflections*) (Hong Kong: Oxford University Press, 1996), 4.
9. For more on the differences between "networking" and "contact," see Samuel Delany, *Times Square Red/Times Square Blue* (New York: New York University Press, 2001). The culmination of such erasure in Delany's case is Mayor Rudy Giuliani's cleaning up of Times Square in the 1990s.
10. For a more thorough examination of "pre-gay/post-queer" identities and politics, see Peter Jackson, "Pre-Gay, Post-Queer: Thai Perspectives on Proliferating Gender/Sex diversity in Isia," *Journal of Homosexuality* 40, no. 3–4 (2001): 1–25.
11. See Leslie Chung, "Moon River," in *Leslie Chung Live in Concert 97*, VCD (Hong Kong: Rock, 1997), disc 2, track 8.
12. See Eve Kosofsky Sedgwick, *Epistemology of the Closet* (Berkeley: University of California Press, 1991); and David Harvey, *The Condition of Postmodernity* (Oxford: Wiley-Blackwell, 1991).
13. Nayan Shah's research on Chinese immigrants in San Francisco and their representation as medical menace provides us with useful tools for reading the relationship between medicalizing discourse, racism, and heteronormative justifications of government policy around containment. See *Contagious Divides: Epidemics and Race in San Francisco's Chinatown* (Berkeley: University of California Press, 2001).

14. Some examples of work on queer temporality and their relationship to race, class, and nationalism are Judith Halberstam, *In a Queer Time and Place: Transgender Bodies, Subcultural Lives* (New York: New York University Press, 2005); Bliss Cua Lim, *Translating Time: Cinema, the Fantastic, and Temporal Critique* (Durham, NC: Duke University Press, 2009); and Kara Keeling, "Looking for M—: Queer Temporality, Black Political Possibility, and Poetry from the Future," *GLQ* 15 (2009): 565–82.
15. See Pheng Cheah, *Inhuman Conditions: On Cosmopolitanism and Human Rights* (Cambridge, MA: Harvard University Press, 2006), 11.
16. Cheah, *Inhuman*, 11.

Books in Brief

MAYBE MIDLIFE, BUT NO CRISIS:
QUEER THEORY IN ITS THIRD DECADE

Sylvia Mieszkowski

After Sex? On Writing since Queer Theory
Janet Halley and Andrew Parker, editors
Durham, NC: Duke University Press, 2011. 336 pp.

Imagine inviting a bunch of theorists to a round of academic metareflection. Boring? Not so! *After Sex?*, a collection of snapshots on matters queer, is anything but unproductive navel-gazing.[1] "Quo vadis, queer theory?" is the question that twenty-two scholars in the field have been asked to explore. Implicitly dedicated to the late Eve Kosofsky Sedgwick, *After Sex?* presents the mosaic of their answers to how "all kinds of excitement remain possible" (4) even though queer theory has obtained a past. Some of the authors allow themselves to be guided closely by the editors' brief catalog of queries, which contains such questions as, "Does the distinction between the sexual and the non-sexual matter to queer thinking, and if so, when, where, and how?" (2). Other contributors stray farther afield as they allow readers a glimpse of what queer theory does these days, by presenting their own work as case studies. The overall result is a kaleidoscopic collection that rotates around the personal-is-political-is-personal axis of denormativization.

According to Lauren Berlant, what materializes in *After Sex?* is a "desire not to be stuck" (80). Those among the authors who do not dismiss the afterness of sex, sexuality, sexual/gay identity right away deconstruct the volume's provoking title. Both in historicist projects and beyond, the strategic "complicat[ion] of temporalities of before and after" and "the ass-backwardness of queer," in Neville Hoad's words, are major issues (137, 139). Carla Freccero devotes attention to "queer spectrality," which she defines as "ghostly returns suffused with affective materiality" (22). Jonathan Goldberg insists on "temporal multiplicity" in his work on early modern materialism (36). For Lee Edelman, the title question implies a linearity that feeds directly into "'futurism.'" Having shown how this ideologically saturated logic supports and drives heteronormativity, he fervently dismisses "after sex?" in favor of queer "*ever* aftering" (117). Michael Lucey comments on the danger of queer ideas "coalescing into normative dogma" (223). Using Pierre Bourdieu's description of "the *synchronization* of crises latent in different fields," he attempts to explain both the "queer moment" of the 1990s and the present "sense of afterness" as a "loss of contemporaneity as the energies that coincided for a moment . . . continue on different paths" (221, 222).[2] Weighing queer theory's "weird ability to touch almost everything" against the effectiveness of an expansive theory of sexuality, Heather Love answers back to accusations of "elitism" and "imperial ambitions" by reemphasizing queer theory's promise of a coalition against normative forces (182, 181, 183).

Couple critique, which resonates with Lee Edelman's theory of "sinthomosexuality" (113), is offered by Michael Cobb, who identifies "the single . . . as the most despised sexual minority position" (208). Making use of Hannah Arendt's and Giorgio Agamben's concepts of totalitarianism and nonrelation, respectively, he singles out the sexless and invites us to critically reconsider the totalitarian dimension of heteronormative society, which uses the couple as its (biopolitical) foundation.

For Richard Thompson Ford, queer theory offers "a way to take race politics back from the professionals" (127). While the vast majority finds "race" "too useful a fiction to dispense with" (125), queer theory's destabilizing agenda of anti-identitarianism provides tools for fighting the notion that it is *more* than a discursive construction. Granting center stage to questions of sovereignty, Bethany Schneider explores merits and limits of intersectionality between "'sexuality/desire'" and "'ethnicity.'" Taking Craig Womack as her case study, she reminds readers how colonialist discourse translates "'the queer'" into "'the Indian'" and vice versa. Her interests touch with Joseph Litvak's project of "keeping 'sex' and 'politics' strategically entangled." While his object of analysis is blacklisting in the United States since 1947 (which makes "'the Jew'" translatable into "'the queer'" and vice versa), his chosen means is "sycoanalysis": the "psychoanalysis of a social order . . . in which the sycophant . . . is the model citizen" (48).

Having made a case for studying the culture of shame, Leo Bersani points to parallels between the rhetoric of post-AIDS barebacking and "'pure love'" in seventeenth-century mysticism. In a re-vision of his own classic article on the annihilated self, he is joined by Jeff Nunokawa, who aims to put forward "less totalizing, less totalitarian ideas of what binds self to society" (251).[3]

Ann Cvetkovich sees the investigation of affect (available for analysis even in societies where explicit sexuality is *not*) as a useful contribution to queer theory. Her exploration of "how affective categories ranging from desire to shame and loss get sexualized" (172) provides Richard Rambuss's question — "what . . . does it mean . . . to use the sexual . . . to express what is supposed to be nonsexual?" (198) — with a frame that is more extensive, and more explicitly political. The greatest merit of queer theory, for Cvetkovich, lies in its ability to "move across historical and geographical boundaries, away from the recent history of gay and lesbian identities and communities in the Western metropolis" (173).

Queer theory, in short, is alive and kicking. Having proliferated, branched out, and, so far, resisted ossification, it provides space for diversity and disagreement. Testifying to this, the contributions to *After Sex?* make an illuminating and, yes, entertaining read. It is legitimate, of course, to inquire after queer theory by asking twenty-two US scholars, one of whom teaches in Canada, to take its pulse. Another way to assess whether queer research is stagnating, declining, or thriving might be to look at what is happening outside the North American academy. This challenge hopefully will be taken up sooner rather than later.

Notes

1. The volume is a revised and expanded version of a special issue of the journal *South Atlantic Quarterly* 106, no. 3 (2007).
2. Pierre Bourdieu, *Homo Academicus* (Cambridge: Polity, 1988), 173.
3. On the annihilated self, see Leo Bersani, "Is the Rectum a Grave?," *October* 43 (Winter 1987): 197–222.

Sylvia Mieszkowski teaches film studies and English literature at Amsterdam University College.

DOI 10.1215/10642684-1472962

UNCHOSEN FAMILIES

Ellen Lewin

Not in This Family: Gays and the Meaning of Kinship in Postwar North America
Heather Murray
Philadelphia: University of Pennsylvania Press, 2010. xvii + 289 pp.

Those of us who study issues of family and kinship hear a lot about how lesbians and gay men do not — or should not — have families. Indeed, there was a time when the words *family* and *gay* were understood to be polar opposites, words that applied to inherently distinctive domains.[1] This separation was understood to operate on a number of levels. First, people in gay communities and in the larger society tended to assume that coming out as gay or lesbian would inevitably lead to distancing, if not outright expulsion, from one's family of origin. Beyond this, lesbians and gays were not expected to create their own families, that is, reproduction was either logically or morally outside their experience. And finally, family and gay were seen to constitute culturally antagonistic universes, with the values of each set against one another almost as mortal enemies. Being gay, in this reading, was all about individualism and being liberated from the confines of kin demands; being in a family was, well, the opposite. Recent framings of these issues in the work of many queer scholars take a similar position, often based on a different moral calculus: the desire to preserve or establish familial bonds may reveal the power of heteronormativity, a rejection of the insurrectionary foundation of queerness, and thus a kind of capitulation to the forces of straight convention.

Historian Heather Murray's book *Not in This Family* poses a significant challenge to these congenial truths. Instead of relegating issues of sexual difference and family to different universes, she meticulously examines the post–World War II historical record, innovatively reading kin relations during this period. Most important, she focuses not just on what gay men and lesbians said about family but on what their families, especially their parents, said about them and thus on how having a gay or lesbian child shaped parental notions of responsibility and love. Her account parallels the progression of gay consciousness after the war, as gay men and lesbians formed self-conscious communities and increasingly articulated a discourse organized around civil rights and collective pride, showing that parallel shifts also occurred in the lives of parents.

Murray argues that throughout this period gays organized much of their self-awareness in a dialogue that required the presence of family, particularly parents, as interlocutors. Psychological theories of the 1950s and 1960s gave parents a starring role in shaping their children's sexuality, and whether gays and lesbians sought cures for their perceived deviance or demanded dignity, responsibility still rested with their parents, especially their mothers. Letters written by gays during the immediate postwar years reveal a nostalgia for family and a longing to return to the fold, suggesting that the breach between gays and their kin was never easily healed. Liberation movements that emerged in the 1960s and 1970s echoed many of these concerns, not least in the central metaphor of lesbian feminism, sisterhood, which drew on widely shared ideas about mother-daughter relationships.

Ironically, as liberation movements developed in the 1980s, gay men and lesbians embraced the notion that gender roles and sexual orientations were social constructions, while their parents located explanations in nature. If their children were gay because of some irresistible force of nature, then rejecting them would mean resisting nature itself, perhaps even the will of God. Parents began to craft discourses that would help relieve other parents of feelings of blame for their children's sexuality, providing the foundation for the creation of Parents and Friends of Lesbians and Gays (PFLAG). Their insistence that homosexuality was not a conscious choice generated a conflict with the politics of the New Right, leading parents to see not only their children but themselves as victims of homophobic rhetoric.

PFLAG's rhetoric drew on the increasing popularity of self-revelation in memoirs and other public personal accounts while also revealing the influence of self-help movements, particularly as they developed to confront issues of sexuality, mental health, and other personal problems. These accounts, usually written by mothers, often focused on experiences of revealing their children's sexuality to others, framed as a "coming out" process as risky and emotionally problematic as that undergone by their children. Thus the civil rights agenda of the earliest years of parental organizing shifted to more therapeutic goals. If parents could reconcile themselves to gayness being natural, real, and permanent, PFLAG's work suggested, then much of the sadness they faced when they learned their child was gay would be eased.

In what is probably her most compelling chapter, Murray explores parental responses to the AIDS epidemic. Popular accounts of the responses of gay and lesbian communities — friends or "chosen families" — to the needs of those who contracted the disease are the predominant discourse in the history of the period, yet

Murray argues that the biological family also emerged as a vital player during the epidemic, both as a cultural force and as a source of care for the sick.[2] AIDS in the family made the reality of gay sexuality an inescapable part of families' experience. Defending children meant confronting the language of blame even more sharply than before. True, many families rejected their AIDS-afflicted children or refused to accept the reason for their illness. But others provided end-of-life care and were motivated to demand dignity for their children and their memory. Parents wrote touching memoirs about their sick and dying children, and many gay people came to place a renewed value on the kind of nurturance biological family might provide.

Murray's book offers a distinctive reading of the postwar period and of North American family history, one that emphasizes the parallels between the struggles of gay men and lesbians and their kin. By putting family members' views in the spotlight, she challenges stereotypes about families as solely sources of stress and rejection. The story of gay men and lesbians and their biological families is far more nuanced, and the formation of queer cultures, along with the growing centrality of family in lesbian and gay political agendas, must be interpreted through the lens of their varied realities.

Notes

1. Esther Newton, *Cherry Grove, Fire Island: Sixty Years in America's First Lesbian and Gay Town* (Boston: Beacon, 1993).
2. Kath Weston, *Families We Choose: Lesbians, Gays, Kinship* (New York: Columbia University Press, 1991).

Ellen Lewin is professor in the Departments of Gender, Women's, and Sexuality Studies and Anthropology at the University of Iowa.

DOI 10.1215/10642684-1472971

A NEW LOOK AT QUEER TEMPORALITY

Petrus Liu

*Backward Glances: Contemporary Chinese Cultures
and the Female Homoerotic Imaginary*
Fran Martin
Durham, NC: Duke University Press, 2010. xi + 290 pp.

Fran Martin's *Backward Glances* presents a long overdue and startlingly original analysis of the female homoerotic imaginary in contemporary Chinese cultures, written with the rarest kind of conceptual acuity, penetrating insight, and meticulous research. Since the publication of her *Situating Sexualities* (Hong Kong University Press) in 2003, Martin has established herself as one of the most dynamic critics working at the fertile meeting point of queer theory and Chinese cultural studies. Whereas Martin's first two books, *Situating Sexualities* and *Embodied Modernities*, respond to the demands of local specificity with a fairly general poststructuralist argument—that sexual subjectivities must be understood in translocal contexts that are internally contradictory and multiply determined—*Backward Glances* represents what I see as a major breakthrough in Martin's work, offering a much more concrete argument about the distinctive patterns of Chinese queer cultures: that contemporary Chinese representations of female same-sex relations are dominated by an analeptic or backward-looking temporal logic, which at once frames female homoeroticism in youth as a universal and even ennobling experience and asserts its impossibility in adulthood. My sense is that everyone writing on comparative and modern Chinese queer studies will soon have to reckon with this powerfully precise and marvelously provocative argument.

Compared with Martin's earlier works, *Backward Glances* is much more expansive in scope and vision. *Backward Glances* explores the recurring narrative and ideological patterns of female homoeroticism common to mainland China, Taiwan, and Hong Kong. Turning her attention away from elite literature to women's mass culture (which includes telemovie, teenpic, pulp fiction, and melodrama), Martin discovers the remarkable pervasiveness of the memorial mode of narrating same-sex love. This cultural logic subtends a structure of feeling that permeates both the "schoolgirl romance" genre (whose genealogy from early twentieth-century

Republican Chinese literary culture to contemporary reincarnations in Chu T'ien-Hsin, Wong Bikwan, and Liu Suola is the topic of the first three chapters) and the "tomboy melodrama" genre (analyzed in chapter 4). By revealing the pervasiveness of this cultural logic, Martin in turn stakes a claim for the centrality of the female homoerotic imaginary to the making of modern Chinese cultures as a whole.

Martin's argument has profound ramifications, and her work intersects with contemporary queer conversations in at least two important ways. The first has to do with the possibility of writing queer historiography outside Europe. This project invariably produces essentialist works that reduce a complex array of values and practices to a singular attitude, such as Chou Wah-shan's postulation of a "Chinese tradition of tolerance."[1] Adroitly sidestepping the question of negative and positive evaluations (homophobia or tolerance), Martin offers a nuanced formulation that is wonderfully complex and lucid at the same time: female same-sex relations in youth are represented as both cherished and forcibly given up, both properly feminine and necessarily corralled in the past. Accordingly, while this narrative encodes critical queer agency, its proliferation also reflects the social prohibition on adult lesbianism. The second important intersection lies in the way her historically grounded study deepens our understanding of the tension between universalizing and minoritizing discourses of sexual difference. Martin skillfully shows that memorial narratives that represent women's homoerotic experiences as universal and legitimate have conservative consequences as well, in that such narratives risk derealizing lesbian possibilities. This risk is precisely what the rise of New Chinese lesbian cinema (examined in chapter 6) comes to challenge through its "critical presentism"—an attempt to define a self-consciously minoritizing lesbian identity, here and now. Martin's marvelous readings of Li Yu, Chen Jofei, and Mak Yan Yan show their works to be elaborating an image of lesbian presentness by interweaving the horizontal (narrative) dimension of time with the vertical (lyrical or melodramatic) dimension of female homoerotic time.

What I find missing in this otherwise carefully researched and thoughtfully written study is an account of the relation between fictional representations of queer temporality and concrete historical changes—social transformations, economic developments, and political policies. Insofar as there has been a concrete, vibrant queer social movement in China, Taiwan, and Hong Kong since the 1980s, the historical relation between the fictional and the contextual deserves perhaps more attention than the book has allowed. While Martin advocates for the study of popular culture and emphasizes that her texts are "consumed" by both mainstream heterosexual and queer-identified women, the relation between consumption, cultural labors, and sexual identity remains underdeveloped. Lastly, whereas Tze-lan Sang's earlier *The Emerging Lesbian*, for example, emphatically presents itself as a corrective to the gender-blindness of previous studies in queer Chinese cultures, Martin is surprisingly silent on the historical and ideological relation of female homoeroticism to male same-sex culture and to queer subjectivities in general. Surely love between women is not experienced or imagined in a social vacuum. In what sense is the female homoerotic imaginary constructed in relation or even opposition to the male and the queer, and in what ways is it inhibited or facilitated by a broader social imaginary of nonnormative sexualities that would include not just same-sex desire but also transgender, sex work, AIDS/HIV, and polygamy?

As a study of queer temporality, *Backward Glances* makes a timely contribution to an explosive growth of literature that includes Lee Edelman's *No Future*, Judith Halberstam's *In a Queer Time and Place*, Geeta Patel's "Ghostly Appearances," Heather Love's *Feeling Backward*, Carla Freccero's "Queer Times," and Elizabeth Freeman's *Time Binds*, to name just a few.[2] Martin's powerfully original analysis asks why love between women must be represented as temporally anterior and available only through memory's mediation. *Backward Glances* is a must-read for anyone interested in cross-cultural studies of sexuality and theories of queer temporality. Its true impact is something only time will tell, but I anticipate that critics will soon find the insights of *Backward Glances* forward looking, precocious, and paradigm shifting.

Notes

1. See Chou Wah-shan, *Houshimim tognzhi* (*The Postcolonial Tongzhi*) (Hong Kong: Hong Kong tongzhi yanjiushe, 1997).
2. See Lee Edelman, *No Future: Queer Theory and the Death Drive* (Durham, NC: Duke University Press, 2004); Judith Halberstam, *In a Queer Time and Place: Transgender Bodies, Subcultural Lives* (New York: New York University Press, 2005); Geeta Patel, "Ghostly Appearances," in *Secularisms*, ed. Janet Jakobsen (Durham, NC: Duke University Press, 2008), 226–46; Heather Love, *Feeling Backward: Loss and the Politics of Queer History* (Cambridge, MA: Harvard University Press, 2009); Carla Freccero, "Queer Times," in *After Sex: On Writing Since Queer Theory*, ed. Janet Halley and Andrew Parker (Durham, NC: Duke University Press, 2010), 17–26; and Elizabeth Freeman, *Time Binds: Queer Temporalities, Queer Histories* (Durham, NC: Duke University Press, 2010).

Petrus Liu is assistant professor of comparative literature at Cornell University.

DOI 10.1215/10642684-1472980

SOVEREIGNTY, THE QUEER CONDITION

Scott Lauria Morgensen

When Did Indians Become Straight? Kinship, the History of Sexuality, and Native Sovereignty
Mark Rifkin
Oxford: Oxford University Press, 2011. viii + 436 pp.

In *When Did Indians Become Straight?* Mark Rifkin shatters expectations that a non-Native scholar will argue for the inclusion of "Indians" in queer studies by instead holding himself and the field accountable to Native sovereignty. Rifkin's compelling accounts of literary texts and historical cases from the nineteenth and twentieth centuries decidedly demonstrate that the history of sexuality in the United States is conditioned by Native sovereignty and by colonial efforts to contravene it. We learn that the "coalescence in the United States . . . of the ideal of the nuclear, sentimental family" traces an "imperial hegemony that helped legitimize the exertion of settler state authority over indigenous peoples and territory" (47). In contrast, interrelationships of Native peoples, land, and governance — what Native theorists critically redefine as *kinship* — show that what is "at stake in the racialization of native peoples . . . is not just their reduction to a subordinate population within the codes of citizenship . . . but the consolidation of a familial norm that elides native kinship structures which challenged the jurisdictional imaginary of the incipient settler state" (48). Rifkin's indispensable contribution frames the queer history of the United States as a colonial history of heteronormativity defining Native-settler relations, with Native sovereignty presenting a critique of heteronormativity to which queer studies must respond.

Rifkin's intervention follows two arguments. First, we encounter the techniques whereby settler heteronormativity addresses "anxieties over how to cohere national territoriality in the face of the continued presence of indigenous peoples" (98). One technique hails Native people with "the bribe of straightness" (23) by ameliorating colonial violence if Natives mask the nonheteronormativity that threatens the subject of settler modernity. Second, Rifkin links this process to settlers seeking liberation by adopting a sexualized "Indianness" of their imagining that erases Native governance. Colonialism thus invents heteronormativity not merely to control Native peoples but to produce settlers as subjects who require authority over Native difference to attain sexual modernity. Rifkin's arguments develop within meticulously detailed cases that will benefit scholars, while they still merit translation into language that will address and inform broader audiences. Rifkin's queer critiques significantly advance theories of settler colonialism and Indigenous governance. He correctly names Native sovereignty as a target of the biopolitics of the modern racial state and suggests that biopolitics is an elision of the *geopolitics* of Native sovereignty and of settler societies that displace it (47–48). While in a recent article Rifkin examines geopolitics in relation to the work of Giorgio Agamben, the term's unindexed usage in this book invites closer attention to its compatibility with the intricacies of Michel Foucault's theory of biopolitics.[1] A powerful implication of Rifkin's argument is that instantiating heteronormativity in Native nations follows the "recognition" of Native self-governance by settler states (182–83). If heteronormativity as colonial governmentality produces the self-governed Native subject compatibly with what Elizabeth Povinelli calls the "autological" subject of liberal modernity, then here we meet a strikingly queer extension of Glen Coulthard's critique of "recognition" in which Rifkin centers heteronormativity for Indigenous governance to contest.[2]

Among Rifkin's more unsettling messages for queer studies is his rendering of Native sovereignty along "the topology of kinship" (208). Addressing "what happens when the rhetoric of 'kinship' is taken as indexing a history of indigenous-settler struggle rather than as merely describing particular arrangements of *home* and *family*" (11), Rifkin revisits David Schneider's work to transcend both its citation justifying gay and lesbian kinship and critically queer rejections of family and marriage. Instead, Rifkin asks how Native governance displaces kinship's association with "blood" to specify *relations* of Native people to nations and lands while disrupting settlers' intention to replace them. Queer studies then must study kinship among all who seemingly bear no relation to Native sovereignty while answering Native critics who argue that all subjects in settler societies do in fact bear this relation. Reading works by Beth Brant and Craig Womack, Rifkin argues that their responses to colonial violence articulate Native queer people with their own nations so that their liberation renews kinship as a sovereign challenge to settler rule.

Rifkin most strikingly elucidates how settler subjects arise by imagining queer ties to indigeneity. In a reading of Catherine Maria Sedgwick's *Hope Leslie*, Rifkin provocatively argues that US settler identity effectively queered European civilizationalism by adopting its revolutionary difference from an "Indianness" of its imagining that erases Native sovereignty (101). That is, if settler heteronormativity arises on *colonial* terms in a queer relation to Europe, then queer critics must explain colonial violence as the first queer act in a US history of modern sexuality. Rifkin extends this argument in a brilliant reading of Leslie Feinberg's *Stone Butch Blues*. Answering Feinberg's queer and trans radicalism, Rifkin correctly identifies settler modernity as the horizon of the novel's anticolonialism (239). In an especially powerful sequence, Rifkin then situates relations among Seneca women and Jess, the novel's protagonist, in a broader history of US colonization of Seneca people and of the Six Nations of the Haudenosaunee. Feinberg references these histories tangentially or omits them from the times the novel recounts, while narrating Indigenous characters and histories to help queer and trans non-Natives realize personal and collective liberations. Rifkin thus presents the landed contexts of Seneca and Haudenosaunee sovereignty as the absented condition of antiracist, working-class, feminist, queer, and trans aspirations for liberation, among Feinberg's characters and presumptive audiences. Rifkin's many arguments join here to educate queer and trans non-Natives — including many readers of *GLQ* — that your radicalism *is* your settler colonialism when it proves incapable of theorizing its ever-present conditioning by Native sovereignty. What would happen — in queer studies or the colonial spaces of gender/sexual politics — if responsibility to Native sovereignty defined the subjectivities and critiques of Natives *and* non-Natives, and for queer settlers, not as an external quality but as a precondition of that subject's existence?

Notes

1. Mark Rifkin, "Indigenizing Agamben: Rethinking Sovereignty in Light of the 'Peculiar' Status of Native Peoples," *Cultural Critique* 73 (2009): 88–124.
2. Glen Coulthard, "Subjects of Empire: Indigenous Peoples and the 'Politics of Recognition' in Canada," *Contemporary Political Theory* 6 (2007): 437–60; Elizabeth Povinelli, *The Empire of Love: Toward a Theory of Intimacy, Genealogy, and Carnality* (Durham, NC: Duke University Press, 2006).

Scott Lauria Morgensen is assistant professor of gender studies at Queen's University.

DOI 10.1215/10642684-1472989

MARRIAGE EQUALS DEATH... SERIOUSLY

Karma R. Chávez

Against Equality: Queer Critiques of Gay Marriage
Ryan Conrad, editor
Lewiston, ME: Against Equality Publishing Collective, 2010. 84 pp.

Marriage and the millions of dollars that follow it continue to dominate the mainstream LGBT rights agenda. Meanwhile, radical activists are silenced and chastised for their opposition to marriage, and those working on other community issues have increasingly found their funding cut, which takes food, shelter, and medicine from the hands of those queer and trans people who need it most. Marriage, then, is not just a distraction; it literally kills our "community," argues the Against Equality Collective, a radical arts and publishing group and online archive committed to pushing back on the mainstream LGBT agenda that emphasizes marriage, the military, and hate crimes legislation. Founded in 2009 by Ryan Conrad, Against Equality's first self-published book, cleverly titled *Against Equality*, features writings of prominent and diverse queer and trans activists from the United States who challenge the focus on marriage. Other than Chicago activist Yasmin Nair's introduction, all the essays have been previously published in blogs, zines, journals, and other venues, but Conrad brings them together to collectively capture the myriad voices speaking against marriage in contemporary times. Pocket-sized and featuring the cover art of Oakland artist Chris Vargas, *Against Equality* is a quick and easy resource that packs a pedagogical punch. Moreover, it reflects some of the diversity among queer perspectives, many outside academia, that want something different from queer politics.

Nair's introduction sets the platform as she questions the conventional wisdom of the marriage equality movement, which maintains that marriage will provide queers with access to important benefits and promote a culture where queers are no longer subject to violence. Nair argues against such logics, noting that marriage "remains the neoliberal state's most efficient way to corral the family as a source of revenue and to place upon it the ultimate responsibility for guaranteeing basic benefits like healthcare" (4). She further avers that the suggestion that marriage will lead to more justice actually condones prejudice: "Are we not explicitly telling queer teens and adults that non-conformity can and should lead to death?" (3). Thus Nair makes an impassioned plea for a radical queer critique that understands how capitalism dictates family structure and how certain gay identities get co-opted in the service of capitalism.

The other ten short essays pick up different dimensions of the antimarriage argument. Two of the most salient dimensions include challenging the state and advocating intersectionality. First, several essays question why the marriage movement calls on the state to provide freedom. Eric Stanley's essay, "Marriage Is Murder," offers a series of answers to common questions that marriage sympathizers might ask a leftist who is against marriage. Stanley advocates for the "abolishment of State sanctioned coupling," since it promotes institutionalized exploitation of some in order to benefit others (16). Kate and Deeg echo this point, remarking that rather than fighting for eleven hundred benefits for *some* people, we should be advocating rights for all people. Highlighting one of the ironies of the marriage movement in relation to the state, John D'Emilio explains how the movement "has created a vast body of *new* antigay law" (37). For others, the critique of calls to the state is more overt. Martha Jane Kaufman and Katie Miles lament, "The US military is continuing its path of destruction, and gays want to be allowed to fight. Cops are killing unarmed black men and bashing queers, and gays want more policing. More and more Americans are suffering and dying because they can't get decent health care, and gays want weddings. What happened to us?" (59).

A second theme within the essays reflects the lack of intersectional thinking within the marriage equality movement. Kenyon Farrow asks, "Is Gay Marriage Anti Black???" Farrow depicts the complex racial politics that underlie the marriage movement. He shows how the Christian Right pits blacks against gays by positioning gays as only upper middle class and white. He then discusses the related problems with the "gay civil rights"/"black civil rights" analogies that organizations like the Human Rights Campaign use, which have similarly placed black people in an awkward position, making them seem automatically homophobic if they reject the simplistic analogy. Both sorts of arguments virtually erase queers of color. In describing the campaign for marriage equality in Maine, Conrad denounces its classism. The campaign raised millions of dollars in this very poor state, even as vital service agencies for marginalized queer and HIV-positive people have shut their doors because of funding shortages. Dean Spade and Craig Willse frame their concerns as a very direct question relating to the passage of Proposition 8 in California: "Why isn't Prop 8's passage framed as evidence of the mainstream gay agenda's failure to ally with people of color on issues that are central to racial and economic justice in the US?" (19).

Each of the short essays in *Against Equality* raises important questions for marriage equality movement sympathizers to consider. While the theoretical contribution of this collection may not surprise the academic queer theorist, its pedagogical and political significance cannot be overstated. Because of the length of the entire collection, and the brevity of the individual contributions, *Against Equality* is ideal for student and nonacademic audiences. The diversity of the writers and the coherence of the collection's perspective create a persuasive argument against the marriage equality movement. When I used the text with graduates and undergraduates in a queer theory class, many who adamantly supported marriage equality expected to be completely put off by the book (and the subsequent invited lecture by Conrad). Instead, students found the Against Equality perspective to be inviting, realistic, and important. Conrad's decision to leave the essays in their original form to reflect the time period in which they were written is perhaps the text's only major shortcoming: it led to a lot of repetition of ideas. This quibble aside, *Against Equality* represents a vital voice in the cacophonous contemporary milieu.

Karma R. Chávez is assistant professor of rhetoric in the Department of Communication Arts at the University of Wisconsin, Madison.

DOI 10.1215/10642684-1472998

About the Contributors

Vanessa Agard-Jones is a PhD candidate in the joint program in anthropology and French studies at New York University. With the late historian Manning Marable, she is coeditor of *Transnational Blackness: Navigating the Global Color Line* (2008).

Jafari S. Allen is assistant professor of anthropology and African American studies at Yale University, where he also teaches in the lesbian, gay, bisexual, and transgender studies program. He is the author of *¡Venceremos? The Erotics of Black Self-Making in Cuba* (2011). Allen's ethnographic and critical work has been published widely, and he is conducting research for a new book project, "Black Queer Here and There: Sociality and Movement in the Americas."

Robert G. Diaz is assistant professor in the Women and Gender Studies Program at Wilfrid Laurier University. He was also a Mellon Sawyer Postdoctoral Fellow at UCLA and an Andrew Mellon Fellow at USC. His current book project, "Reparative Acts: Redressive Nationalisms and Queer Filipino Politics," examines how queer Filipinos in the diaspora contest reparation's relationship to marginalizing practices of colonialism and imperialism.

Lyndon K. Gill received his PhD in African American studies and anthropology from Harvard University. He has held postdoctoral fellowships in anthropology and African American studies at Princeton University and the University of Pennsylvania. Beginning in the fall of 2012, he will be assistant professor of African and African diaspora studies at the University of Texas at Austin.

Ana-Maurine Lara is an award-winning novelist, playwright, and poet. A Cave Canem Fellow and a member of the Austin Project, a collaborative workshop between artists, activists, and scholars at the University of Texas, Austin, Lara coordinates We Are the Magicians, the Path-Breakers, the Dream-Makers LGBTQ-POC Oral History Project. She is pursuing a PhD in African American studies and anthropology at Yale University.

Xavier Livermon is assistant professor of Africana studies at Wayne State University. His research interests include gender and sexuality in the African diaspora, black cultural studies, and music and performance cultures of the African diaspora. He has recently begun a project examining sexual citizenship in postapartheid South Africa, looking at the intersection of legal discourse, popular culture, and lived experiences of black queer men.

Matt Richardson is assistant professor in the Departments of English and African and African Diaspora Studies and the Center for Gender and Women's Studies at the University of Texas at Austin. He has published articles in the *Journal of Women's History* and *Black Camera*. He has also participated in a dialogue on trans activism with Susan Stryker and Kris Hayashi in the *Journal of Sexuality Research and Social Policy* and coauthored an article with Enoch Page titled "On the Fear of Small Numbers: A 21st Century Prolegomenon of the US Black Transgender Experience," in *Black Sexualities: Probing Powers, Passions, Practices, and Policies*, ed. Juan Battle and Sandra L. Barnes (New Brunswick, NJ: Rutgers University Press, 2009). His book *Listening to the Archives: Black Lesbian Literature and Queer Memory* is forthcoming from Ohio State University Press.

Omise'eke Tinsley is associate professor of English at the University of Minnesota. Her book *Thiefing Sugar: Eroticism between Women in Caribbean Literature* (2010) traces how Caribbean women writers queer landscape-as-female-beloved metaphors to imagine a poetics of decolonization. She is currently at work on a project titled "Ezili's Mirrors: Black Feminism, Afro Atlantic Genders, and the Work of the Imagination," which explores twenty-first-century Caribbean literature, film, and performance, as well as on a historical novel titled "Water, Shoulders, Into the Black Pacific," which explores relationships between black female shipbuilders during World War II.

Keep up-to-date

on new scholarship from this journal.

Email Alerts is a complimentary service that delivers electronic tables of contents straight to your inbox, allowing you to stay current on new scholarship as it is published.

Sign up for free e-mail alerts today at dukejournals.org/cgi/alerts *(no subscription necessary).*

- Complete the free registration process.
- Select your favorite journals to start receiving electronic tables of contents.

DUKE UNIVERSITY PRESS

For more information about Duke University Press journals, visit **dukejournals.org**.

DUKE UNIVERSITY PRESS | University Readers
Custom Publishing Evolved.

Finally, it's easy to customize course materials!

Use the Duke University Press Collection to create materials that fit your course and students' needs

1. Go to the Duke University Press Collection link on the website at http://library.universityreaders.com/

2. Chose from over 1,600 readings

3. Create your complete custom anthology

The **Duke University Press Collection** features authoritative and innovative readings for classroom use. The collection houses 1,200 articles and essays from its journals publishing program, as well as 1,400 book chapters from 115 titles. The content is ideal for graduate and undergraduate courses in a wide variety of disciplines, including Latin American studies, gender and sexuality, ethnic studies, political science, history, literature, and sociology, among many other subjects.

The readings in this collection are pre-cleared, at discounted permission rates, and ready for classroom use. Choose from readings in Duke's collection as well as selections from many other publishers and sources in our library to create the course pack or custom textbook most relevant to your course. University Readers provides complete copyright clearance, print and digital formats, and flexible distribution options to students, all within a quick two-week turnaround for course packs.

For more information go to
http://library.universityreaders.com/?c=duke
800.200.3908 x501 | info@universityreaders.com